REPAIRING BRITISH POLITICS

The first edition of this seminal text was written as a response to the constitutional crisis of 2009, sparked by the 'expenses scandal', which led a general distrust of the UK's entire political order.

A decade on, it is no exaggeration to say that the situation has dramatically deteriorated. The UK's constitutional order faces an existential crisis, with Brexit placing unbearable pressure on the political and legal architecture. All this makes the need for a written Constitution more pronounced. Retaining the easily accessible style of the first edition, this book addresses how this might be put in place.

Part 1 sets out a number of arguments in favour of a written Constitution, as well as the most common objections. Part 2 presents a working draft in the form of one possible model for a Constitution. Observations and explanatory notes are attached to each section of this draft Constitution. This model Constitution is intended as the first stage in a public debate, designed to provoke further discussion about the content and method of legislating into law a written Constitution. Part 3 contains the draft of the Act of Parliament that would be needed to introduce any form of constitutional change.

Rarely has a book been more timely or essential.

Repairing British Politics

A Blueprint for Constitutional Change

Second Edition

Richard Gordon KC

•HART•
OXFORD • LONDON • NEW YORK • NEW DELHI • SYDNEY

HART PUBLISHING

Bloomsbury Publishing Plc

Kemp House, Chawley Park, Cumnor Hill, Oxford, OX2 9PH, UK

1385 Broadway, New York, NY 10018, USA

29 Earlsfort Terrace, Dublin 2, Ireland

HART PUBLISHING, the Hart/Stag logo, BLOOMSBURY and the Diana logo are trademarks of Bloomsbury Publishing Plc

First published in Great Britain 2025

A catalogue record for this book is available from the British Library.

A catalogue record for this book is available from the Library of Congress.

Library of Congress Control Number: 2024946795

ISBN: PB: 978-1-50993-343-3
ePDF: 978-1-50993-345-7
ePub: 978-1-50993-344-0

Typeset by Compuscript Ltd, Shannon
Printed and bound in Great Britain by CPI Group (UK) Ltd, Croydon CR0 4YY

FSC www.fsc.org MIX Paper | Supporting responsible forestry FSC® C013604

To find out more about our authors and books visit www.hartpublishing.co.uk. Here you will find extracts, author information, details of forthcoming events and the option to sign up for our newsletters.

Civilization is a thin and precarious crust, erected by the personality and will of a very few, and only maintained by rules and conventions skilfully put across and guilefully preserved.

John Maynard Keynes ('My Early Beliefs', 1938)

Acknowledgements

I would like to thank those people again who contributed to the first edition including Professor Swati Jhaveri, Glen Davis (now a KC), my old history teacher Patrick Tobin, David Walter, Professor Stuart Weir (the last three dead), Mark Hofman, Stephen Hockman KC, Professor Sir Vernon Bogdanor, Professor Sir David Edwards, Professor Andrew Le Sueur, Professor Brickson, Lord Justice Rabinder Singh, Jemima Stratford KC, Noemi Byrd, Sarah Naylor, and Christopher Knight.

Turning now to the second edition. I met Nat le Roux at the launch of the first edition and he introduced me to the work of the Constitution Society. Through the Constitution Society to which I spoke and read frequently I met many politicians and academics of all kinds including Sir Malcolm Jack, Professor Andrew Blick, Professor Sir John Baker KC, Professor Sionaidh Douglas-Scott, The Rt Hon Mark Harper MP, the Rt Hon the Lord Howarth of Newport, Professor David Howarth, Dame Eleanor Laing MP, Sir Thomas Legg, Professor Rick Rawlings, and the Rt Hon the Lord Tyler. I spoke at a number of conferences at Ditchley Park with speakers as diverse as Lord Maude of Horsham and Labour MP Chris Bryant.

All the above have contributed in some fashion (whether expected or not) to the Constitution that I have suggested in this edition.

My thanks are also owed to Hart and to the wonderful editors to work so hard in producing the book. In particular, I want to thank Sinead Moloney, Kate Whetter, Verity Stuart and Maria Skrzypiec.

Most of all I wanted to thank my wife Jane, whose support and encouragement since I suffered a stroke in March 2019 has been invaluable.

Jane alone has worked ceaselessly to ensure that the second edition is a worthy successor to its predecessor.

Any errors of fact or law are mine alone.

Contents

Glossary of Essential Terms

Accountability

In the context of this book, this embodies the concept of **responsibility** of either executive government or of the **judiciary** for their acts and omissions. In electoral terms it is usually taken to mean accountability to voters but the **executive** is also accountable to **Parliament** and the judiciary is subject to control by the Legal Services Ombudsman.

Act of Parliament

A law passed as primary **legislation** by **Parliament**.

Address by Parliament

A statement of the wishes or opinions of one or both of the Houses of Parliament delivered to the sovereign. It is a necessary prerequisite for the removal of a senior judge from office.

Amending Constitutions

The process of changing the terms of a written constitution. It is usually set at a high threshold so that provisions of a written constitution are often said to be 'entrenched', compared to the ability of **Parliament** to make and unmake laws by simple majority vote.

Attorney-General

The main legal adviser to the Government.

Bills

Bill are draft stages for new laws. If they pass every stage of scrutiny in the **House of Commons** and the **House of Lords** and receive Royal Assent they become **Acts of Parliament**.

Bill of Rights

A statement of fundamental rights and privileges considered essential to afford protections to citizens of a state.

Domestic Bill of Rights

A Bill of Rights that is the product of an **Act of Parliament** and does not depend on **international treaties** such as the **ECHR**, part of which has still not been **incorporated** into domestic law. Like any piece of domestic **legislation**, a domestic Bill of Rights can be repealed by **Parliament** at any time, under the doctrine of **parliamentary sovereignty**, unless it is 'entrenched' in a written constitution.

Brexit and its aftermath

The Brexit decision, conducted after a nationwide **referendum**, had a number of constitutional effects. Briefly summarised, they were: (i) the effect on law-making, (ii) the effect on devolution, (iii) the effect on reform of the House of Lords, (iv) the effect on reforming constitutional conventions, (v) the effect on referendums. All of these effects are analysed in this book.

Brexit referendum

The outcome of the Brexit **referendum** was to split the UK. England and Wales opted to leave; Scotland and Northern Ireland opted to remain. The voting was marginal, with 51.9 per cent voting to leave and Scotland and Northern Ireland held the whip hand since in both Scotland and Northern Ireland there were many who had decided in leave the EU. The lessons learned from the Brexit referendum are few but important. There is a need to look at the threshold requirement for these kinds of important decisions. There is also the need to consider whether two consecutive referendums would be more appropriate for such important issues, as it is impossible to have a complete picture until certain key information becomes available.

British Constitution

An uncodified series of laws and conventions, developed over many centuries and with only limited 'separation of powers'. **Parliamentary sovereignty** is a total bar to the UK ever having a true constitution.

British Overseas Territories and Crown Dependencies

British Overseas Territories are 14 territories with a constitutional and historical link with the UK; they do not form part of the UK itself. These territories all have the Crown as their Head of State and the UK is responsible for defence and foreign relations. The Crown Dependencies (ie the Bailiwick of Jersey, the Bailiwick of Guernsey and the Isle of Man) have never been colonies of the UK. Nor are they British. The Crown Dependencies are not part of the UK. This means that they have their own directly-elected legislative assemblies, fiscal and legal systems.

By-elections

An election that is held to fill a political office that has become vacant between general elections.

Cabinet

The committee of senior government Ministers at the heart of executive government and the supreme decision-maker in government.

Cabinet Manual

A record of what counts as an 'essential guide to our system of government'. The problem is that too much of the UK's constitution is omitted from the Manual and too much of the content is outdated. The Cabinet Manual was intended to be for the executive alone and this may account for its undoubted flaws.

Charter of Fundamental Rights of the European Union

An international document which introduces many economic and social rights that do not appear in the **ECHR**. It is referred to in the Treaty of Lisbon, which came into force on 1 December 2009. However, the Charter applies only to the implementation of **EU** law and is not a general charter of rights.

Citizens' Branch

One of the branches of government which could be in a written constitution reflecting citizen power. Mention of a Citizens' Branch in written constitutions is, however, unusual.

Civil list

The civil list details the amount appropriated by Parliament to pay the annual expenses of the Sovereign and his or her household.

Civil Service

A branch of public service entrusted with the administration of the state and for providing impartial (ie non-party political) advice to government but which does not form part of the three traditionally recognised arms of government: **executive**, **legislature** or **judiciary**.

Coalition Government

When two parties govern together because they did not secure enough seats for a government majority on their own. The Conservatives and Liberal Democrats formed a coalition government between 2010 and 2015.

Codes of practice

A code of written rules which explains how people working in a particular profession (here, for example, politics or the civil service) should behave.

Coke LCJ

Sir Edmund Coke (1552–1634) argued that the judges of the common law were those most suited to making law, followed by Parliament. The monarch was subject to the law.

Common law

The body of law created by judges in legal decisions over a period of time.

Compulsory voting

This is the legal requirement that registered voters participate in elections. Failure to vote will be penalised with a statutory penalty (in most cases and in the Draft Constitution included in this book) such as disenfranchisement for a permitted period. There are arguments for and against this practice but the experience of most countries that have tried it is that voting numbers do increase, and that numbers diminish when the voting is not mandatory.

Constituency

An electoral area that elects an **MP** to the House of Commons.

Single-member constituency

A constituency that returns one elected candidate to **Parliament.**

Two-member constituency

A constituency that returns two elected candidates to **Parliament.**

Multi-member constituency

A constituency that returns more than two elected candidates to **Parliament.**

Constituency link

The link between an individual **MP** and electors in a particular **constituency.** This link is broken by most, if not all, forms of **proportional representation.**

Constitution

A device setting out the role and functions of the branches of government. Constitutions may be written or unwritten but all modern democracies (the UK, New Zealand and Israel excepted) have written constitutions.

Codification

The process of reducing a constitution to a single written document.

Dignified constitution

A term coined by the political theorist Walter Bagehot (1826–77) to denote those parts of the UK's unwritten constitution which inspired reverence (notably, the **monarchy**) rather than performing efficient functions.

Efficient constitution

A term coined by the political theorist Walter Bagehot (1826–77) to denote those parts of government playing a functional role in the day-to-day business of government (most notably, the **executive** and **Parliament**).

Unspoken Constitution

A satirical account, published by Democratic Audit in 2009, of the current rules by which the UK is governed in the form of a mock written Constitution.

Unwritten constitution

As used in this book, the term means a constitution where the rules by which society is organised, including the institutions of government, have not been codified. In this sense the UK can certainly be said to have an unwritten constitution since the roles and functions of government are contained in various different sources including informal **constitutional conventions**. However, the absence of a written constitution means that the doctrine of **parliamentary sovereignty** survives intact. Conversely, a written constitution, by reference to which the powers of the branches of government would be constrained, is incompatible with the retention of parliamentary sovereignty.

Constitution Committee

The Constitution Committee is a House of Lords Committee which examines all public bills for constitutional implications and investigates broad constitutional issues.

(Constitutional) convention

In the constitutional context, a convention is a set of agreed or generally accepted political standards or practices which are treated as binding. The full term 'constitutional convention' is used to denote a gathering for the purposes of drafting a written Constitution. In *Miller 1* [2017] UKSC 5 the Supreme Court held that constitutional conventions cannot be adjudicated upon by the court.

Salisbury Convention

A constitutional convention preventing the House of Lords from vetoing the second or third parliamentary reading of any government **legislation** promised in its election manifesto.

Sewel Convention

A constitutional convention that the Westminster **Parliament** will only legislate on reserved matters (ie matters reserved to the Westminster Parliament) and will not legislate on devolved matters (ie matters delegated to the Scottish Parliament) without first seeking the consent of the Scottish Parliament.

Constitutional documents

A term sometimes used to denote the documents that make up the informal and uncodified constitution of the UK. The documents often referred to in this phrase include Magna Carta (1215), the Bill of Rights (1689), the Act of Settlement (1701), the Acts of Union 1707 and 1800, the Representation of the People Act 1832, the Parliament Acts 1911 and 1949, the European Communities Act 1972 and the Human Rights Act 1998. To these must be added all the various Acts to disentangle the UK from the EU.

Constitutional moment

A point of national crisis which prompts a state to draft a written, codified constitution.

Constitutional monarchy

This term has been used in a variety of ways. However, here it means a **monarchy** in which the power of the monarch is limited by a written constitution. In a wider sense the term is sometimes used to denote a form of constitutional government where the monarch wields autocratic power and is the sole source of political power.

Contractarian theories of government

Theories of government which postulate a theoretical **social contract** between people and government. Generally, such theories (espoused by, amongst others, Thomas Hobbes (1588–1679) and John Rawls (1921–2002)) do not suggest any legal 'contract' but, rather, a rationale for the existence of such a contract.

Crown prerogative

Legal powers using the royal prerogative are those which do not require parliamentary consent. All these powers would have been exercised by the monarch directly but over time the majority have been abolished, delegated to ministers or replaced by statute. These are often exercised by the Prime Minister acting alone or in cabinet.

Counter-majoritarian dilemma

The dilemma arising where laws are made by judges without popular mandate. The term was coined by the jurist Robert Bork (1927–2012).

Declaration

A legal remedy whereby a court states (declares) what the law is.

Democracy

A system of government in which citizens govern either directly or, more commonly, by elected representatives of the people.

Deliberative democracy

A mixture of direct democracy and representative democracy in which popular consultation is used to formulate political policy.

Direct democracy

A system of government in which the process of government is undertaken directly by the citizens. It is often said to derive from ancient Athens.

Representative democracy

A system of government in which citizens elect individuals to represent them in government. It is to be distinguished from direct democracy in which the citizens participate directly in the business of government. It is argued here that a representative democracy underpinned by **parliamentary sovereignty** is necessarily less 'representative' than one underpinned by constitutional or popular sovereignty, since only in the latter is power conferred by the people as opposed to being imposed on the people.

Derogation

An exemption from or relaxation of a rule of law.

Devolution

The granting of power by central government to government at a local level. The devolution settlement includes those rights which are devolved (that is **transferred powers** or, in the case of Northern Ireland, **excepted powers**) apart from a residual power in the English Parliament to vote. However, the so-called **Sewel Convention** stipulates that the English Parliament will not normally vote unless there is legislative consent from the relevant assembly. There is a further category of **reserved or exempted rights** over which the English Parliament has full control. In the UK there have been significant devolution reforms leading to the establishment of the Scottish Parliament and the Welsh and Northern Irish Assemblies, which exercise, in different ways, power ('devolved power') formerly attaching to central government in Westminster. The outcome of the **Brexit referendum** has given the Scottish National Party (SNP) and the various parties in Northern Ireland material for demanding a referendum in the next few years.

Devo-max

A form of devolution which grants full fiscal autonomy to the devolved administrations instead of the block-grant which they receive from the UK Exchequer at present. Advocates of a full federal system usually promote devo-max as a realistic alternative to full devolution.

Dictatorship

The form of government in which one person or group of persons possess absolute power without effective constitutional limitations.

Election primaries

An adaptation by UK **political parties** of the US system of primaries whereby potential candidates for election are voted on by the public in the **constituency** rather than being chosen by the party machine. A **by-election** was conducted by the Conservative Party in Totnes using this procedure in 2009.

Elective dictatorship

A graphic phrase used by the former Lord Chancellor, Lord Hailsham (LC 1970–74), to describe the dominance of the **executive** over **Parliament**, reflecting the fact that once elected on a general political manifesto the government of the day will usually be able to pass whatever **legislation** it wishes.

Emergency debate

Emergency debate is a debate called at short notice in the **House of Commons** on a matter that should have urgent consideration.

Emergency powers

Powers of central government to act outside its normal powers in an emergency such as war or armed rebellion.

Entrenching provisions

Provisions firmly established in a constitution so that it would be difficult to change them.

Erskine May

Parliament's rule book, featuring a collection of hard conventions dictating behaviour in the Chambers of the **House of Commons** and the **House of Lords**.

European Convention on Human Rights (ECHR)

An **international treaty** to protect human rights and fundamental freedoms. Many of its provisions have been **incorporated** into UK domestic law by the Human Rights Act 1998, which came into force on 2 October 2000. However, the existence of **parliamentary sovereignty** in the UK means that Parliament may violate fundamental rights protected by the ECHR if it chooses to do so using clear language.

European Union (EU)

A group of 27 Member States regulated by a number of **international treaties** which are primarily designed to ensure economic integration. EU law is a system of law operated directly by the institutions of the EU (EU Commission (Brussels), EU Parliament (Brussels and Strasbourg) and the Court of Justice of the European Union (sitting in Luxembourg)) and was formerly **incorporated** into UK law by the European Communities Act 1972. It has supremacy in each of the Member States (including, prior to Brexit, the UK). The effect of this is that **parliamentary sovereignty** was powerless to resist EU law overriding laws enacted by **Parliament.** The only way parliamentary sovereignty could assert itself in an EU context would be by complete withdrawal from the EU, which occurred on 31 January 2020. In *Miller (1)* [2011] UKSC 5 the Supreme Court held (by a majority) that EU law was a source of the constitution and that ministers had no power unilaterally to withdraw from the EU law without the assent of Parliament.

The European Union (**Withdrawal**) **Act 2018 as amended by The European Union** (**Withdrawal Agreement**) **Act 2020**

The EU (Withdrawal) Act provides both for repeal of the European Communities Act 1972 and for Parliament's approval to be required for any withdrawal agreement. The Act is designed to enable 'cutting off the source of EU law in the UK … and remove the competence of EU institutions to legislate for the UK'. To provide for legal continuity the Act enables the transposition of directly-applicable already existing EU law into UK law thereby creating 'a new category of domestic law for the UK: retained EU law'.

The Retained EU Law (**Revocation and Reform**) **Act 2023**

The broadly removes some 600 pieces of uncontentious legislation but the constitutional framework established by the 2018 Act is subtly dispensed with by: (i) revoking all direct effective EU law; (ii) revoking the supremacy of EU law; (iii) revoking the retained general principles of EU law; (iv) renaming 'retained EU law' as 'assimilated law'. Additionally, the Act introduces less stringent tests for review of what was formerly EU law by national courts, by ministers/civil servants by: (1) permitting lower courts more often to depart from legacy case law of the Court of Justice of the European Union; (ii) conferring power to update assimilated law in light of technological and scientific developments; and (iii) relaxing the rule of scrutiny for modifying or revoking assimilated laws.

Executive

A constitutional organ of government that is responsible for the daily administration of the state. The executive comprises the Crown and the Government, including the Prime Minster and Cabinet Ministers.

Executive power

Executive authority means the power and the right to issue executive functions.

Expenses crisis

The name given to the political scandal triggered in 2009 when it was discovered, following disclosures under the Freedom of Information Act, that **MPs** had in a great many cases misused their permitted allowances and expenses. The crisis came to light when the *Daily Telegraph* leaked on a day-by-day basis the names of particular MPs who had apparently exaggerated their expenses claims.

Federation

A federation is a political entity marked by a union of partially self-governing provinces, states or other regions under a central federal government.

First-past-the-post (FPTP)

The electoral system currently used for **general elections** in the UK, whereby the candidate with a simple majority (ie more than 50 per cent) of votes in each **constituency** is elected to **Parliament**.

Fixed-term parliament

A regime whereby **general elections** are called within a stipulated time, as opposed to the situation at present where the **Prime Minister** is free to decide the date of a general election under prerogative powers.

Fusion of powers

The political theorist UK Kingdom **constitution** from the traditional **separation of powers** doctrine because of the fact that one arm of government (the **executive**) was selected from another arm (the **legislature** (**Parliament**)) and so instead of being separate they were inextricably fused.

General election

In a general election **MPs** are elected to the **House of Commons** in each of the constituencies of the UK. **General elections** are required to take place every five years but are usually held earlier, on a date decided by the Prime Minister.

Green paper

A consultation paper issued by the Government to test opinion on a legislative proposal that is couched in fairly general terms.

Head of state

The Crown is nominally the Head of state.

Henry VIII power

A delegated power which allows a Minister to change an existing Act of Parliament.

Hereditary peer

A person who is a member of the Peerage by inheritance. Only 92 hereditary peers (out of 800) sit in the House of Lords, being elected from their number (House of Lords Act 1999).

House of Commons

The House of Commons is an elected Chamber comprising 650 MPs selected through a first-past-the-post voting system in local constituencies. The House of Commons (the House of Representatives in the Constitution) is the main legislation arm of government. Procedures in the House of Commons require reform.

House of Lords

The House of Lords (the Senate in this Constitution) is one of the two places where Bills are promulgated. Procedures in the House of Lords need to be reformed. The House of Lords is a revision chamber tasked with improving legislation but it can only delay such legislation. Peers currently sit in the House of Lords.

Incorporation/incorporated

The process by which an obligation of the state in international law is enacted into domestic law.

Instrument of Government

The 'Instrument of Government' (the new written Constitution of 1653) placed great power in the hands of the executive formed by the Protector and the Council of State.

International treaties

International treaties are not part of national law unless **incorporated** into national law by **Act of Parliament.** This is as true of EU treaties and the **ECHR** as it is of any other international treaty. Unincorporated international treaties do not present any challenge to the doctrine of **parliamentary sovereignty**.

Interpretation

Interpretation covers the following essential aspects of a constitution. The first is the **Constitution** itself. The second is all the **Acts** (**Acts of Parliament and delegated legislation**) that affect how the UK is governed.

Interregnum

In this book, this term describes the period of parliamentary and military rule under the Commonwealth of England following the English Civil War and the ascent to power of Oliver Cromwell (1649–1660).

Judicial independence

The idea that judges should be free of interference from the other organs of government.

Judicial review

This refers to the type of case where a judge or judges review the lawfulness of a decision or action taken by a public authority.

Judiciary

The system of judges and courts charged with interpreting and applying the law.

Justiciable

The meaning of justiciable in the present context is whether or not the matter before the court is capable of being pronounced upon.

King (or Queen) in Parliament

A term referring to the Crown in its legislative capacity acting with the advice and consent of **Parliament**. The King's (or Queen's) speech involves setting out government's legislative agenda for the year ahead.

Legislation

Laws passed by a legislature or other governing body.

Primary legislation

Laws passed by **Parliament** in the form of **Acts of Parliament**. Prior to being enacted (following the formality of Royal Assent by the monarch) the draft law is called a **Bill**.

Secondary legislation

Sometimes called subordinate or delegated legislation, secondary legislation is a law made under authority contained in primary legislation.

Legislation that compels the violation of principles of public international law

'The rule of law requires compliance by the state with its obligations in international law as in national law' (Lord Bingham summarised this as the eighth and final principle in *The Rule of Law*).

Legislature

The law-making body in a state. In the UK, **Parliament** is the relevant law-making body.

Bicameral legislature

The practice of having two legislative bodies. In the United Kingdom there is a bicameral legislature consisting of the (elected) House of Commons and the (currently unelected) House of Lords.

Unicameral legislature

The practice of having only one legislative body.

Life peers

Members of the House of Lords whose peerage cannot be inherited.

Majority vote

The vote which, according to the voting system that is followed, produces the desired candidate or candidates.

Member of Parliament (MP)

A person elected to the House of Commons to represent his or her **constituency**.

Moment of interruption

The moment of interruption is the time at which debate must stop and the question is decided at the end of the main business of the **House of Commons**. The time at which the debate must stop on each weekday is set down in the House of Commons **Standing Orders**. If the Government wants extended time for a debate it must ask the House to agree to a special business motion.

Monarch

Hereditary **Head of State**. Referred to in the text of the Constitution as 'Sovereign'. See also **Constitutional monarchy**.

Montesquieu

French judge, historian and philosopher (1689–1755). He is the principal source of the theory of separation of powers.

Motion

A motion is a proposal put forwards for debate or decision in the House of Commons or the House of Lords. A motion must be proposed by an MP or peer before any debate or vote can take place in Parliament.

Order in Council

Orders in Council are made by the King/Queen acting on the advice of the Privy Council and are approved in person by the monarch.

Originalism

The theory that the interpretation of a written constitution should be consistent with the intentions of those drafting the **Constitution** and that its meaning depends on the meaning ascribed to it at the time of drafting. Justice Scalia (1936–2016) and Robert Bork (1927–2012) are often associated with this view.

Parliament

The legislative body (the **legislature**) of the UK, consisting of the **House of Commons** and the **House of Lords**.

Parliament Acts

These are the generic name for two Acts of Parliament (1911 and 1949) which limited the former legislative veto of the **House of Lords** and the ability of the House of Lords to delay Bills passing into law.

Parliamentary Business and Legislation Committee

Set up to monitor the Government's parliamentary business, including delivery of its legislative programme.

Passage of legislation

This phrase means the passage of laws through both Houses of Parliament.

Pluralism

The existence of different types of people who have different beliefs and opinions. The UK has moved towards political, religious and cultural pluralism.

Political party

A body that seeks to attain and maintain political power in government consistently with a published political manifesto. The major parties in Great Britain now are the Conservative Party, Labour, the Liberal Democrats, and the Scottish National Party,

Preamble

An introductory or explanatory statement in a document (such as a Constitution) that explains the document's purpose and underlying philosophy.

Prime Minister

The Prime Minister is the leader of His Majesty's Government chosen because of internal party arrangements and is ultimately responsible for the policy and decisions of the government (senior members of which form **the Cabinet**). The Prime Minister also: (i) chooses members of the government; (ii) oversees operation of the civil service and government agencies. As Minister of the Union the Prime Minister works to ensure that the government is working on behalf of the entire UK.

Private Members' Bill

A Bill introduced into **Parliament** by backbench **MPs** (members of Parliament who do not hold government office) or peers. Such Bills have very little prospect of becoming law because of the inadequate parliamentary time devoted to debating them.

Proportional representation (PR)

An electoral system designed to ensure a close approximation between the percentage of votes cast and the number of seats allocated. Most forms of PR break the **constituency link.**

Alternative vote (AV)

Not a form of proportional representation, but often confused with it, AV is an electoral system designed for single-winner elections in which voters rank candidates in order of preference. A candidate with over 50 per cent of the votes wins. If there is no such candidate, the second-preference votes of the candidate finishing last are redistributed. This process continues until there is a candidate with more than 50 per cent of the votes. Some maintain that AV is less proportional than **first-past-the-post** (see above).

Alternative vote plus (AV+)

A combination of AV and diluted proportional representation. It involves electing most **MPs** from constituencies in the normal way (albeit under AV rather than **first-past-the-post**). However, constituents also elect 15–20% of MPs from regions containing 'top-up' lists of parties determined by the vote share of the parties. AV+ was recommended in the 1998 Jenkins Report but was never implemented.

Party list

A form of proportional representation in which a list of candidates is prepared by each of the political parties in a multi-member **constituency** with seats being allocated to each party in proportion to the number of votes received, which may, depending on the type of list system employed, be cast for a party, for candidates or for a list.

Single transferable vote

A system of proportional representation used in multi-member constituencies in which voters have only one vote but can rank the candidates in order of preference. Their vote may be transferred to another candidate (their second preference) when their first preference candidate has too few votes to be elected or where their first choice candidate does not need their vote.

Prorogation

The ending of a parliamentary session, which triggers a period of inactivity ahead of the state opening of Parliament that begins the next session. Usually a procedural formality, but it was found to have been used unlawfully by Boris Johnson in 2019.

Putney Debates

From 28 October to 9 November 1647, the soldiers and officers of Oliver Crowell's New Model Army, including civilian representation, held discussions on the constitution and future of England.

Recall

A means of removing an **MP** from office by a vote when a certain threshold of dissatisfaction has been reached. Since publication of the first edition, it is noted that Parliament has passed the Recall of MP's Act 2015 which stipulates a threshold requirement of 10 per cent of the voters requiring a by-election for three categories of misconduct. The Draft Constitution also requires a threshold requirement of 10 per cent for the holding of a by-election but leaves it to the voters to determine the seriousness of the misconduct.

Referendum

A vote by the electorate on a specific proposal, usually of a significant or constitutional nature. Sometimes called a plebiscite.

Reform of the House of Lords

There has been much talk but little action in respect of reforming the **House of Lords**. The lengthy wrangle about the alternating policies is summarised in this book. But the outcome of the **Brexit referendum** has made it imperative to take some steps (if it is not too late) to regulate representation in the House of Lords (or a pre-structured body) that allows the devolved legislatures to play a greater role in representing the Union than is currently the position.

Report stage

Report stage gives MPs the opportunity (on the floor of the House) to consider further amendments to a Bill that has been examined in committee. Report stage is normally followed by the third reading of the Bill in the House of Commons.

Republic

A state without a **monarch** as head of state, and which usually has an elected President.

Responsibility

The obligations, whether legal or moral, owed by citizens to each other or to the state. There is an issue as to which, if any, civic responsibilities should be inserted in a domestic **Bill of Rights**.

Royal prerogative

The formal powers of the **monarch**, such as declaring war or appointing ministers. The powers are non-statutory and many are outside the control of the courts. In modern times the prerogative powers have been delegated to central government but many are still exercised on a non-statutory basis. Many consider that all prerogative power should now be placed on a statutory footing and brought within the control of the courts.

Rule of law

The principle that all are subject to the law and that the law is publicly and prospectively promulgated and publicly administered in the courts.

Scrutiny of Bills

Scrutiny of Bills takes place in the Commons and the Lords and both on the floor of the Chamber and in various kinds of committees.

Second ballot

A run-off electoral system whereby a single vote is cast. If no candidate receives an absolute majority of votes only the two candidates with the most votes go forward and a second round of voting takes place.

Second-past-the-post

An electoral system in which the first two candidates securing the most votes are elected to **Parliament**. This is not a system currently practised in the UK and would require two-member **constituencies.**

Select committee

A committee composed of parliamentary members appointed to deal with specific issues.

Separation of powers

The constitutional doctrine that divides governmental power into separate organs of state so that no one branch acquires a monopoly of power over another. In the UK it is sometimes thought that there is a separation of powers as between the **executive**, **legislature** and **judiciary**. However, in reality, the UK has a fused system in which the executive and legislative branches of government are not truly separate and in which, increasingly, central government (the executive) dominates the legislature from which it is selected (**Parliament**).

Skeleton Act/Framework Bill

Several Committees of the Houses of Parliament have expressed concern about the increasing use of skeleton Acts (or framework Bills). These set out the principles for a policy but leave it to Ministers to fill in the relevant detail. Because these powers are subject to less rigorous scrutiny than bills there have been calls for the use of such Acts to be restricted.

Social contract

A key notion in much political theory. Its premise is a theoretical agreement between the people leading to the surrender of autonomy in return for governmental protection. Social contract theory cannot be used to justify **parliamentary sovereignty** because whereas the former presupposes legislative power coming from the people, the latter is incompatible with any superior constraint on the powers of Parliament.

Sovereignty

Government free from external control.

Constitutional sovereignty

Under constitutional sovereignty (used interchangeably with 'popular sovereignty'), the legitimacy of a government is determined by the consent of the people in a written constitution. This doctrine is the antithesis of parliamentary sovereignty, which (see below) is conferred either by unelected judges or is derived from the claims of the English **Parliament** as reflected in the Bill of Rights 1689.

Parliamentary sovereignty

A constitutional doctrine that, as outlined by the Victorian jurist AV Dicey (1835–1922) provides for the absolute legislative supremacy of **Parliament**. The effect of this is that Parliament may, with no constitutional restraint at all, make whatever laws it chooses, and may change or repeal earlier Acts of Parliament. It has also been taken to mean that the validity of Acts of Parliament cannot be challenged in the domestic courts. The origins of the doctrine are obscure. Although the claims of Parliament to rule without royal interference were made in the Bill of Rights 1689, many believe that the doctrine of parliamentary sovereignty is judge-made.

Speaker

The chair of proceedings in the **House of Commons/Lords**. They rule on points of order and select MPs to speak.

Special adviser

Colloquially known as 'spads'. They are political appointees hired to support Ministers. It would be inappropriate for the civil service to provide such advisers because, other things aside, it would destroy the civil service's political impartiality.

Standing orders

Standing orders are the written rules that regulate the proceedings of each House.

Statute of Westminster 1931

This Act established legislative equality between the self-governing dominions of the British Empire and the UK. It sets the basis for the continuing constitutional relationship between the Commonwealth States and the Crown.

Statutory instrument

The main form in which secondary **legislation** is made in the UK.

Supremacy of the common law

There are some who believe the common law (that is judge-made law) is supreme.

Sunset clause

A sunset provision is a clause in a statute or regulation that expires automatically on a specified date.

Supreme Court

The highest court in the UK, possessing final jurisdiction to hear appeals. In many countries, such as the US, the Supreme Court exercises constitutional power and may strike down **legislation.** A Supreme Court was established in the UK in October 2009, to replace the former judicial jurisdiction of the House of Lords. Currently, it possesses no powers comparable to that of the US Supreme Court although some have suggested that it will develop such powers incrementally. The Draft Constitution in this book confers such powers.

Treaty

A formally concluded and ratified agreement between states.

Urgent question

Request by an MP to ask a question of the relevant minister in the Commons. The urgent question became a key part of the Speaker's toolkit during the Bercow era and remains so today.

US Declaration of Independence

The is the founding document of the US. It was adopted on 4 July 1776 and it explains to the world why the 13 colonies regarded themselves as independent sovereign states no longer subject to British colonial rule.

West Lothian question

An apparent anomaly whereby Scottish **MPs** can vote on issues affecting England, whereas English MPs cannot vote on issues affecting Scotland.

Whip

A role in party politics designed to ensure control over attendance by **MPs** at votes and compliance with the wishes of the Party as to the vote cast, on pain of sanction. Defiance of a three-line whip is regarded as very serious and career demotion and even expulsion from the party are the likely consequences of such a breach.

White paper

White papers are a way that the Government can introduce policy preferences before it introduces legislation.

Wright Committee

A committee established in 2010 to explore avenues for reform of Commons procedure. Its recommendations were only partially implemented.

Written Constitution

See notes on the term 'Constitution'.

1

Setting the Scene

IN HIS *RIGHTS of Man*, published in 1791, Thomas Paine argues for a radical brand of republicanism that will sweep away the old order; the dead hand of hierarchical authority embodied in the autocracy of George III. His target is the conservative Edmund Burke, the defender of tradition, experience and precedent as guardian of an unwritten constitution.

Paine wants to start again with a *tabula rasa*. With the examples of the American and French revolutions fresh in his mind, and as a direct participant in many of the dramatic events that were unfolding in those countries, his approach is uncompromising:

> Man has no property in man; neither has any generation property in the generations which are to follow ... I am contending for the rights of the *living*, and against their being willed away by the manuscript assumed authority of the dead.[1]

It may be thought that we need some of Paine's iconoclasm today as the UK has experienced a series of constitutional incidents since, at least, the mid-seventies of the twentieth century[2] – a situation that is getting worse, not better.

Britain is rightly proud of its own democratic tradition and supports democracies throughout the world as being the best form of power-sharing that has been devised for any state because it provides a structure for respecting the individual and taking account of diverse views and minority interests. Recent surveys have found that the majority of the population in the UK approve of the idea of democracy, but not in the way that it is reflected in our institutions,[3] which have lasted for several hundreds of years with passive acquiescence but without any obvious popular endorsement. So it is suggested here that one way of ensuring the continuation of the best in our democratic system would be to entrench it in a written constitution and thus appeal to the higher authority of

[1] Thomas Paine, *Rights of Man* (1791–92) (Oxford, Oxford World's Classics, 2008) 92.

[2] I acknowledge that many will prefer Edmund Burke over Thomas Paine as a standard-bearer. Paine's values certainly influenced the Declaration of Independence, but the leaders of the American Revolution rejected Paine's ideals as the rule of 'the worst over the best'. John Maynard Keynes was a fervent admirer of Burke, of whom Keynes observed, 'He does not think of the race as marching through blood and fire to some great and glorious good in the distant future': see Robert Skidelsky, *John Maynard Keynes: Volume 1, Hopes Betrayed* (Harmondsworth, Penguin, 1994) 154–57. However, as will be seen, *Repairing British Politics* has strong Burkean elements in seeking to preserve the continuity of the most valuable elements of our existing institutions.

[3] Survey by the Pew Research Centre, report dated 27 February 2020. Approval ratings in the UK went down from 66% to 44% in the space of the years since the previous survey, conducted in 2002.

the constitution rather than merely the views of whichever government happens to be in power at any particular time.

In the words of Abraham Lincoln, the value of democracy is that it is 'government of the people, by the people for the people'.[4] It is usually characterised as government chosen by the people through fair and free elections. But the reality is that this definition should be more nuanced to avoid the creation of an 'elective dictatorship'[5] because it leaves out the influence that the people have between elections. For example, once elected, some governments – untrammeled by the need to seek immediate popular approval – try to accrue power to themselves.[6]

Democracy is articulated in many different ways from the Athenians in the fifth century BC to the Swiss in the twentieth century. A factor they have in common is that they all give opportunity to different voices. As Professor Ben Ansell[7] said in his 2023 Reith Lectures:

> So for democracy to succeed, it must permit us to resolve our disagreements peacefully. But that doesn't mean we'll feel happy about it because agreeable disagreement means winners and it means losers. It means competing priorities, clashing ideals and vocal dissent. So our democratic systems have a dual function. Yes, they need to be agreeable to prevent spilling over into violence, but they also need to encourage disagreement, to avoid a blunt tyranny of the majority because a simple electoral majoritarianism can make decisions for us in a world of disagreement, sure, that kind of mere democracy is not enough because it's unstable and volatile … We can't govern by daily opinion poll, constant referendums will be neverendums, it'll been like having a Brexit vote every week …

The value of democracy is in the recognition of individuals as against the governing elite thus although Ansell may mention 'clashing ideals and vocal dissent' room has to be created whereby they can be expressed whilst avoiding violence and reaching a consensus which will enable a functioning government to operate. I would argue that a written constitution would facilitate this.

What is needed is public discussion of the ground rules by which we want to live and be governed. There has never been encouragement for, or proposed organisation of, such public debate. *Repairing British Politics* is intended as a modest first step in that process. How do we approach the arrangements for the governance of our country? Would a written constitution help to solve many of the issues that have arisen in the twentieth-first century?

The Constitution drafted in this book is intended as a suggestion for consideration on how we could better organise our system of government.

[4] Abraham Lincoln, speech delivered on the afternoon of 19 November 1863 at the dedication of the Soldiers' National Cemetery.

[5] Lord Hailsham in his BBC Richard Dimbleby Lecture titled 'The Elective Dictatorship' in October 1976.

[6] Indira Gandhi comes to mind. Her state of emergency lasted from 1975–1977 and was accompanied by mass arrests of opposition politicans.

[7] Professor Ben Ansell, *The Future of Democracy*, 29 November 2023. See also Ben Ansell, *Why Politics Fails* (Viking, 2023). For a lighter touch see Erica Benner's *Adventures in Democracy* (Allen Lane, 2023).

Even if there were strong support for a written constitution,[8] the drafting begun here and many of the solutions are likely to be discarded or amended during a debate. But such debate has not happened. It will *never* happen without a clear focal point around which certain threshold questions can be confronted. I would suggest that there are three preliminary questions:

— Should the *principle* of a written constitution be endorsed?
— (If so,) what should be the *content* of that constitution?
— What *process* should be undertaken to answer the previous two questions?

I. OUTLINE OF THE BOOK

The central idea behind *Repairing British Politics* is to provide a focus for a debate on the attractions of a written constitution by providing the framework for a draft constitution for the UK, underpinned by a new principle of constitutional (or popular) sovereignty in place of the traditional principle of parliamentary sovereignty.

The book is divided into three parts. Part 1 briefly sets out the ideas that might drive and be included in a written constitution, as well as a short background analysis which puts these ideas in context. The core of the analysis is that, despite its original virtues in effecting a transfer of power from absolute monarch to parliament, the doctrine of parliamentary sovereignty is responsible for perpetuating a hierarchical, top-down system of government in Britain that obstructs rather than reflects representative democracy, or impedes giving (to use the more demotic phrase) *power to the people.* It is a problem that has been recognised for many years. As long ago as 2009, Shirley Williams, speaking in a television interview, went so far as to say that 'it's a huge revolution in the wings if we're going to save representative democracy'.[9]

The simple replacement of one constitutional norm (parliamentary sovereignty) by another (constitutional sovereignty) will not, at a stroke, change the nature of the institutions by which we are governed. However, what I argue it will do, by engendering a proper separation of powers and much greater citizen participation in politics, is to promote greater trust in the democratic process and to create a number of policing mechanisms which will make each of the organs of government (including the citizenry itself) more responsible and more accountable.

[8] There is, for example, support for the opposite premise, articulated in works such as Adam Tomkins, *Our Republican Constitution* (Oxford, Hart Publishing, 2005), namely that parliamentary sovereignty is alive and kicking and has a contemporary constitutional basis (albeit a weak one). For further discussion of some practical arguments against a written constitution see Stephen Sedley, 'No Ordinary Law' *London Review of Books*, 5 June 2008, 20–23.

[9] Baroness Williams, *The Andrew Marr Show*, BBC, 20 September 2009. In the same interview Shirley Williams described the House of Commons as 'an excessively exclusive place'.

The meat of the book is in Part 2 (A Draft Constitution for the United Kingdom). In devising a prototype constitution some positions may, to some, appear extreme, but care has been taken to preserve our main institutions, including the monarchy (as a constitutional monarchy), to as great an extent as is logically compatible with the ideas behind the new constitution.

That there is a need for continuity alongside change is undeniable. Continuity is essential both from a jurisprudential point of view (the incremental development of the common law) and from a practical perspective. Political mechanisms and institutions (and, as importantly, the people behind the institutions) require time and space to catch up with the changes introduced by a new system.

Therefore, the aim has been to collate in written form much of our existing informal constitution and to add a number of possible changes which would have the effect of altering the underlying basis of our constitutional arrangements. In many cases the pros and cons of particular proposals are canvassed in the Observations and Explanatory Notes which accompany each section.

Finally, Part 3 contains a working draft of the Act of Parliament that would be needed to introduce any form of constitutional change. The Constitution of Britain (Referendums) Act sets out a step-by-step approach for (if necessary) *two* national referendums. The first referendum would, in the absence of any clear commitment to introduce a written constitution, canvass opinion as to the idea of such a constitution in principle.[10] If the idea of a written constitution were approved, there would be a second referendum to approve content. On the safe hypothesis that the model constitution drafted in this book would not itself be approved, it could at least serve to mark the start of a process of drafting a new written constitution with the widest possible public participation. The Act also contains a requirement for public education and debate preceding the first referendum so that those voting on whether we should have a written constitution are as well informed as possible about the issues involved.

I now want to revisit some of the ground just covered in order to sketch outs the main themes that led me to write this book.

II. WHY WE NEED A WRITTEN CONSTITUTION[11]

This book has a specific thesis. It suggests that our profound disillusionment with politics can only get worse with the 'constitution' we have – a 'constitution'

[10] From the point of view of the arguments advanced in *Repairing British Politics*, it would of course be preferable if the election manifestos of the various parties accepted the idea of a written constitution, thus bypassing the need for a first referendum. If that were done, the structure of the Act proposed here would be different. The two-step approach is suggested on the basis that *as a minimum* each of the parties campaigning for office should make a commitment to hold a referendum on the idea of a written constitution for the UK.

[11] The non-specialist reader may find it helpful at this stage to consult the Glossary of Essential Terms at the front of this book, for a brief explanation of some of the most important terms used in the book.

which is out of touch with the reality of the modern world; a loose unwritten constitution. Our disaffection with politics is exacerbated by a constitutional settlement in which the spoils of victory following the power struggle between Parliament and the monarchy (which claimed absolute power) went to Parliament but in which the people were left out. This has developed into the system of parliamentary sovereignty by virtue of which Parliament has the power to change any law it wishes, regardless of when or why the previous law was enacted leaving us in a position whereby no value or safeguard is sacred. This has provided a limited form of democracy because the people can never be the masters. In contrast, a written constitution would specifically acknowledge the people as masters. It is argued, therefore, that a written constitution is not merely a desirable objective; it is in fact a constitutional necessity if true representative democracy is to be achieved in Britain.

The current apathy that seems to have triggered rapidly declining electoral voting patterns is part of a more general malaise in which we, as citizens, feel powerless to affect events about which we feel strongly but over which we have no control (the Iraq War being an example); a malaise in which the top-down government that we have – itself the legacy of our history of absolute monarchy – leaves us politically disillusioned and at times (the MPs' expenses scandal of 2008 being a notable example) profoundly mistrustful of the good intentions of those who exercise power over us.

The argument advanced in *Repairing British Politics* is that a written constitution for the UK would change our lives for the better by making politicians more accountable to the people. Empowerment of the people could be achieved by the introduction of the principle of constitutional or popular sovereignty in place of the existing doctrine of parliamentary sovereignty. The latter has taken us a long way in extricating us from the successive eras of feudal monarchy, Henrician despotism, and botched Stuart absolutism to the calmer waters of parliamentary representation (though the ruling monarch, in theory at least, continues to hold a measure of power over Parliament). From a practical point of view, parliamentary sovereignty works best when the constitution is balanced and where none of the organs of government is dominant. This was the position in the nineteenth century. But things changed with the weakening of the House of Lords by the Parliament Acts of 1911 and 1949 and by the growth of the modern party system[12] and associated increase in executive power. Parliamentary sovereignty, in constitutional terms, should be viewed as but one stage in the course of society's political development, rather than as a necessary end-point.

[12] See The Hon Mr Justice Beatson, 'Reforming an Unwritten Constitution', 31st Blackstone Lecture (2010) 126 *Law Quarterly Review* 48. Tellingly, the lecture cites Andrew Adonis, *Making Aristocracy Work: The Peerage and the Political System in Britain 1884–1914* (Oxford, Oxford University Press, 1993) 278: 'Only once since the Napoleonic wars – the great Reform Act of 1832 – has far reaching constitutional change come as a direct response to popular pressure …'.

Traditionally it has been argued that the institutions that have developed in the UK over time and that make up most of our unwritten 'constitution' reflect, in part, a characteristic British pragmatism. They have evolved organically and adapted to circumstances. In that way we have been able to distance ourselves from the revolution and social unrest that characterises our European neighbours' constitutional histories. After a fashion, our constitution – haphazard as it may be – 'works'. To move from an informal arrangement of that kind to a formal written constitution, itself usually the product of a crisis in national affairs, may seem at best pointless and at worst threatening.

In contrast, implicit in the thesis presented here is that, with a written constitution defining our overarching values, we would become a more responsible, more accountable society, and that with greater citizen involvement in the form of a Citizens' Branch of government, we would also be more inclusive. Despite this, I should make it clear that I do not advocate that 'the people' should simply be able to vote on anything and everything affecting the process of government. That would be unrealistic. Any constitution needs checks and balances to maintain an equilibrium in which government can operate under the rule of law. An unrestrained system of public voting would not provide this and would itself have to be tempered to avoid the risk of instability caused by swings in popular sentiment. My argument is that the constitutional principles that govern our informal, unwritten constitution have themselves got out of control and have ceased to provide the best mechanism for good and effective government.

If the changes suggested in this book are to escape the fate of merely providing food for thought at middle-class dinner parties, the ideas of 'responsibility, 'accountability' and 'inclusiveness' (popular political buzzwords, often used to secure electoral advantage) need to be made real – things to which people as a whole can relate on a personal level. We are not individually *responsible* if we play no part in political decisions. MPs are not *accountable* if they can simply hide behind the notion of parliamentary sovereignty to resist controls over their actions or to prevent us having at least a measure of control over the other ways in which they exercise power. As a society we are not *inclusive* if we break off into atomistic groups (environmentalists, religious fundamentalists, bankers etc) driven to different degrees of opposition (depending on the group) by herd instinct and self-interest.

A written constitution would not immediately change these things, but it would contribute to improving them by providing the people with more say in how they are governed and thus mitigate against the apathy and indifference that fester like a cancer in British politics. A blueprint for constitutional change of the kind found in a written constitution could be a first step towards a greater awareness of our system of government. If general education in schools and universities included a consideration of the principles underlying a written constitution they could become embedded in the nation's culture and thus raise awareness. This would contribute to ensuring the adherence to proper standards by public office-holders, thus replacing the current position whereby changes only come about as the result of outrage at the inappropriate behaviour of parliamentarians or deployment of parliamentary resources. A written constitution of which the general population is aware helps to embed standards of conduct among public figures.

We are not an oppressed society like those in South Africa or India who at the time that they had to devise their own written constitutions started more or less from scratch. In contrast Britain has evolved a form of democracy which encompasses many ancient traditions and institutions but these have been increasingly challenged in recent years and without a written constitution they can be slowly eroded and need to be protected. When complacency exists in which our freedoms are taken for granted they can be at most risk of being sacrificed. A political climate in which things seem to work and so is tolerated can quickly become hostile and threatening, encroaching on freedoms and leaving the population powerless to resist, such as occurred when Hitler converted Germany into a legal dictatorship by introducing the Enabling Act in 1933. Today it might be prolonged detention of terror suspects without charge or draconian libel laws – which do not affect most people. But tomorrow it could be wholesale invasion of our privacy (a national DNA database) or abandonment of the rule of law[13] as we have come to recognise it, for example, scrapping the presumption of innocence in criminal trials.

A written constitution would set the parameters of the function of each organ of government which would ensure a balance of power and thus temper any tendency to corruption afforded by the excessive power of any single government entity. The theory of parliamentary sovereignty in the UK, on the other hand, entails a claim to absolute power on the part of Parliament. The logic of those who defend it is to endorse the position whereby parliamentarians are free to make or unmake any laws they wish.

A government could use this power if elected with a large majority to take the first steps towards a true dictatorship, witness Boris Johnson's attempts to reduce scrutiny of his planned changes to the civil service and Parliament after winning a landslide 80 seat majority in the 2019 election. This power can also be extended to the personal gains of MPs. For example, some claim that to introduce an external monitoring system to oversee MPs' expenses would involve their surrendering control and thus violate parliamentary sovereignty.

[13] It is impossible to give any comprehensive definition of the term 'rule of law'. In his 2006 Sir David Williams Lecture titled 'The Rule of Law' (2007) 66 *Cambridge Law Journal* 67 Lord Bingham suggested that the term connotes that 'all persons and authorities within the state, whether public or private, should be bound by and entitled to the benefit of laws publicly and prospectively promulgated and publicly administered in the courts'. For a further definition of 'the rule of law' see T Bingham, *The Rule of Law* (London, Penguin, 2011).

The same logic would resist a UK Supreme Court having stronger powers to protect fundamental rights on the basis that this would offend parliamentary sovereignty by offering 'its own subtle challenges to constitutional norms'.[14]

The British Constitution is based on power: at first royal power, then the power of Parliament and then the power of the executive. In most civilised Western nations that power imbalance has been cured by a written constitution. The constitution in written form assists in the stabilisation of the power impulse because it means that those carrying out functions under the constitution have a standard to reach which is enforced by an independent judiciary. It also helps to entrench the fundamental values of a society which should be upheld regardless of the party or government in power. These can be agreed and thought out in advance rather than being a knee-jerk reaction to events.

However, in the UK, the nations that drafted constitutions for much of the world to follow, the power imbalance has continued. In the UK it is Parliament (and in reality the executive) who dictate through the principle of parliamentary sovereignty the laws that must be followed and if another Parliament changes those laws they replace the old laws. Of course, the people can throw out the rascals every five years or so but those rascals have only been replaced by other rascals. Under parliamentary sovereignty they could change the nature of elections themselves. David Cameron, for example, introduced the Fixed-term Parliaments Act 2011, an Act which was subsequently repealed by the Dissolution and Calling of Parliament Act 2022. The basic problem is one of standards. The two major parties have ruled now for just over a century and in that time – in the absence of a higher threshold upheld by a written constitution – there is no benchmark. Thus, for the most part, problems are only addressed retrospectively. The sole standard is what will get an individual elected.

Lord Sumption in his Reith Lectures (2019) argues that the answer to this is to rely on the political process rather than the legalistive process because (see his fifth lecture):[15]

> … it must, I suggest, be obvious that adopting a written constitution to serve as our supreme law will not make any difference. It will simply produce a partial shift of power from an elective and removable aristocracy of knowledge to a core of professional judges which is just as remote, less representative and neither elective nor removable.

But Jonathan Sumption's analysis in the same lecture showed the weakness of that view. To demonstrate the fickleness of politicians to obtain power he used as an example the Liberal Democrats abandonment of its published policy on charging for university fees. In other words he is relying for his vision on the very unreliability of politicians who are swayed by the electorate in the political process.

[14] Colin Kidd, 'The Irresistible Itch' *London Review of Books*, 3 December 2009.
[15] Lord Sumption *Shifting the Foundations* Lecture delivered on 22 June 2019.

He also mischaracterises a democracy under a written constitution because in a constitution which has been drafted to include popular participation, a shift of power to the people would occur and so mitigate against a shift of power to the judges.

In addition, I would argue that an independent judiciary responsible for enforcing violations of the constitution is the strongest way of protecting our democracy. Politicians, once in office, have the strongest reasons for not being over-protective of democracy. 'Power tends to corrupt and absolute power corrupts absolutely'.[16] Although absolute power may not yet be the hallmark of our constitutional legacy, the power implicit, as a result of parliamentary sovereignty, is constantly seeking to rear its head. The conduct of MPs and peers has been the subject of numerous debates and regulation, whereas the conduct of senior judges has rarely surfaced. A specifically trained cadre of judges, secure in their office, would be best placed to make an impartial assessment of failure to comply with issues arising from a predetermined constitution rather than a host of politicians who depend for their position on popular support from the electorate.

III. POWER TO THE PEOPLE

In his penetrating nineteenth-century study of American society, *Democracy in America*, Alexis de Tocqueville complained that, in reality, Britain had no constitution.[17] He was wrong. For centuries Britain has had an uncodified constitution set out in numerous documents, but it is old-fashioned and top-down.

Nearly all democratic states have a *written* (in the sense of a properly codified) constitution. Only Israel and New Zealand join us in relying on a nebulous body of rules, some contained in Acts of Parliament, some in constitutional conventions, others scattered around in the most diverse sources. In addition, the British constitution is underpinned by a doctrine of parliamentary sovereignty, which, I suggest here, should be replaced by constitutional supremacy even though the powers of Parliament itself would, in this draft constitution, be strengthened in relation to executive government to restore the balance between the executive and legislature.

Written constitutions necessarily embody the idea of constitutional supremacy, which is something quite different from parliamentary sovereignty and usually comes from the people. The term *constitutional supremacy* (interchangeable, in the sense intended here, with *popular sovereignty*) expresses the idea that the constitution is the supreme law of the land, is derived from

[16] Lord Acton in a letter to Bishop Mandell Creighton in 1887.

[17] Alexis de Tocqueville, *Democracy in America* (Harmondsworth, Penguin Classics, 2003) vol 1 pt 1 ch 6, 118.

the people, and cannot, at least in its fundamental features, be altered save (if at all) by wide popular consent. This means that in principle the constitution 'trumps' any laws that are inconsistent with it. A constitution in this sense has the effect of *entrenching* its provisions so that they cannot simply be repealed by Parliament, as happens with existing laws under the current system. This general constitutional principle, adopted by almost all democratic states, is one that I argue should now be established in the UK in place of parliamentary sovereignty.

Before moving to popular sovereignty's antithesis – parliamentary sovereignty – I should make clear what I do not include as part of 'popular sovereignty' in the context of a written constitution. I am not advocating mere plebiscitary consent by majority vote without controls in the form of constitutional checks or balances. Although the exact nature of such controls will need to be debated, there are obvious dangers in simply leaving the fundamentals of political decision-making to a popular vote.

A written constitution must contain control mechanisms that ensure a broad separation of effective power among the institutions of government. The nature of those control mechanisms should not, I believe, be decided by a simple majority vote; if it were, there could be no practical guarantee that a constitutional settlement was being devised that would best protect minority interests and secure an enduring moral and ethical dimension to our constitutional arrangements.[18] Both the initial control mechanisms and provisions for amendment that are laid out here are based on the premise that there are fundamental values in a western liberal democracy that need to be entrenched. They include, but are not limited to, the rule *of* law (as opposed to rule *by* law) and respect for and enforcement of fundamental rights. These values form the fabric of our democratic society which is organised according to due process and respects all individuals.

None of this, however, is incompatible with a greatly enhanced role for public participation in deciding how we are governed, nor – subject to the necessary constitutional checks and balances – to the explicit recognition that power is conferred by the people on government rather than government simply imposing its authority on the people.

If this form of constitutional supremacy replaced parliamentary sovereignty, the focus would (because a written constitution would compel greater institutional balance) shift – a shift that would be welcome, marking a true separation of powers as the organising constitutional principle used to explain the division of power among the various branches of government. Without such a constitution, we have, as Bagehot recognised,[19] not a *separation* of powers in the UK but a *fusion* of powers, by which, in reality, the executive – essentially selected by the Prime Minister from the governing political party in

[18] Unrestrained decision-making by 'the people' could otherwise be used to subvert democracy and promote extremism if a cause were sufficiently populist in nature.

[19] Walter Bagehot, *The English Constitution* (Oxford, Oxford University Press, 2009) 11.

Parliament – controls Parliament. The move towards increased separation of powers would involve both strengthening Parliament in its relations with executive government and providing enhanced checks from a stronger judiciary, as well as from a new Citizens' Branch of the constitution.

Parliamentary sovereignty is quite different. In theory, at least, it admits of no superior authority and does not achieve a true separation of powers. A written constitution that retained parliamentary sovereignty could be repealed by Parliament at any time. This is because the idea underpinning parliamentary sovereignty, as articulated most clearly by the great Victorian lawyer AV Dicey,[20] is that Parliament can make (and change at any time) whatever laws it pleases. This would appear to be the position however unjust, however arbitrary those laws may be. It is at both first and second sight terrifying. Its origins are controversial and the source of its supposed authority is wholly unclear. Its consequences in the twenty-first century are, anyway, belied by the political reality that it is not Parliament (one part of which – the House of Lords – is still wholly unelected[21]) but, with the rise of the first-past-the-post electoral system, executive government (and – to some extent included in that – unelected special advisers) which holds real and potentially arbitrary power. A former Lord Chancellor, Lord Hailsham, accurately stigmatised this in his celebrated 1976 Dimbleby Lecture as *elective dictatorship*.

Any idea of *legislative* sovereignty – whether that of Parliament or executive government – is at odds with the notion of *constitutional* supremacy, which provides by far the strongest foundation for representative democracy. Put shortly, constitutional supremacy makes it clear that power resides in the people and that they have delegated a defined measure of that power to government. This type of popular sovereignty is usually forgotten in this country until elections are imminent. Exceptionally, in the wake of the mistrust engendered by the expenses furore in 2009, it was given voice by several leading politicians, who suggested that, as Parliament's role is to represent the people, more power should be given to the people.[22]

In fact, the slogan *Power to the People* is probably better known as the title of a John Lennon song than as a real political aspiration in Britain. Yet it is the logical result of representative government. As will be suggested later, it is not merely an aspiration but represents the essence of modern constitutionalism. It was also, for the briefest of periods, the express basis on which we were governed.

[20] See AV Dicey, *Introduction to the Study of the Law of the Constitution* (London, Macmillan, 1855). Although a strong advocate of parliamentary sovereignty, it is worth recording that Dicey's opposition to Home Rule for Ireland led him to support the use of the referendum (though not until the eighth edition of his magisterial work and then only in the Introduction).

[21] Only the 'new' hereditary peers are elected from among their dwindling number. But, of course, they were never elected in the first place. The new Labour Government promises to reform the 92 hereditary peers by making them forgo the right to vote and sit in the House of Lords.

[22] See eg David Cameron, 'Giving Power Back to the People' (speech, Imperial College London, 25 June 2009).

The concept of constitutional supremacy is still-born if parliamentary sovereignty survives. It is therefore extremely odd that popular sovereignty is often suggested as a justification for parliamentary sovereignty when it is actually its antithesis.

In approaching constitutional reform, the first task is to show that there is nothing axiomatic in the idea that Parliament can do anything it chooses; nor is it an expression of democratic choice. The seeds of parliamentary sovereignty were sown when the sovereignty of the 'King in Parliament' was established in the 1530s with savage penalties for those who demurred. In more recent times, parliamentary sovereignty has gained passive acceptance as the prevailing constitutional orthodoxy. And this provides the foundation of the unwritten constitution that we currently have. But unlike the written constitutions that Britain has been instrumental in giving to many other countries, in the UK the principles have never been thought through nor have they been endorsed by the people. Crucially, therefore, parliamentary sovereignty has nothing whatsoever to do with an expression of popular sovereignty and cannot be justified on that basis.

Under our present system there is a token gesture to democracy in that MPs are elected at general elections on manifestos which the incumbent government has no duty to abide by. During the course of each Parliament between elections there is nothing self-evidently true in the idea that Parliament has an unfettered right to govern us or to make any laws it chooses and impose them on the people. To quote again from Thomas Paine's *Rights of Man*:

> Sovereignty, as a matter of right, appertains to the Nation only, and not to any individual; and a Nation has at all times an inherent indefeasible right to abolish any form of Government it finds inconvenient, and establish such as accords with its interest, disposition and happiness.[23]

We have accepted for too long that the Emperor is wearing clothes, when the truth is otherwise.

IV. POWER-SUSTAINING DEVICES

Laws and government did not, in general, spring up because of any social contract or collective agreement. Political theories that postulate such models are not usually describing an asserted historical event; rather, they are seeking to justify a set of political arrangements by reference to normative ideas. Thus, for example, John Rawls[24] relies on a social contract which is negotiated under a 'veil of ignorance' under which the individuals negotiating the contract do not know what their position in society – stemming from the terms of the

[23] Paine (n 1) 193.
[24] John Rawls, *A Theory of Justice* (Oxford, Oxford University Press, 1999).

contract – will be. Rawls is not suggesting that such a contract was ever made. It is a purely hypothetical construct designed to suggest a formulation for the content of justice.

Political theories of this kind are, though, divorced from the reality of government. At best they serve as myths to suggest how we should live, rather than reflecting how we actually live.

A different type of myth or social narrative lies in using ideas to legitimate the existing power of government. Governments and the institutions of government have often originated from the brute fact of plunder and conquest. Those who were stronger ended up as tribal chieftains and later (with the development of the nation state) as monarchs or emperors. Those who lost out were (assuming they were lucky enough to survive) enslaved and made subjects. If those who conquered were to retain power, it was convenient to devise associative ideas that would suggest or reinforce the legitimacy of their authority. This association might be a ritual or a doctrine, or even a symbol. It would, necessarily, change over time but would be extremely potent in particular societies. Examples of such legitimating devices include the crowning of Charlemagne as Emperor by the Pope in AD 800 and notions of the divine right of kings in Europe in the sixteenth century.

In his 1919 Vocation Lectures Max Weber suggested that mechanisms of these kinds were designed solely to legitimate acts of violence,[25] but it is equally possible to view what might be termed *power-sustaining devices* more broadly. Political ideology is strewn with concepts serving the ends of those seeking to exercise power in specific ways. Thatcher's and Blair's use of social narrative (market forces, the third way) to explain the sudden rise of their respective visions of the social good is different in degree but not perhaps in kind from Marx's narrative of the dictatorship of the proletariat.

V. PARLIAMENTARY SOVEREIGNTY

A. The Origins of Parliamentary Sovereignty

Parliamentary sovereignty is, I suggest, such a power-sustaining device which has come to form the bedrock of our political constitution today. Valuable though it has proved in marking a transition from monarchical absolutism to a relatively weak form of democracy, it should reflect the middle rather than the end of the constitutional story. In order to see its weaknesses, we need to understand its origins.

[25] Max Weber, *The Vocation Lectures: Science as a Vocation, Politics as a Vocation* (Indianapolis, Hackett, 2004).

The result of the conflict between the common law and the royal prerogative (judge-made law against king-made law) with the judges emerging victorious is usually portrayed as Britain's gift to the civilised world – constitutional liberty.[26] Viewed in this light, the story is one of glowing triumphalism. There is, I suggest, another more realistic way of analysing how we have come to be where we are.

Anglo-Saxon England was in some respects a brutal and bloody place. It was a world in which a triumvirate of superstition, magic and religion held sway.[27] There were published laws, but they were made by the king and there was, save for the reciprocity intrinsic in feudalism, no limit to his power. This remained the position for several hundred years.

Then attempts were made to curb the powers of the king or queen. Magna Carta (1215) is often regarded as our first constitutional document. But in truth, it was the result of a stand-off between King John and his rebellious barons. Its contents were rooted in a specific historical conflict and, side by side with a few general sound-bites about justice being neither denied nor delayed, were many more detailed clauses dealing with a number of vested interests such as those of the barons themselves and the Church.

To view Magna Carta as our first charter of rights is therefore fundamentally misleading (although it did make reference to limited rights which would later be used in the development of more general theories of rights in Britain). However, its undoubted significance lies in the fact that it was the product of historical events which made it necessary to find new ways of explaining governmental power. For the first time the power of the king had been directly challenged. This meant that, although the source of the concessions made in Magna Carta came from the king and could in theory be withdrawn, absolutist notions of kingship had to give way to different power-sustaining devices.

Over the course of the next several hundred years there evolved our current power-sustaining device – the doctrine of parliamentary sovereignty. Before discussing its defects it is important to trace the main elements in its story. Along the way, this country was given not one but two written constitutions.

Much of the essential story of the transition from royal to parliamentary power evolved with attempts by the barons to curb royal power. In the mid-thirteenth century Simon de Montfort led the baronial opposition to Henry III and in the Provisions of Oxford (1258) obliged the king to agree to various terms

[26] See, generally, Peter Kellner, *Democracy: 1,000 Years in Pursuit of British Liberty* (Edinburgh, Mainstream, 2009). The Foreword by John Humphreys is worth reading as a model of the traditional and somewhat self-satisfied take on the merits of our current constitutional arrangements with no hint that they might be less than adequate. It was, however, written before the expenses scandal and might not be drafted in the same way now.

[27] This is to over-simplify. Many of the Anglo-Saxon kings, such as Athelstan and Edgar, were enlightened men who had a strong sense of ruling under 'God'.

and cooperate with a Council of Fifteen. Just a few years later, in 1264, the first rudimentary Parliament was held and (albeit sporadically) many others followed. They were not parliaments as we know them today and, at least to start with, there was not even a suggestion that they were there to represent the people. Nonetheless, even though they were the King's Parliament and therefore, in one sense, a manifestation of royal authority, they also acted increasingly as a curb on royal power.

From about the middle of the fourteenth century claims to absolutist monarchy were being gradually whittled away. As early as 1341 a statute made during the reign of Edward III required annual meetings of Parliament. In 1471 Sir John Fortescue, a former Chief Justice of the Court of King's Bench, published *The Difference between an Absolute and Limited Monarchy as it more particularly regards the English Constitution*[28] in which he extolled the virtues of limited monarchy in England as compared with the absolute power held by the French kings.

However, the curbs on royal power until the seventeenth century were limited. It was not until the accession of James I that the theory became divisive in competing claims for power. James lacked the political skill to avoid conflict with his noblemen. He asserted his authority by resurrecting the doctrine of the divine right of kings. It drove him into conflict with Sir Edward Coke, the supreme lawyer and judge (Lord Chief Justice) of the day.

Coke sided with the Parliamentarians: first by upholding the supremacy of the common law over the royal prerogative; second by discovering a source of legal constraint over the king in Magna Carta; and finally by arguably single-handedly inventing the doctrine of parliamentary sovereignty. He observed in his *Institutes* (1644)[29] that Parliament possessed a 'transcendent and abundant' authority which could not be 'confined … within any bounds'.[30] This short statement has been used to buttress the notion of parliamentary sovereignty ever since.

Later, the resulting increased confidence of Parliamentarians led them to confront Charles I following growing dissatisfaction with his autocratic behaviour. This led to a bloody civil war after which Charles was removed from power and executed in January 1649. Oliver Cromwell then introduced a republic and was responsible for Britain's first written constitution.

[28] It was later published as *The Governance of England*.

[29] For example, his judgment in *Dr Bonham's Case* (1610) suggested that the common law could control Acts of Parliament and render them void.

[30] *The Fourth Part of the Institutes of the Laws of England: Concerning the Jurisdiction of the Courts* (London, W Clarke & Sons, 1817) 36.

B. Cromwell and the Two Written Constitutions

It comes as a surprise to many to learn that we have already had two written constitutions in this country.[31] We are surprised because we have grown so used to swallowing the comfort fodder which tells us that the merits of our informal constitutional arrangements are to be preferred to a codified constitution such as that adopted in the US. The British Constitution, as JAG Griffith once suggested with characteristic realism,[32] is 'what happens'.

Curiously, it occurs to few to look back – only a little over 350 years – to the world's first written constitution, which was actually British. In 1653 the Instrument of Government established Cromwell as Lord Protector of the Commonwealth of England, Scotland and Ireland (on an elective rather than hereditary basis). Power was vested in the Lord Protector, who was assisted by a Council (of between 13 and 21). The Instrument made provision for a triennial Parliament which would sit for five months (Article X provided for 400 persons to be chosen 'within England, Wales, the Isles of Jersey, Guernsey and the town of Berwick-upon-Tweed' and 30 each for Scotland and Ireland as well as a property-based franchise). The Instrument of Government set out a short but comprehensive written framework for how Britain was to be governed, which (somewhat obscurely) separated legislative and executive power. Crucially, it substituted for the authority of the King in Parliament that of the people. Article I expressly provided that supreme authority resided not only in the Lord Protector but also in 'the people assembled in Parliament'.

These were paradigm shifts which – had they lasted – would have led to popular sovereignty as it is preached but not practised today. As mentioned earlier, popular sovereignty is a political theory which embraces the notion that power resides in the people but the people delegate power to a government in order to avoid confronting the practical impossibility of making and enforcing laws themselves.

The Instrument of Government did not give voice to the idea of popular sovereignty by accident. In late 1647, in similar fashion to the way the US Declaration of Independence came to be drafted a century or so later, a series of extended debates on England's constitutional future (the Putney debates) took place, during which, amongst other profound topics, the concept of popular sovereignty and the idea of replacing the monarchy were analysed by leading players, rather in the manner of a modern constitutional convention of the good and the great.

[31] Our second Constitution was called the Humble Petition and Advice and was drawn up in 1657 to replace the Instrument of Government. It was an attempt to limit Cromwell's power and is not relevant to the argument I am advancing here.

[32] JAG Griffith, 'The Political Constitution' (1979) 42 *Modern Law Review* 1, 19.

In Cromwell's time, then, popular sovereignty was becoming a strong political ideology.[33] Had it taken root we might have been living in a very different society today, with a properly codified written constitution. Instead, we are governed by reference to a constitutional principle – that of parliamentary sovereignty – which is not the product of popular sovereignty and which has never received popular endorsement. Worse still, to the extent that Parliament is in thrall to the executive, it is *not* in practice sovereign, even if in terms of prevailing constitutional theory it is supposed to be.

C. Restoration of the Monarchy

The potential significance of what followed the execution of King Charles I is skated over in most school history lessons. The usual version has it that, as both the Restoration and so-called Glorious Revolution of 1688 show, the execution of Charles I by no means heralded the end of faith in the office of king. After a short spell of republicanism with Cromwell (December 1653 to September 1658) the status quo was restored (with the return of the monarch Charles II in 1660) and the new constitution was abandoned. Unlike the radical constitutional revolutions that took place in France and the US in the eighteenth century, the British never witnessed a revolution. What happened instead was the so-called 'bloodless revolution' following Charles II's death in 1685. James II, his successor, was deposed in the Glorious Revolution of 1688 (he tried to impose Catholicism) and William of Orange with his wife, Mary (daughter of James II) became King and Queen in 1689.

It is surprising that so little is made of the fact that in the mid-seventeenth century Britain became a republic and that we had a written constitution which purported to grant legislative power to Parliament from the people. Certainly, the process was incomplete, but a royal (top-down) source of authority was for the first and only time in our history expressly replaced by a popular (bottom-up) one.[34] That could have continued. Indeed, it is how democracy progressed to the next stage in most countries, even if (as in the US and France) it took revolutions to achieve it. It is certainly true that the execution of Charles I dealt at least a temporary body blow to any royal pretensions to absolute power or divine right to rule. But it also resulted in at least the initiation of a process by which power could be transferred to the people. The tearing up of the written constitution and the restoration of royal power in 1660 made it impossible for that process to continue.

[33] It was not, however, the prevailing orthodoxy. Levellers, who espoused popular sovereignty, were themselves viewed as political threats by Cromwell, who was determined not to tolerate Leveller democracy. Poor John Lilburne had his ears nailed to the pillory for such excesses.

[34] It must be conceded that Cromwell himself was constantly improvising between 1649 and 1658 and would have preferred to become king but was deterred from this by the objections of his army.

Whatever its precise origins, the context in which parliamentary sovereignty emerged as a constitutional doctrine was a power struggle between king and Parliament. But the assertion of parliamentary power over the king tells us little about the role of the people in such a constitutional settlement. Importantly, it was not at all obvious at the time that the institution of monarchy would survive and that Britain would cease to be a republic. The events that saw the possibility of a republic vanish were driven more by personality than by anything else. As Jenny Uglow puts it in her study of Charles II:

> [Charles II's] return in May 1660 was a crucial turning point and although the Stuart dynasty would soon lose the crown, the way that Charles played his hand is part of the reason that Britain is still a monarchy today: we call the Commonwealth and Protectorate the 'Interregnum', as if it was a gap in an accepted sequence.[35]

Once royal power was restored it was inescapable that, as a matter of constitutional theory, the king was the ultimate source of authority. We were no longer a republic.

However, following the execution of Charles I the parliamentary cause gradually evolved over the next few centuries into the popular model of representative democracy we enjoy today. James II was deposed because his frequent attempts to prorogue Parliament were seen as an attempt to reintroduce Catholicism to an increasingly Anglican country. His successors, William III and Mary II, became joint monarchs as the result of an invitation from Parliament. They could be called the first constitutional monarchs. They were subject to the provision of the Bill of Rights 1689 and the Act of Settlement 1701, thus reinforcing Coke's earlier principle of parliamentary sovereignty. Just as Magna Carta was a mixed bag of concessions granted by the Crown, so too was the Bill of Rights despite its references to an elected Parliament and despite the increasing power of that Parliament.

The most radical idea of the 1688 Revolution was a contract between ruler and people; a fundamental denial of the Stuart ideology of the divine right of kings/queens to rule. It was a contract founded on the presumption that the people no longer wished to be subjected to arbitrary rule by a king/queen and did not want future monarchs to undermine the Anglican establishment. This development of the doctrine of parliamentary sovereignty led the nineteenth-century lawyer, AV Dicey, to say that Parliament had the power to make any law it wishes. It could not be overridden by anybody and could not bind its successors nor be bound by its predecessors.

D. Recent Developments in Parliamentary Sovereignty

This constitutional arrangement survived, indeed flourished, for several centuries. Initially, parliamentary sovereignty was welcomed as a relief from

[35] Jenny Uglow, *A Gambling Man* (London, Faber and Faber, 2009) 2.

despotic rule. The despotism though, simply changed hands. The despotism of the monarch slowly evolved into the despotism of the executive – a latter incarnation of the supremacy of parliament. True, it was it provided a measure of democracy while at the same time retaining parliamentary control. It was significant in the development of empire. Britain drafted constitutions for other countries but those countries were always subject to the power of Britain.

Things changed during the twentieth century. For a little more than three centuries the country had been ruled by the upper classes based on a severely restricted franchise. If the great British success of the nineteenth century was to integrate the middle classes into the parliamentary system, the failure of the twentieth century was the incomplete translation of liberalism into a more democratic culture. For the voice of the constitution remained an essentially upper-class voice – ironic and private. At the beginning of the twentieth century this attitude trickled down to the upper reaches of the middle classes which enabled laws and conventions to be supported at a time when the need for them was fast becoming outmoded. This was especially true by 1928 when the franchise had been extended to all men and women over the age of 21.

By the 1970s two factors exacerbated the need for a revamp of Britain's constitutional arrangements. First, the majority of the population was educated and had become less deferential and fully prepared to self-assert. The second factor was Margaret Thatcher. Mrs Thatcher had little time for the upper classes, which she blamed for the country's moral and economic decline. But the Thatcherite means were crudely economic rather than political. Her policy of the sale of council houses, for example, helped to increase the property-owning class and with it middle-class aspirations and material values.

Mrs Thatcher could not – or refused to – contemplate the link between a liberal constitution and the encouragement it gives to social mobility, for example, by enshrining equal rights which among other things would provide the ground for liberalising the rules for women's access to top jobs. Instead, the freedom given to her by the doctrine of parliamentary sovereignty enabled her to ruthlessly centralise power and decimate competing centres of power such as that traditionally enjoyed by local government. The disadvantages of parliamentary sovereignty when inappropriately applied were beginning to be starkly exposed. John Major's Government (1990–1997) just continued Thatcher's policies.

If the causes of the disease were relatively easy to diagnose, the solution was not. The people could not be de-educated and the Thatcherite revolution seemed permanent. The Blair government in 1997 produced a flurry of constitutional reforms. Among the reforms was a change to the highest court, which became the Supreme Court. It had previously been part of the House of Lords and thus had failed to ensure the separation of the legislature from the judiciary. The revolution was not in the fact of the change in name nor in the change in location (the new Supreme Court operated in the old Middlesex Guildhall situated in Parliament Square) but in the fact that the change removed any confusion over the role of senior judges exercising judicial power unalloyed by the exercise of governmental power when they sat in their role as members of the House of Lords. The impact of the change was cosmetic rather than substantive because it removed any apparent political influence as judges continued to exercise power neutrally on a legal basis.

A more significant area where Blair's government introduced reform was in the matter of devolution. The objectives of devolution and consequent outcome to give more power to the regions of Britain (though not to England) and perhaps ultimately to a form of federalism were never properly considered. This lack of thinking led to the devolved governments of Scotland and Northern Ireland producing unforeseen tensions, leading to a possible disintegration of the UK. For example, Scotland wanted its increased power to enable it to hold an independence referendum. Although Scotland voted to remain in the UK in 2014, Westminster has retained the ultimate authority and denied a further referendum in 2022. The relationship between Northern Ireland and the Irish republic meant that the constitutional arrangements could not be replicated in all the nations of the UK. This was highlighted in the difficulty experienced since the UK left the European Union (EU) when reaching an agreement in relation to the Irish border. Even Wales, the nation thought to have the most to gain from the continuation of the UK, produced a report from the Independent Commission on the Constitutional Future of Wales on 17 January 2024 in which it treats independence as one of the options it faces.

Nor have Tony Blair's successors resolved the issues satisfactorily. Despite Gordon Brown's interest in constitutional matters he was unable to produce much that was effective. One reason is that he had the misfortune to be in office at the time of the MP's expenses scandal in 2009 when it was revealed that many members of both the House of Commons and House of Lords had misused their parliamentary allowances, leading to many resignations and sackings. This caused widespread anger among the UK public and heavily dented public trust in political institutions. Several members (or former members) of the House of Commons and House of Lords were prosecuted and sentenced to terms of imprisonment. The abuses were possible because parliamentary sovereignty meant that there was no oversight of the actions of parliamentarians. In an attempt to end the self-policing of parliamentarians and to monitor their future activities the Independent Parliamentary Standards Authority (IPSA) was created which is responsible for establishing the level of MPs' salaries and expenses and for paying them. IPSA is also entrusted with the task of investigating complaints about MPs' expenses. IPSA is an addition to various other bodies, such as the Parliamentary Commission on Standards and the Independent Complaints Scheme, which have been created over the years to monitor and control the conduct of parliamentarians. However, none of this removes the fact that all of these bodies exist according to the will of Parliament and can be removed by Parliament at any time.

The Conservative and Liberal Democrats coalition government led by David Cameron was the surprising result of the 2010 general election, forming the first peace-time coalition in the UK since the 1930s. Although the coalition achieved nothing in constitutional terms, it did try to reform the voting system. A condition of the Liberal Democrats' participation was a referendum to introduce a form of proportional representation (alternative vote[36]) which would more accurately tie the number of seats in Parliament to the number of votes cast for each party in an election. A referendum was held on 5 May 2011, with 67 per cent of those that voted rejecting the idea.

Movement affecting the constitution did occur in 2016 when, after winning the 2015 general election, the Conservative Government, again led by David Cameron, offered a referendum on the UK's continued membership of the EU. The leave vote won the referendum, contrary to the Government's advice, and this led to Cameron's resignation. This result necessitated a major change to the UK constitution, in that during its EU membership precedence had been given to EU law whereby decisions of UK courts were subject to rulings of the European Court of Justice sitting in Luxembourg.

The manner in which the referendum was held threw up many problems because of a lack of foresight and any written rules or guidelines on how one should be conducted or implemented. Initially, it was a matter of internal Conservative party politics and an attempt by David Cameron to pacify the Eurosceptics on the right of his party. However, it exposed deep-seated attitudes on each side of the argument which split the nation after a close result in the vote. This ushered in a seachange in the way that politics was conducted. Views that had hitherto been regarded as extreme were regularly voiced and were played out on the floor of the House of Commons.

The way in which the referendum was handled, and its aftermath, raised several constitutional issues. First, David Cameron promised voters that the referendum would be binding. This was not something that he could deliver as, under parliamentary sovereignty, only Parliament could pass a law enacting that the result was binding – although, of course, any subsequent Parliament would be free to revoke it. Second, the vote was by a simple majority. This meant that a single vote could have swept the country into leaving the EU and introduced a seismic constitutional upheaval. Third, the Government deliberately shut the door on the need for consensus from the four nations of the UK. The results from the four nations were a divide right down the middle, with England and Wales voting to leave and Scotland and Northern Ireland voting to remain. Fourth, the Government issued an instruction that the civil service could not prepare for Brexit prior to the referendum. Fifth, the method of implementing Brexit was not made clear to the public beforehand. A second referendum on the details of implementation was not offered. All these issues were foreseeable and could have been covered by a written constitution.

Although the leave vote won the referendum, most MPs voted to remain. David Cameron's successor, Theresa May, was left with the task of bringing the

[36] For the pros and cons of a coalition see Vernon Bogdanor, *The Coalition and the Constitution* (Hart, 2010).

Conservative Party together after such a divisive vote. She tried to exercise the executive prerogative by using the increased powers accumulated by successive governments under parliamentary sovereignty to trigger Article 50 of the Treaty on European Union, instead of seeking the approval of Parliament for this route. This action was challenged in the Supreme Court in *Miller (1)*,[37] where it was held that the prerogative could not be used, as EU law was uniquely one of the sources of the British Constitution and therefore the decision had to be approved by Parliament.

After the resignation of Theresa May, Boris Johnson was elected leader of the Tory party and thus because the Conservative party remained in power, he automatically became Prime Minister. He went on to win a landslide victory with a majority of 80 seats in the December 2019 general election based on the campaign slogan, 'Get Brexit Done'. However, there was no plan for how Brexit would be done. This caused frequent rifts within Parliament. Although a charismatic figure, Johnson had little regard for detail or parliamentary convention, which was particularly relevant in his negotiations with Europe over the border with Northern Ireland.

The failure to note the detail on the Brexit negotiations meant that he had signed up to the trade barriers created by the Northern Ireland protocol but 'hoped' that the EU would not 'apply' them. This led to the threat to introduce a doctrine of necessity under the Northern Ireland Protocol Bill. The Government accepted that this would breach international law but claimed that this was essential to enable the country to unilaterally disapply parts of the Protocol. The Northern Ireland Protocol Bill was, in the event, made unnecessary by the Windsor Framework (though the Democratic Unionist Party voted against it) but it created a new version of Parliamentary sovereignty which sought to include breaches of international law within the doctrine.

Another significant convention that Boris Johnson tried to breach was the convention to prorogue Parliament. Prorogation usually occurs at the end of each session of Parliament and the beginning of the next session at the state opening of Parliament. Prorogation is part of the royal prerogative of the monarch exercised on the advice of the Prime Minister according to law. Since 1979 Parliament has been prorogued for a maximum of three weeks, the typical period being 18 days. Johnson's government proposed to trigger a prorogation lasting five weeks, in order to avoid parliamentary debates on Brexit. Queen Elizabeth II, acting on advice from Mr Johnson, authorised prorogation on 28 August 2019. On 24 September of the same year the Supreme Court in the second case of *R (Miller) v The Prime Minister* and in *Cherry v Advocate General for Scotland*[38] ruled unanimously that this issue was outside the powers of the Prime Minister.

[37] *R (on the application of Miller and another) (Respondents) v Secretary of State for Exiting the European Union (Appellant)* [2017] UKSC 5.

[38] *R (Miller) v The Prime Minister* and *Cherry v Advocate General for Scotland* [2019] UKSC 41.

The Supreme Court held that the advice given by Johnson to Her Majesty was both justiciable (that is capable of being adjudicated upon in court) and unlawful. The Court ruled that any prorogation would be unlawful 'if it has the effect of frustrating or preventing, without reasonable justification, the ability of Parliament to carry on its constitutional functions as a legislature'. The Court further ruled that in this instance the prorogation of Parliament did have the effect of frustrating Parliament's constitutional functions. The Court found that the suspension of Parliament in the prelude to the 'fundamental [constitutional] change' of Brexit had an 'extreme' effect on the 'fundamentals of democracy'. The Court also found that the Government had not provided a justification for the intended prorogation, nor for its length or its effect on the requirement for parliamentary scrutiny of any withdrawal agreement under the terms of the European Union (Withdrawal) Act 2018. As a result the Court quashed the relevant Order in Council, which meant that the legal result of the royal proclamation of prorogation had the effect of 'a blank piece of paper'.

Boris Johnson's period in No 10 lasted only three years despite his huge majority because of a perception of his lack of personal integrity and his loose attitude towards rules. The latter was demonstrated by the Owen Paterson affair, where Conservative MPs were ordered by the party whips not to back the all-party standard committee's call for Mr Paterson to be suspended for 30 days – a ban which could have seen him face a recall petition from his constituents. A planned yes-no vote on Mr Paterson's suspension was superseded by Tory MP, Dame Andrea Leadsom's amendment to establish a new Tory-led committee to reconsider both Mr Paterson's case and whether a new standards committee was needed. Backed by Downing Street, Tory MPs were told to vote for the Leadsom amendment. Although the Tories won the vote it was not implemented because Labour, the SNP and Liberal Democrats voted to boycott it, depriving the new panel of any real cross-party authority. In an apparent climb down for a Tory dominated committee to rewrite the conduct rules the Commons leader told MPs that he would now seek cross-party talks on reform. Boris Johnson clearly was prepared to use his large majority to bend the conduct rules laid out in Parliamentary standing orders to suit himself and his friends

Further examples of Johnson's conduct which under a written constitution could have been subject to control with less upheaval are a series of events colloquially known as 'partygate'. They culminated in Johnson being fined for breaching restrictions on social gatherings during the lockdowns imposed during the Covid-19 pandemic. The House of Commons referred him to its Privileges Committee for allegedly misleading Parliament (the Privileges Committee produced a report on 15 June 2023). Sue Gray, appointed separately by Johnson to investigate the affair, wrote in her official report that 'the senior leadership at the centre, both political and official, must bear responsibility'.

The resignation of Deputy Chief Whip, Chris Pincher, and No 10's bungled reaction to it, finally brought the Prime Minister down. Pincher was accused of sexually assaulting two men when he was drunk. Johnson was said to have known about the allegations and to have ignored them when appointing Pincher. This, coming at the end of a series of events which was tearing the Tory party apart, led to the resignation of 31 ministers by 6 July 2022 and ultimately to Johnson's resignation on 7 July 2022.

At present, a change of leader in the majority party in Parliament does not give rise to the need to call a general election. This was highlighted by the fiasco that occurred after Johnson's resignation. A new leader and consequently a new Prime Minister was elected solely by paid-up members of the Conservative party. As membership numbers of parties have declined their members have increasingly comprised hardcore supporters. Liz Truss received 57 per cent of the valid votes cast compared with her rival Rishi Sunak who received 43 per cent of the votes. She lasted just 44 days, making her the shortest-serving Prime Minister in the history of the UK. She was appointed by Queen Elizabeth II on 6 September 2022 (two days before the death of the Queen) and resigned after her chancellor, Kwasi Kwarteng, introduced a 'mini-budget' containing £45bn of unfunded tax cuts, which sent the financial markets into a tailspin.

Rishi Sunak was the fourth Conservative prime minister to be in office without the people being given an opportunity to have a say. Although he and his chancellor Jeremy Hunt helped to restore financial stability to the country by reversing many of Truss's policies, he was not elected by either the membership of the Conservative Party nor by the country at a general election but was appointed by the Tory membership unopposed without a ballot of MPs or party members after Truss resigned. Thus, once more, the British public were ignored in the transfer of power. A written constitution could ensure that the voice of the people is heard by providing for a general election within six months of such a situation arising.

Now that the General Election is over – held on 4 July 2024 – a new Labour Government has been elected. One can only hope that a different attitude to politics will prevail. Despite the constitutional vulnerability in the past decades it is unlikely, though, that Sir Keir Starmer will introduce measures designed to safeguard our constitutional rights. The sad reality is that since the period of Thatcher engineered social dynamics the question has arisen of how this country's constitution can best reflect the needs and aspirations of a modern society and if so what is the best way of ensuring this actually happens.

VI. NO-ONE EVER VOTED FOR PARLIAMENTARY SOVEREIGNTY

It is at precisely this point that we need to pause and ask one of the great 'what ifs?' of history. What if Britain's spell of 'republicanism' had actually taken root?

Theories have a habit of catching fire. They then endure as a means of labelling events and, as I have already suggested in the context of politics, are sometimes used as power-sustaining devices. This is exemplified by the attempt to link parliamentary and popular sovereignty.

There are at least two reasons why it appears that popular sovereignty is used as the basis for propping up parliamentary sovereignty. The first is that without it there would be no obvious *democratic* justification for the assertion of parliamentary sovereignty at all. Put another way, it would raise the question, 'Who gave Parliament authority to legislate as it chose?' – to which there could, without popular consent, be no answer that would withstand democratic scrutiny. As suggested in this section, there has never been any endorsement of the doctrine of parliamentary sovereignty by the people.[39]

The second reason why popular sovereignty is used to defend parliamentary sovereignty is that the idea of consensual endorsement of the Government by the people fits in with the contract-based political theory that developed from the seventeenth century in the ideas of Hobbes, Locke, Rousseau and others. This is not the place for a detailed account of such theories. However, each of them, in their own way, advances a theory of government that presupposes a voluntary cession of rights in exchange for governmental power exercised for the public good – albeit with different views of that aspect of human nature which compels such action. On the basis of such a pact it is an easy (if misplaced) assumption that parliamentary sovereignty represents the fruits of that exchange.

But if there is in fact no popular consent to parliamentary sovereignty, this type of reasoning becomes circular and suffers from the fact (as suggested above) that contract-based theories of government are (save, perhaps, in exceptional cases) hypothetical constructs divorced from the reality of government rather than a description of how governmental power has come to be exercised over time.

The fact that we are allowed to vote at the ballot box for a political party with specific policies is completely different from endorsement by the people of the way in which power may be exercised by any government that is voted in. Thus, the fact that our present electoral system (including the limitation on the powers of the unelected House of Lords) can be traced back to the elections of 1910 and the subsequent Parliament Act of 1911 or the fact that, since 1928, there has been universal adult suffrage is neither here nor there. The simple point is that we have never been invited to vote on whether we should be ruled by a principle of parliamentary sovereignty.

The American colonists looked back to Locke and other radical English thinkers for inspiration when drafting the Declaration of Independence and the US Constitution. They were right to do so. What the proponents of consensus as the underlying basis of government tell us is that popular sovereignty is a necessary rationale for good government. They neither state not imply, however, that a doctrine such as parliamentary sovereignty is in any way to be derived from some form of social contract.

[39] A point implicitly endorsed by Thomas Paine in his *Rights of Man* (n 1) 140: 'The Parliament in England, in both its branches, was erected by patents from the descendants of the Conqueror. The House of Commons did not originate as a matter of right in the people to delegate or elect, but as a grant or boon.' Not only did Parliament not originate from popular election; the proposition that Parliament is sovereign is claimed as a creation of the judges (see below).

It is clear that in England the electoral franchise was not reformed even as a matter of theory until the the Representation of the People Act 1832. The reform itself also needs to be put in perspective. Once the 1832 Act came into force, it had the effect of enfranchising only around one in five *males* (women were still almost a century away from getting the vote on equal terms with men – that only happened with the passing of the Representation of the People Act in 1928). The difficulty, therefore, with seeking to locate a doctrine of parliamentary sovereignty in popular sovereignty is that as we have seen, Sir Edward Coke was bandying the idea around in 1644, nearly two hundred years before the Representation of the People Act 1832, as if it were an axiomatic truth. No-one had ever bothered to seek the endorsement of the people to its establishment.

Since parliamentary sovereignty has never been voted on, neither its origins nor its survival has anything to do with an expression of popular will.[40] As explained above, no solace can be taken in political theorists such as Locke or Rawls who provide at best a general rationale for government rather than any specific doctrinal basis on which the people have consented to be governed.

In reality, a doctrine of parliamentary sovereignty was the reflection of gradual institutional changes[41] that came about as a consequence of the conflict between king and Parliament. This was facilitated by the dissolving of religious or charismatic notions of governmental authority into secular ones,[42] which made it possible for the judges to start setting limits on the scope of royal authority by reference to the superior authority of Parliament. But popular sovereignty has never had anything to do with the origins or continuation of parliamentary sovereignty. We are, therefore, left with a doctrine that is said to underpin our unwritten constitution but which, in fact, lacks any representative democratic foundation.

In the absence of any democratic foundation for the doctrine of parliamentary sovereignty, attempts to justify it must be found elsewhere.

If parliamentary sovereignty is not an expression of the popular will, it can only reflect the claims of an assertive but undemocratic Parliament, as enacted in the Bill of Rights 1689, to legislate as it chose without royal interference.[43] Otherwise it is a creation of the common law by unelected judges.

[40] This is not to say that it would be impossible for profound constitutional change to be foreshadowed in an election manifesto. Even though it served the interests of the executive, the erosion of the House of Lords' power to veto proposed legislation was set out in the Parliament Act 1911. It was a very explicit and radical constitutional change preceded by two general elections in which the proposals were foreshadowed.

[41] Many abstract political ideas appear to develop in this way: see generally Raymond Geuss, *Philosophy and Real Politics* (Princeton NJ, Princeton University Press, 2008).

[42] See eg John Neville Figgis, *The Divine Right of Kings*, 2nd edn (Bristol, Thoemess Press, facsimile (March 1997) of 1914 edition).

[43] A particular historical difficulty arises in relation to Scotland. When the Bill of Rights was enacted in 1689, Scotland had its own distinct Parliament. The Acts of Union were not enacted until 1707, some 18 years later. There is no clear evidence that parliamentary sovereignty was being asserted by the Scottish Parliament.

The latter is indeed what the judges are starting to say. In a House of Lords[44] case, Lord Steyn made these comments:

> The classic account given by Dicey of the doctrine of the supremacy of Parliament, pure and absolute as it was, can now be seen to be out of place in the modern United Kingdom. Nevertheless, the supremacy of Parliament is still the general principle of our constitution. It is a construct of the common law. The judges created this principle. If that is so, it is not unthinkable that circumstances could arise where the courts may have to qualify a principle established on a different hypothesis of constitutionalism.

What Lord Steyn said (and he is not alone)[45] is that parliamentary sovereignty was created by the judges and could as easily be abolished by the judges. This is truly alarming, as it suggests that it is the unelected judges who lay down the ground rules of our constitution.[46]

The suggestion that unelected judges may create new and binding constitutional principles under the umbrella of the common law is as unfathomable in terms of representative democracy as the proposition enshrined in parliamentary sovereignty that Parliament can make and unmake any laws it wants because it is sovereign.

Whether created by the judges or not, parliamentary sovereignty as a doctrine is profoundly undemocratic (because it is divorced from popular sovereignty). If our judges have the power both to invent and to change that principle with a wave of their common law wands this compounds the problem, for in that event all of our constitutional principles are at the mercy of the judges. This is, since we do not elect judges, even less democratic than the assertion of unlimited power by Parliament. Some form of 'countermajoritarian difficulty'[47] cannot ultimately be evaded, in that no power should be unfettered and there must be a need for at least some judicial checks and legal norms if governmental absolutism is to be curbed. However, judges should not have unrestricted freedom to select our constitutional norms as and when they choose.

[44] *Jackson v Attorney-General* [2006] 1 AC 262.

[45] See eg Lord Hope's speech in the same case at para 107; H Woolf, 'Droit Public – English Style' [1995] *Public Law* 57; J Laws, 'Law and Democracy' [1995] *Public Law* 80. Lord Justice Sedley, writing extra-judicially, suggests that 'It is now widely accepted … that the doctrine of parliamentary supremacy is itself an artefact of the common law, growing out of the historic compromise between the three limbs of the crown – legislative, judicial and executive – which was reached in the course of the 17th century and has been developed in modern concepts of the rule of law': Stephen Sedley, 'On the Move' *London Review of Books*, 8 October 2009, 3–5. For a directly contrary view which expressly disagrees with Lord Steyn and Lord Hope, see Tom Bingham, 'The Rule of Law and the Sovereignty of Parliament' (2008) 19(2) *King's Law Journal* 223.

[46] This alarming consequence may also be the position as far as the US Constitution is concerned if Chief Justice Charles Evans Hughes was right when he observed that 'the Constitution is what the judges say it is'.

[47] This phrase was coined by the American scholar Robert Bork to defend the thesis of originalism, which, put shortly, is the notion that, consistent with the requirements of democracy, constitutional adjudication by the judiciary may only take place by reference to the understanding of those who originally drafted the US Constitution.

Constitutionally, we are in a muddle. We claim to be a democracy and yet the touchstone of our constitutional arrangements (parliamentary sovereignty) has no democratic foundation or even clear historical starting point. That does not deprive it of any status as a constitutional principle. Nor does it mean that if it is a sound principle, we should not retain it. But it does mean that we should not be inhibited from trying to find a better principle and one more in tune with the nature of a representative democracy as the starting point for a new constitutional settlement.

But the stumbling block in searching for that settlement may be parliamentary sovereignty itself. Taken at face value, it seems to inhibit any entrenched changes as well as failing to confront the reality of modern politics. I will briefly suggest why.

VII. WHY PARLIAMENTARY SOVEREIGNTY DOESN'T WORK

A codified constitution is one that contains, amongst other features, at least some entrenched provisions of a fundamental kind that are incapable of being changed without invoking a specific amendment procedure set out in the constitution itself.[48]

Taking the US Constitution as an illustration of how popular sovereignty works in practice, the starting point is a formal delegation of power by the people by reference to particular ground rules (the Constitution). This is made clear in the Preamble:

> We the People of the United States, in Order to form a more perfect Union, establish Justice, insure domestic Tranquility, provide for the common defence, promote the general Welfare, and secure the Blessings of Liberty to ourselves and our Posterity, do ordain and establish this Constitution for the United States of America.

There follows a series of articles which lay down both the scope and, as importantly, the limits of legislative, executive and judicial power under the Constitution. Also encompassed in a number of amendments at the end of the main provisions is a Bill of Rights containing important fundamental rights.

This structure exemplifies the essence of most written constitutions. It can immediately be seen that the structure is inconsistent with parliamentary sovereignty in two important respects.

[48] See eg Art V of the US Constitution: 'The Congress, whenever two thirds of both Houses shall deem it necessary, shall propose amendments to this Constitution, or, on the application of the legislatures of two thirds of the several states, shall call a convention for proposing amendments, which, in either case, shall be valid to all intents and purposes, as part of this Constitution, when ratified by the legislatures of three fourths of the several states, or by conventions in three fourths thereof, as the one or the other mode of ratification may be proposed by the Congress; provided that no amendment which may be made prior to the year one thousand eight hundred and eight shall in any manner affect the first and fourth clauses in the ninth section of the first article; and that no state, without its consent, shall be deprived of its equal suffrage in the Senate.'

First, parliamentary sovereignty rejects all constraints on the exercise of legislative power. It follows that no constitutional provision can ever be entrenched because the effect of entrenchment is to fetter Parliament's absolute right to make and unmake laws as it pleases. Second, parliamentary sovereignty is incompatible with popular sovereignty for the reasons already given.

These are insuperable obstacles to constitutional reform only if parliamentary sovereignty is elevated from its true status as a constitutional principle of the moment to one that is treated by those who wield the ultimate source of power (the people) as an immutable yardstick against which all constitutional reform must be assessed. For many hundreds of years we have wrongly treated parliamentary sovereignty as sacrosanct when it is merely a constitutional principle of undemocratic origin which can be changed.

There are several indicators which suggest that – despite the benefits it once had – parliamentary sovereignty is now outmoded as a doctrine. First, even as a concept it threatens to obstruct, and certainly does not facilitate, important national changes.[49] Second, because of the dominance of the two major parties, not only does parliamentary sovereignty serve no practical purpose, it actually weakens representative democracy by enabling executive government to pass whatever legislation it wishes, often in defiance of the pluralism that should be intrinsic in any democracy. Third, if, as I argue, a written constitution would be a distinct improvement on what we have now, the survival of parliamentary sovereignty is incompatible with a written constitution for the reasons already discussed.[50]

I shall address each of these objections to the retention of parliamentary sovereignty in the paragraphs that follow. When coming to the third reason I will focus on the subsidiary question that is thrown up – is a written constitution better than the system we have?

When a constitutional principle which is designed to enhance legislative supremacy threatens instead to subvert it, something has gone badly wrong. This is certainly what has been happening with parliamentary sovereignty in the context of Europe.

The UK's entry into the EU in 1972[51] was, in all but name, a surrender of parliamentary sovereignty to Brussels. It is no part of my argument here to

[49] In addition to the difficulties encountered in reconciling the idea of parliamentary sovereignty with our membership of the EU (see below), Britain's loss of empire presents further problems. How, for example, could Parliament legitimately pass laws with any effect over any independent Commonwealth country?

[50] This incompatibility can take an extreme form. It is sometimes suggested that parliamentary sovereignty cannot be 'repealed' by Act of Parliament because, by its very nature, Parliament cannot legislate to destroy its own legislative competence. If correct, that would prevent any written constitution from ever being drawn up. But the fallacy is to treat parliamentary sovereignty as binding merely because of its own precepts. For an illuminating discussion of the academic issues see Michael Gordon, 'The Conceptual Foundations of Parliamentary Sovereignty: Reconsidering Jennings and Wade' [2009] *Public Law* 519.

[51] Brexit was on 31 January 2020.

debate the pros and cons of joining Europe. Whatever the merits or demerits of the decision, it was what the Government of the day wanted to do. The difficulty, as many opponents perceived, was that joining Europe meant that the EU institutions would control what future laws Parliament could enact; this was a direct affront to parliamentary sovereignty.

Following the enactment of the European Communities Act 1972, Parliament had no legislative power to do anything it wanted if it conflicted with EU law, *unless it pulled out of Europe*. By the very fact of doing what it wanted in joining Europe, legal constraints were placed on Parliament's own sovereignty in the future because in legal terms the EU's institutions pulled the strings. This change was the automatic result of the doctrine of the supremacy of EU law as laid down by the European Court of Justice in Luxembourg (a court whose rulings the UK courts were bound to follow during UK membership). It means that EU law always prevails over inconsistent national law and that the UK must always prefer and apply EU law even when it conflicts with national law. As a principle, EU legal supremacy is unequivocal and unyielding. In the words of one commentator, it has the effect that 'the most minor piece of technical Community legislation ranks above the most cherished constitutional norm'.[52]

A graphic illustration of EU law's supremacy over parliamentary sovereignty[53] was afforded by a case in the courts called *Factortame*.[54] At stake was the constitutionality of a law passed by Parliament which prevented foreign-owned vessels from fishing in British waters (the Merchant Shipping Act 1988). Before our entry into the EU, parliamentary sovereignty would have made it impossible for a law enacted by Parliament to be the subject of challenge in a domestic court. But the legality of a national law – the Merchant Shipping Act – was ultimately challenged before the European Court of Justice in Luxembourg and was held by that court to be materially incompatible with EU law. The result was that the House of Lords was required to dis-apply it even though Parliament had enacted it.

Unsurprisingly, attempts have been made to get round what is an insurmountable problem. For example, it has been suggested that Parliament can, if it so chooses, limit its own sovereignty. But this contradicts the essence of parliamentary sovereignty, which is that Parliament can make and *unmake* whatever laws it chooses. What happens therefore if at some hypothetical future point

[52] S Weatherill, *Law and Integration in the European Union* (Oxford, Oxford University Press, 1995) 106.

[53] The extent to which joining the EU involved loss of sovereignty was not stressed at the time of the UK's entry, but the legal position was acknowledged in July 1990 by Hoffmann J: 'The EEC Treaty is the supreme law of this country, taking precedence over Acts of Parliament. Our entry into the European Economic Community meant that (subject to our undoubted but probably theoretical right to withdraw from the Community altogether) Parliament surrendered its sovereign right to legislate contrary to the provisions of the Treaty on the matters of social and economic policy which it regulated. The entry into the Community was in itself a high act of social and economic policy, by which the partial surrender of sovereignty was seen as more than compensated by the advantages of membership.' *Stoke-on-Trent City Council v B & Q plc* [1991] Ch 48.

[54] *R v Secretary of State for Transport, ex p Factortame* [1991] 1 AC 603.

(hypothetical because the UK has chosen to leave the EU) Parliament wished to legislate contrary to EU law? Plainly it could not do so while we remained a member of the EU. It would not have had power to do so, because the courts would be bound to dis-apply such a law. This is inconsistent with the notion of the unfettered constitutional freedom of Parliament, as expounded by Dicey, not only to make laws but also to unmake them at any time.

The ratification of the Lisbon Treaty, which came into force on 1 December 2009, illustrates the impotence of parliamentary sovereignty when opposed by the superior might of EU law.[55] David Cameron was thought to have offered a 'cast iron guarantee' to hold a referendum on the Lisbon Treaty. But this 'guarantee' could never be honoured once Lisbon had been ratified by all Member States (as it was once the Czech Republic's President Klaus signed up to it). It then became part of EU law and, as such, superior to all national law (including the outcome of any national referendum). Without pulling out of Europe, David Cameron (whose fault is not lack of integrity but lack of knowledge of EU law) could no more honour his 'guarantee' than he could commit his party to pulling out of Europe.

In the wake of Lisbon, the European Union Amendment Act 2011 (now repealed) was passed. This Act required that any future amendment of the Treaty on European Union or the Treaty on the Functioning of the European Union made by treaty (and any use of a passerelle provision) be approved by an Act of Parliament and that a referendum must be held in certain specific cases. To the extent that the proposed Sovereignty Amendment Act requires a people's mandate before new far-reaching international obligations are entered into *which are not themselves required by EU law* it is difficult to fault. But there is a danger in confusing that over which Parliament retains legitimate control with the assertion that parliamentary sovereignty could have any superiority over EU law while we remained a member of the EU. The following media report, referring to the Conservative proposal for an Amendment Act (telling in its reference to a written constitution), illustrates the scope for possible confusion:

> 'Unlike many other European countries, Britain does not have a written constitution,' said Mr Cameron. 'Given the increasing amount of EU law with which we have to deal, we would amend the law … to make it explicit that ultimately Britain's parliament is sovereign.[56]

It was, in fact, fear of usurpation of parliamentary sovereignty that prevented earlier incorporation of the European Convention on Human Rights (ECHR),

[55] See Christopher Booker, 'The End of the Great Deception' *Sunday Telegraph*, 8 November 2009. It is true that the UK had negotiated certain opt-outs from the Lisbon Treaty. Their legal effect was not always clear. But an opt-out is weaker than a veto and, in any case, the negotiation of an opt-out has no relevance to the impotence of parliamentary sovereignty once confronted with the requirements of an existing treaty obligation governed by EU law after it has been entered into. In particular, the opt-outs did not in any meaningful sense mean that British law overrode EU law.

[56] *Daily Telegraph*, 8 November 2009.

which guaranteed the most elementary of human rights, into national law. The ECHR was drafted as long ago as 1950 and was ratified by the UK in 1951. But it remained an international treaty that had not been incorporated into national law by Act of Parliament and was therefore not enforceable in the UK's courts. It was not until 2 October 2000, with the passing of the Human Rights Act 1998, that the ECHR was, in substance, incorporated into national law.

Despite the backing of the judges who had been informally lobbying for incorporation for many years, a draft human rights bill introduced by Lord Lester of Herne Hill fell by the wayside in 1995. The fear was that a home-grown Bill of Rights would allow judges to strike down legislation as unconstitutional if it offended against fundamental rights.[57] This could not, it was argued, be reconciled with parliamentary sovereignty.

The Human Rights Act 1998 tries to square the circle by, in essence, incorporating the ECHR into domestic law but then permitting primary legislation which breaches the ECHR to remain on the statute book with full legal validity, leaving it to Parliament to change the law only if it wishes to do so.[58]

These contortions grapple with monsters that need not exist. The slogan 'Bringing Rights Home' was the name of the consultation document published before the 1997 general election, which advanced the case for the Human Rights Act. But a statute does not bring rights home in any meaningful sense if Parliament is free, with impunity, to breach the very rights that it has introduced.

At best, sustained adherence to the supposed sovereignty of Parliament in the European context produces laws whose effect when they conflict with it must be denied, and 'guarantees' which in those circumstances cannot be honoured, or else the conflict must allow sovereignty to triumph so that the law cannot do what is necessary. This can only produce bad law, even if (as appears to be the case with the Human Rights Act) Parliament complies with rulings of the European Court of Human Rights and changes laws when they offend against fundamental rights.[59]

At worst, though, purely domestic laws left at the mercy of a doctrine of unchecked parliamentary sovereignty may, in theory, be wholly unreasonable or – however fundamental in nature – may be changed at the whim of an incoming government. In a written, properly codified constitution this could not happen because laws would be subject to the constitution.[60]

[57] This fear was apparently shared in Hong Kong by the last Chief Justice under British rule, who warned the Chinese Government that the Hong Kong Bill of Rights would lead to chaos due to judges striking down legislation: see 'Chief's Warning over Hong Kong Bill' *Financial Times*, 19 November 1995.

[58] The country is of course party to the ECHR and nothing in Brexit overrides this.

[59] For an analogue, consider the law on assisted suicide, which, though still a crime (see Suicide Act 1961, s 2), co-exists with the fact that conduct which assists suicide is in some circumstances (clarified by the Director of Public Prosecutions) very unlikely to be prosecuted. The logical position ought surely to be that in those circumstances the law should not stigmatise such conduct as a crime.

[60] It seems distinctly possible that, for example, a Conservative Government would in future seek to repeal the Human Rights Act 1998, replacing it with legislation that emphasises our responsibilities

There is a further practical consequence of retaining parliamentary sovereignty in the UK with its combined brand of first-past-the-post voting and strong party discipline through the whips. Save in a hung Parliament, the majority party controls the House of Commons and usually implements its policies in full without fear of effective parliamentary opposition. It may be, as we are constantly told by the majority parties, that there are some virtues in strong government. But, whatever those virtues may be, strong government is *executive* sovereignty. It is not, even taking into account the independence but relative powerlessness of the unelected House of Lords, a manifestation of the sovereignty of *Parliament*. The two ought not to be confused. Whatever its other demerits, the notion that Parliament is elected to legislate and the executive to govern is one that lends some democratic legitimacy to the organic constitutional arrangements that we have which are, in theory at least, meant to reflect the separation of powers so admired by Montesquieu.

In reality, there is no true separation of powers in the UK. Indeed, it was only in October 2009 that a new Supreme Court was created in order to remedy a different issue over separation of powers – the judiciary, at its highest level (the Law Lords), being part of the legislature (the House of Lords) and entitled to vote on proposed laws.

The vice of executive sovereignty masquerading as parliamentary sovereignty is that an overly strong executive dominating Parliament weakens the pluralism that is intrinsic in representative democracy. It is emphasised that this is not so much a question of extreme policies dividing society; it is more one of policies reflecting the wishes of those in power rather than the wishes of the people.

As is explained more fully in the Notes to the Constitution in Part 2 below, our current political system consists of, in essence, a struggle for power between the two main parties. The minority parties are squeezed out so that they lack any effective representative influence. The Conservative and Labour Parties are engaged not in *representative* politics but in *power* politics. Thus, the major parties may well agree on a number of policies. They may, though, not properly consider a policy – electoral reform being a case in point – which the electorate would almost certainly support.

So, even if – as proved to be the position during the expenses scandal – politicians are forced by the collective public anger at least to be seen to be doing *something*, that something in a first-past-the-post voting system need be very little indeed. This is because the only effective choice that the electorate has at a general election is to vote for one of the two main parties.[61]

rather than our rights. See, for example, the then Secretary of State's (Dominic Raab) attempts to introduce a Bill – The Human Rights Bill – into Parliament that would have violated the Human Rights Act 1998. See, for example, of the many voices of criticism, Professor Mark Elliott 'The UK's (new) Bill of Rights' *Public Law for Everyone*, 22 June 2022. The Bill was abandoned by Liz Truss in September 2022.

[61] It should, however, be noted that in his speech to the Labour Party Conference in 2009 Gordon Brown promised a national referendum should Labour win the 2010 general election on

In all but name, parliamentary sovereignty (because under our modern electoral system it tends to *elective dictatorship*) can wreak havoc on pluralism because, in order to work, pluralism involves choices that must at least be *available*. In modern Britain there simply is no real choice involved in much of what passes as an electoral 'mandate'. Not only may neither main party offer a real choice at all; even if it does, the electorate faces a binary-computer electoral model in which votes are cast for a party rather than for a policy. It follows that voters may agree with some of the policies of one party and some of the policies of another but can only, in the end, vote for one party.

VIII. THE NEED FOR A PUBLIC DEBATE

As explained earlier, parliamentary sovereignty is incompatible with a written constitution derived from the will of the people which imposes legal constraints on each of the institutions of government. Despite this, if a written constitution offered nothing better than the doctrine of parliamentary sovereignty, there would not seem to be much point in jettisoning that doctrine as the basis of our current constitutional arrangements.

If a referendum were to be held offering people the choice between parliamentary sovereignty and a written constitution, it would be meaningful, in constitutional terms, for the people to reject a written constitution and to embrace parliamentary sovereignty.[62] However, that has never happened. The fact that when presented with an electoral choice, the people vote by putting a cross beside a name on their ballot paper does not mean – and cannot be taken to mean – that they have endorsed any underlying principle of parliamentary sovereignty.

Unless, therefore, one subscribes to the view that the people should simply have no choice in the matter, parliamentary sovereignty cannot be defended on the basis of popular sovereignty unless and until the people have voted on it. It is not easy to see how democratic theory sits easily beside a view of parliamentary sovereignty that is not linked in some way to popular sovereignty since, if parliamentary sovereignty is not founded on popular sovereignty, it is founded on no clear constitutional doctrine at all.

The starting point is, therefore, that whether or not parliamentary sovereignty has advantages over a written constitution, the issue should be put to the

whether our current majority vote in constituencies – 'first-past-the-post' – should be replaced by the 'alternative vote'. The nature of alternative vote and other types of electoral system are discussed further in the Notes to the Constitution in Part 2. It should be observed that the Conservative–Liberal coalition did issue a voting referendum the following year, titled the '2011 Alternative Vote Referendum'. The result was a defeat for the advocates of an alternative vote solution.

[62] There would, though, as Thomas Paine pointed out in a different context, be some difficulty in saddling future generations with that choice (see Notes to the Constitution in Part 2).

people in a referendum. There may be those who believe that a weakening of parliamentary sovereignty will also weaken executive power and so lead to less rather than more effective government.[63] In a representative democracy those views may prevail. However, that does not remove the need for a fully informed public debate as to how we should be governed.

IX. THE VIRTUES OF REPRESENTATIVE DEMOCRACY

Repairing British Politics advances the proposition that a written constitution deriving its authority from the people and founded on principles of representative democracy based on popular sovereignty has incomparable advantages over our current organic constitutional arrangements.

That said, there is a potential difficulty inherent in the notion of 'power to the people'.[64] Letting the people decide is by no means always guaranteed to result in the most informed decision-making. It was for this reason that, according to Plato, Socrates, in his classification of governments, put democracy well down the list and below both the philosopher-kings and the oligarchs (ending up only just above the tyrants). The basis for this was that in a pure democracy (Socrates was considering the Greek brand of direct democracy whereby all citizens were required to participate in political decision-making) the people as a whole would be likely to become slaves to their own desires. In Plato's somewhat emotive words, such persons might spend their days 'winebibbing and abandoning [themselves] to the lascivious pleasures of the flute'.[65]

Although the dangers of excessive flute-playing could, no doubt, be borne with equanimity, from a twenty-first century perspective the risks of reaching uninformed decisions are potentially considerable. It might be considered unfortunate if decisions of this kind were made on the basis of less than fully informed public opinion. On the other hand withdrawal from, say, the Ukrainian war on the basis of that public opinion risks ignoring the political consequences of withdrawal.[66] Although there is a compelling case to be made for leaving important decisions such as these to persons or bodies with greater

[63] History provides examples of cases where the strongest forms of democratic government have been considered necessary. When, for example, De Gaulle emerged as the saviour of France it was on the understanding that the Fifth Republic would alter the constitutional balance in favour of a strong executive President after the inherently unstable Fourth Republic.

[64] Coming from another direction, a rather different issue with empowering the people lies in the fact that empowerment needs to distinguish between abstract measures such as more decentralisation and the need to account for the resources that people need to lead dignified lives. See Daniel Leighton, 'What Power the People?' *The Guardian*, 19 December 2009.

[65] *The Republic*, 561c. *The Collected Dialogues of Plato*, Edith Hamilton and Huntington Cairns (eds) (Princeton NJ, Princeton University Press, 1963) 789.

[66] See, for example, the helpful analsis by Tim Willasey-Wilsey, 'What lies ahead for the war in 2024' *The Guardian*, 2 January 2024.

specialist knowledge than the general populace, this is not inconsistent with establishing a true separation of powers through a new principle of constitutional supremacy.

As suggested earlier, it is crucial to put in place constitutional mechanisms that entrench the protection of minority interests. The idea that those interests should be protected should not itself be a majority voting issue; it is simply a premise underlying civilised society, certainly in western liberal democracies. Similar considerations attach to the need to ensure that certain areas of decision-making are delegated to those who have the expertise to make such decisions. No complex modern society could operate if every aspect of decision-making had to be taken by a majority vote. Constitutional supremacy would, however, make the exercise of political power more accountable by putting in place greater checks on its legitimacy and enabling citizens, in cases where the exercise of power was wholly out of kilter with the mood of the people, to prevent its continuation by recourse to constraining constitutional mechanisms such as referendums where triggered by a sufficiently large proportion of the electorate.

It is in the light of these considerations that Part 3 of *Repairing British Politics* sets out a mechanism whereby referendums can be held on whether we wish to continue with parliamentary sovereignty or embrace a new principle of constitutional supremacy (the first referendum)[67] and how – if we support constitutional supremacy – we should bring it into effect (the second referendum).

In seeking to devise a 'good' constitution (with a small 'c') we have few tools at our disposal other than the aggregation of individual reason directed towards finding *better* (not ideal, not even always the *best*) ways of solving our common predicament in the light of what we know about ourselves and each other.

I argue that one need only look to the theoretical alternatives to collective reason for the creation of effective constitutional arrangements to see how inadequate any other regulating principle would be. Any principle other than the collective wisdom of the people reflected in a representative democracy fails a threshold question, namely what is to happen when the interests of an authority accepted *outside* that collective wisdom conflicts with the interests of the people. Unquestioning obeisance to monarchical authority fails this test. Parliamentary sovereignty fails this test. No-one suggests that there is any other basis such as tyranny or oligarchy for our giving others power over us. The sleight-of-hand has been to equate parliamentary sovereignty with popular sovereignty. For the reasons set out above, that elision is a false one.

The fact that every other liberal democracy apart from Israel and New Zealand has a written and codified constitution should give us pause for

[67] There is, of course, a concealed danger here. If one generation votes against parliamentary sovereignty, why should the next generation not embrace it? The answer to this must be that provided that basic democratic values are preserved, the basis on which we are governed must be susceptible to review.

thought. All the more so, perhaps, when it is realised that New Zealand retains the British monarch as Head of State and Israel is in the process of devising a written constitution.

X. DRAFTING A WRITTEN CONSTITUTION: THE PRACTICALITIES

The difficulties inherent in devising a written constitution founded on rational principles and reflecting a representative democracy lie, perhaps, not so much in selecting the appropriate constitutional theory as in the practice. It would be tempting to dismiss these difficulties, as de Tocqueville arguably did in describing the newly-minted US republic as:

> … the slow and tranquil action of society on itself. It is an orderly state truly founded in reality upon the enlightened will of the nation … Republicans in the United States value customs, respect beliefs, recognize rights.[68]

However, even if the British collective popular will is 'enlightened', there are many different versions of enlightenment. It is here that the mechanism enabling, and the quality of, a public debate is so critical.

The approach of this book in offering a possible model for a constitution has been first to adhere to the central principle that the constitution is meant to reflect as strongly as possible a representative democracy. This entails a number of highly specific suggested changes, discussed in the Observations and Explanatory Notes that accompany the provisions of the Draft Constitution in Part 2 below.

Against that overarching principle two further principles have been followed. First, given that the changes proposed here are not derived from some external precipitating event (a 'constitutional moment') but involve major changes to an existing, albeit 'organic', constitutional structure, they are tailored as far as possible to fit in with that existing structure. The most obvious example is that of the monarchy. Making a written constitution the supreme law is, in theory, more compatible with a republic than with any form of monarchy. If one were starting with a blank piece of paper it is unlikely that a constitutional monarchy would be created.

But, if there is a sense in which the monarchy in modern Britain has arguably become anachronistic, it is an anachronism with which we are comfortably familiar. Even if the possible wisdom of Bagehot's warning not to 'let in daylight upon magic'[69] by ceasing to 'reverence' the monarchy has been tested over the years by marital difficulties in the Royal Family and by caricature fictionalisation in films such as Stephen Frears' *The Queen*, the Crown – as a totemic symbol – still arguably forms part of our national identity. In some ways, along with red

[68] de Tocqueville (n 17) vol 1 pt 2 ch 10, 464–65.
[69] Bagehot (n 19) 54.

pillar boxes, the Union Jack and the traditional pint, the Royal Family is an emblem of Britain that, in an era of bland anonymity, provides distinctiveness and historical continuity. Some would go further and defend the monarchy as being essential as a protection against the dangers of social dislocation or even tyranny.

It cannot be denied that King Charles III (and formerly his mother Queen Elizabeth II) is widely respected and a considerable asset in terms of our relations on the international scene, thus demonstrating that a monarch with no formal political role may yet wield considerable symbolic, even moral, authority and be widely revered as a unifying figure.[70] Provided, therefore, that the monarchy can, as an institution, be made to fit in with the principles of a representative democracy, there is considerable justification for retaining a constitutional monarchy with a clear symbolic rather than political function. That is the proposal suggested in the draft constitution.

The final principle adhered to in devising this constitution is more abstract and requires separate consideration. It is the need to search for pragmatic solutions to specific issues rather than for some ideal of a perfect constitution.

Whatever else it does, a written constitution should reflect the principles of a just society. That statement is unlikely to be controversial. It is when we start to think about what constitutes justice that we get into difficulties. It was clear to the framers of the US Declaration of Independence, drafted in 1776, what justice meant. Its declamatory second sentence asserts that:

> We hold these truths to be self-evident, that all men are created equal, that they are endowed by their Creator with certain unalienable Rights, that among these are Life, Liberty and the pursuit of Happiness.

From this it can immediately be seen that what may have been self-evident to those who drafted the US Declaration is not necessarily so obvious more than two centuries later. For one thing, the reference to a 'Creator' (in the French Declaration of the Rights of Man drafted in 1789 it was a *Supreme Being*) as the author of fundamental rights is, to put it neutrally, now very far from obvious. For another, though in the twenty-first century we would probably agree that the right to life is inalienable, we recognise certain constraints on the right to liberty, and the ECHR, at least, recognises the possibility of even derogating from Article 8 (right to respect for private and family life), which is the Convention right most directly linked to the pursuit of happiness.

Of course, if our supposed creator is *not* the source of fundamental rights, a second difficulty arises. Even if identifiable fundamental rights exist, where do

[70] Consider, for example, the words of General Dannatt, who observed in a debate that the British Army, with its mix of religions, works 'because we all owe our allegiance to Her Majesty The Queen and endeavour to live our lives by a core set of values that are themselves essentially British': 'It's Still Great to be British' *Country Life* 27 July 2009, www.countrylife.co.uk/news/its-still-great-to-be-british-28155.

they come from? To the renowned utilitarian Jeremy Bentham the answer was obvious:

> ... is the child of law; from real laws come real rights; from imaginary laws, from laws of nature, fancied and Right invented by poets, rhetoricians, and dealers in moral and intellectual poisons, come imaginary rights, a bastard brood of monsters.[71]

To Bentham, therefore, it was clear that any idea of 'natural rights' amounted to 'rhetorical nonsense', or, in his more memorable phrase, 'nonsense upon stilts'. It is easy to become trapped by Bentham's logic into conceding that if divine natural law is an illusion, it follows that the only source of entitlement to fundamental rights is to be derived from law. This is a false dichotomy if we accept that certain moral events or situations are, at least at the present time, obviously wrong. For example, it is surely obvious that murder is morally wrong. It is certainly obvious now, and became increasingly so in the course of the nineteenth century, that slavery is morally wrong.

But certain things are not as clear. In fact they may not be clear at all. In his book *The Idea of Justice*[72] Amartya Sen provides a helpful illustration of this. In his example of three children who each claim entitlement to a flute on different grounds, Child A claims entitlement because she is the only one who can play the flute. Child B claims entitlement on the ground of poverty – he has no toys of his own. Child C claims entitlement because the flute is the product of her labour – she made it. As Sen points out, a Marxist would certainly incline to Child C's claim. The economic egalitarian would favour Child B. A utilitarian hedonist might support Child A.

The example illustrates perfectly the genuinely different views that reason – which the French celebrated so enthusiastically at Notre Dame de Paris in 1793 – might supply for the resolution of moral dilemmas for which there can be more than one answer.

Two consequences seem to flow from this. First, the fact that reason may come up with different answers to moral dilemmas means that the search for an 'ideal' formulation of fundamental rights, or other constitutional obligations and responsibilities, is probably doomed to fail. Amartya Sen's principal criticism of the so-called 'original position' of the liberal thinker John Rawls

[71] Jeremy Bentham, 'Anarchical Fantasies' in AI Melden (ed), *Human Rights* (London, Wadsworth, 1970) 28, 30–34.

[72] Amartya Sen, *The Idea of Justice* (London, Allen Lane, 2009) 12 ff. For a treatment of justice that makes this point in different and illuminating ways see Michael Sandel, *Justice: What's the Right Thing to Do?* (London, Allen Lane, 2009). Sandel argues, amongst other things, that contemporary western reliance on the free market credo has tended either to obscure the necessity of making moral judgements about justice or has detrimentally informed some of the moral judgements that have been made. The conclusion to which Sen and Sandel implicitly subscribe is that philosophies such as those of the free market or libertarianism or utilitarianism or communitarianism are metaprinciples, none of which can authoritatively determine how a just constitution should be ordered. Indeed, they may well be in conflict one with another – for example, economic freedom versus social justice.

is precisely that Rawls appears to imagine that there is only one liberal solution to justice,[73] and that his contractarian model of political thought (shared with others such as Hobbes and Locke) ignores the practical objection that it may not – even in theory – be easy to persuade sufficient numbers to add their names to the contract.

The second consequence of reason providing not one but a number of possible resolutions to moral dilemmas is that it supports, rather than negates, the proposition that reason is a valuable aid for examining these issues. How else could such examination be conducted? Nonetheless, it is equally consistent with the societal truth that, ultimately, decisions are made in a social context rather than in some philosophical vacuum.

The power of ideas fuelled by reason but needing to be accepted in the social marketplace before they acquire more than transient validity was recognised by Justice Oliver Wendell Holmes in his strong dissenting opinion in *Abrams v United States*.[74] He said this:

> Persecution for the expression of opinions seems to me perfectly logical. If you have no doubt of your premises or your power and want a certain result with all your heart you naturally express your wishes in law and sweep away all opposition … But when men have realized that time has upset many fighting faiths, they may come to believe even more than they believe the very foundations of their own conduct that the ultimate good desired is better reached by free trade in ideas … that the best test of truth is the power of the thought to get itself accepted in the competition of the market, and that truth is the only ground upon which their wishes safely can be carried out. That at any rate is the theory of our Constitution.

Holmes' reference, in the context of free expression, to free trade in ideas being 'the theory of our Constitution' (by which he means *underlying* theory) is also the necessary theory behind *any* written constitution. A debate reflecting Holmes' 'free trade in ideas' must be the starting point for considering how best to draw up a written constitution. Some ideas will fall by the wayside; others will triumph in the marketplace of ideas.[75]

In order to triumph in that context, it seems clear that ideas must be practical and attract a consensus. If they are impractical they will attract little consensus, and if they do not attract consensus they will never be generally accepted. In a representative democracy those kinds of ideas will not find their way into a written constitution.

That is the reasoning underpinning my third and final drafting principle. This is not to suggest that *any* of the ideas set out in this constitution will find

[73] Sen's argument is more complex than this and he acknowledges a huge debt to Rawls, but the essence of his critique is that Rawls fails to address the many different ways in which the search for just solutions may be resolved.

[74] *Abrams v United States* (1919) 250 US 616.

[75] Holmes' market in ideas can, however, be carried too far and could never be used to justify eroding fundamental values such as the protection (and advancement) of minority interests.

acceptance. But the drafting focuses, for the most part, on ideas which have found some support from various groups in the past. They are put forward for further debate, following which the best ideas may survive.

The methodology followed, then, in drafting this constitution for the UK has been to start from the central premise of representative democracy and to advance a personal statement of how, informed by reason but respecting the traditions that have developed over the centuries, this might be achieved in 21st century UK.

XI. CONTENTS OF A WRITTEN CONSTITUTION

Yet, even if there were to be widespread support for a written constitution *in principle*, its detailed content would present another, entirely different set of issues. Should we simply catch up with the organic unwritten constitution that is modern Britain and put it in writing?[76] Or should we strike out boldly in new directions and, if so, what new areas should a written constitution encompass? In this book I suggest that the time is ripe for us to chart a new course. External 'constitutional moments' in which momentum for change exists are extremely rare and can be very divisive. Further, no written constitution can co-exist with parliamentary sovereignty. The two are mutually exclusive because the institutions of government are bound by the terms of such constitution and, therefore, no single institution can possess potentially unlimited sovereignty particularly under a written constitution which has made the *people* sovereign. So, charting a new course is inevitable once it is accepted that there should be a written constitution making the people sovereign. By the very act of adopting such a constitution, we cast ourselves into a new constitutional settlement in which the overarching principles affecting government are different.

The overarching principles of a new constitutional settlement would make it clear that power rested with the people instead of with Parliament. A citizen's assembly would be introduced which would reinforce the notion that the people delegated power to Parliament. A revision of the electoral system from the current first-past-the-post system to one of proportional representation would be more inclusive by acknowledging a greater proportion of the views of the electorate and so encourage greater involvement. Democracy would be better served by enshrining in the constitution the clear principles by which government would be carried out with a programme of enforcement action for a violation of the constitution. Checks and balances would also exist to maintain the distribution of power between the different organs of government. Those principles would be reinforced by an independent judiciary and civil service which in themselves would be overseen by independent regulators.

[76] For a brilliant lampoon of what our present 'constitution' might look like reduced to writing, see *The Unspoken Constitution* (Democratic Audit, October 2009).

These, then, are the shapes of the main *arguments*. But obtaining any consensus on the principle about the possible content of a written UK constitution will take much time. There is bound to be disagreement along the way.

XII. REPAIRING BRITISH POLITICS: THE PROPOSALS

The draft Constitution contains a Preamble and 14 Parts. It consists of a 17-point blueprint for constitutional reform as follows:

- The creation of a sovereign, democratic, secular state with power conferred by the people according to the terms of a written, codified Constitution and disestablishment of the Church of England.
- Making that written Constitution the supreme law with a duty on all the organs of state (including the courts and a newly-created Citizens' Branch) to apply and to implement its provisions.
- The scrapping of parliamentary sovereignty as a constitutional doctrine applicable to the UK and its replacement with a doctrine of constitutional supremacy.
- Renaming the Houses of Parliament the House of Representatives (formerly the House of Commons) and the Senate (formerly the House of Lords) and reforming the Senate by making it 50 per cent elected and 50 per cent appointed.
- Fixed-term Parliaments of four years with major electoral reform from first past-the-post to a system of proportional representation or alternative vote and with a constitutional requirement that there should, as far as possible, be an equal number of elected men and women in Parliament.
- Tight control of MPs' financial interests and conduct with strict consequences for breaches of the rules, including mandatory loss of seat and provision for the recall of MPs if a sufficient number of their constituents are dissatisfied with their performance.
- Transferring most prerogative power from the Crown to executive government and subjecting those powers to control by both Parliament and the courts.
- Converting the Crown into a constitutional monarchy with recognition of the symbolic authority the monarch wields as Head of State but with a duty to swear an oath of allegiance to the Constitution as a condition of assuming office.
- Strengthening Parliament in its relations with executive government by enabling Parliament to veto the exercise of certain executive powers, including the appointment of special advisers, reforming the system for

membership of select committees, and empowering Parliament to initiate legislation and public inquiries.

— Empowering the Supreme Court with major new constitutional responsibilities, including power to declare laws that violate the Constitution to be unconstitutional with the effect that such laws are invalid, which the Supreme Court may, nonetheless, declare to be incompatible with the Constitution.
— Creating a Bill of Rights for the UK which strengthens the existing protections, including those contained in the Human Rights Act 1998, and introduces a number of 'third generation' social and economic rights.
— Introducing the notion of civic responsibilities under the Constitution.
— Creating a clear regime for the exercise of emergency powers which may not be used to derogate from a wide range of fundamental rights.
— Introducing state funding of political parties but also permitting the Supreme Court in certain circumstances to declare parties which threaten to subvert democracy to be unconstitutional and, in certain cases, making temporary banning orders.
— Creating a new Citizens' Branch of the Constitution selected annually at random from the electoral register and the election by the Citizens' Branch of a small Citizens' Council to initiate legislation and public inquiries (where a referendum shows sufficient support) and to make applications direct to the Supreme Court on questions of constitutional interpretation.
— Making important changes to the civil service, the army, the police and local authorities, including the principle of progressive strengthening of local authority power and self-financing.
— Creating a mechanism for the holding of citizens' referendums to determine important constitutional and legislative developments.

XIII. TOWARDS THE FUTURE

The bitterest argument will be whether we should change anything at all. This is amply illustrated by the furore that arose over the creation of a Supreme Court in the UK in October 2009.

We simply cannot have anything like a separation of powers without a Supreme Court. Other countries with written constitutions have a Supreme Court which can pronounce laws to be constitutionally invalid. That is one of the very points of separating judicial power from legislative power. There is something quaint and very British about having our top judges sitting in a legislative body (the House of Lords). But it is constitutionally inept. The fact that the system has creaked along over the centuries is neither here nor there in terms of what a modern constitution in a modern state should contain.

Yet the fears that surfaced shortly before the opening of the Supreme Court show how little prepared we are for change. Lord Neuberger of Abbotsbury, when Master of the Rolls, had this to say about the new Court:

> The danger is that you muck around with a constitution like the British constitution at your peril because you do not know what the consequences of any change will be.[77]

That is, of course, true. But if it were applied literally, our constitution could never change. If an inbuilt fear of change had deterred, say, the 13 colonies, there would have been no US Constitution or, indeed, any constitutional progress of any kind, anywhere.

In *Great Expectations* the wealthy spinster Miss Havisham will never remove her wedding dress nor move her wedding cake – leaving it uneaten on the table – nor change the clocks from the time of her betrayal at the altar. She lives alone in a decaying mansion in a doomed attempt to reverse history by denying what actually happened. Resistance to the idea of change would lead to a fate little different on the national scale from that of the individual fate of Miss Havisham. Sadly, it is obvious that without a written constitution Britain will be driven increasingly to supporting the fiction of parliamentary sovereignty by more and ever greater subterfuges as the reality of a global, secular and multicultural society discredits it more and more openly.

It seems unlikely that the policies of either the Conservative or Labour Parties will, without considerable popular pressure, contain any meaningful proposals in respect of a written constitution or that, therefore, the British people will ever be given the opportunity to consider them.

Yet, what the evidence shows is that the fabric of our so-called constitution could easily unravel. It is like the proverbial house of cards. Unlike the US Constitution, no-one has ever drawn up plans, commissioned an architect or even taken a step back to consider what the house might look like.

But the evidence also shows us that it is when things go wrong that a space is opened up for change. As the evidence mounts for a debate on constitutional change, that opportunity should not be lost.

One of our deepest intuitions as far as the process of government is concerned is the idea of the social contract. It has never come to fruition. Political philosophers have suggested theoretical models for what might go into such a contract, were one ever to be concluded. But these models lag behind reality because, without a movement for change, there is no sensible prospect of the people ever being offered a contract for government. We will have to be content with what we have. And what we have is the outmoded doctrine of parliamentary sovereignty, the palest of shadows of the popular sovereignty to which we are entitled if we want it.

[77] Joshua Rozenberg, 'Fear Oover Supreme Court Impact' *BBC News*, 8 September 2009.

KEY POINTS

Why Parliamentary Sovereignty is Useless in a Written Constitution

- Parliamentary sovereignty is a doctrine that stresses absolute power. Absolute state power is the trajectory of any power of the state in a country without a constitution.
- As part of that doctrine, parliamentary sovereignty in its sharpest form (the form currently adopted by the UK Government) is that Government can both make and unmake laws at will. It is the making and unmaking of laws that is the central flaw in parliamentary sovereignty.
- If the Government can unmake laws at will the Government will never be able to guarantee the constitutional rights that it has purported to grant – because the Government will never be able to entrench laws.

Why Democracy Viewed Through a Constitutional Lens is Best

- The trouble with most definitions of what constitutes good government is that it depends on the authority of one man or a group of men who want power; the trouble with democracy – so it has been thought – is that all men want power.
- A constitution stops that relentless urge for power because it imposes standards of good government imposed by the judges.
- The people vote on the constitution prepared by those with specialist knowledge but always with thought for the community as a whole.

Then and Now

- The English Civil War raged for nine years (1642–1651), during which King Charles I was executed (1649). The War might have had a different result if Cromwell's two written constitutions had endured, but they only lasted until his death.
- For a long time parliamentary sovereignty survived as a doctrine because Parliament was kept alive by a small group of people acting as a clique – England had had a 'bloodless revolution' (the change of monarch in 1688 from James II to William of Orange) but this meant that an aristocracy was acting in what it perceived to be the best interests of society and the King/Queen was gradually losing power.
- This survival of parliamentary sovereignty for nearly 400 years was testament to the cohesiveness of this group but it also coincided with the slow

emergence of democracy and the sometimes brutal build-up of empire. Also, the people enjoyed the diminution of power in the monarch.

- But parliamentary sovereignty was effectively bankrupted when two things happened – first, the British population was now educated; second, Margaret Thatcher's assault on upper-class values, which had a crudely economic but not a political effect, leading people to want to be included in the so-called liberal system of politics.

Why Parliamentary Sovereignty Doesn't Work

- Parliamentary sovereignty is based upon a fiction, that Parliament will always have authority to make and unmake laws. Sometimes this is obvious (as when – when we were still members – the EU makes laws directly or indirectly); sometimes it is clear that whatever the theory, the doctrine of parliamentary sovereignty doesn't work because Parliament does not have that authority (for example, when the issue is about a private company) or because others are involved (eg the Commonwealth). The origin of sovereignty as a theory is obscure, but its attractions are obvious to those in power.
- Nobody ever voted for parliamentary sovereignty: the sovereignty of Parliament is a given, but the problem is that it was given by Parliament rather than from the people.

2

A Draft Constitution for the United Kingdom

CONTENTS

PREAMBLE

WHEREAS the peoples who have come to these islands over the centuries share a common belief in and aspiration towards principles of liberty, fairness, tolerance and economic well-being for all;

Whereas the Constitution of the United Kingdom of Great Britain[1] and Northern Ireland has developed piecemeal and has, in particular, evolved without systematic review of the effectiveness of its institutions or of its constitutional and democratic principles;

[1] There is often confusion as to the exact meaning of the terms 'Britain', 'Great Britain' and 'the UK'. The United Kingdom ('the United Kingdom of Great Britain and Northern Ireland') was formed as a union of England and Wales (Laws in Wales Act 1536) with Scotland, forming Great Britain (Union with Scotland Act 1707) and Northern Ireland (Union with Ireland Act 1800, Government of Ireland Act 1920). It does not include the Crown Dependencies (the Channel Islands and the Isle of Man). In legislation, 'United Kingdom' means 'Great Britain and Northern Ireland' (Interpretation Act 1978, Sch 1) and 'British Islands' means the United Kingdom, the Channel Islands and the Isle of Man (ibid). Although Gibraltar is not part of the UK for most purposes, the UK is responsible for its external relations. In popular usage 'Britain' and 'the UK' are interchangeable terms and include England, Scotland, Wales and Northern Ireland. However, Great Britain should be used to encompass only England, Scotland and Wales.

Whereas, in particular, the principle of parliamentary sovereignty[2] has not proved sufficiently effective to continue to protect fully the interests of the people of the United Kingdom and other persons residing in or otherwise living in the United Kingdom;

Whereas the nature of society in the United Kingdom has undergone many social and political changes such that it is now multicultural and its citizens practise a variety of faiths, as well as having decentralised legislative bodies in Northern Ireland, Scotland and Wales,[3] with the result that its different backgrounds, cultures, faiths and beliefs are no longer best reflected in the present constitutional arrangements;

Whereas it is now necessary that the United Kingdom adopts a new written Constitution[4] to remedy these and other concerns so as to establish clear constitutional and representative democratic principles for the exercise of legislative, executive, judicial and citizen power and, thereby, to ensure the fullest protection of the human, political, legal, social and economic rights and general welfare of all the people of the United Kingdom and all those otherwise subject to its laws;

We the people of the United Kingdom[5] therefore establish and adopt this Constitution for the United Kingdom.

[2] The doctrine of parliamentary sovereignty is expressed by AV Dicey in his *Introduction to the Study of the Law of the Constitution* (London, Macmillan, 1855): 'Parliament ... has ... the right to make or unmake any law whatever; and further ... no person or body is recognised by the law of England as having a right to override or set aside the legislation of Parliament. Parliament is not bound by its predecessor'. Thus, parliamentary sovereignty and the supremacy intrinsic in a written constitution are incompatible. This incompatibility is discussed further in the Notes immediately below and in Chapter 1 'Setting the Scene', above. Parliamentary sovereignty also allows a government to include as parliamentary reform aspects of its policy when in truth the reforms are party policy rather than reform, or to do nothing at all.

[3] There are, as a result of specific devolution reforms, many detailed issues that could become relevant in drafting a written constitution. Some of them are relevant to the drafting of a domestic Bill of Rights (see Part 9). Such issues could arise as the result of devolving certain matters to the respective legislative bodies of Scotland, Wales and Northern Ireland while at the same time reserving certain matters to the Westminster Parliament. The final detail of a written constitution may therefore, as a matter of practicality, have to make allowance for this division of functions.

[4] The word 'new' is inserted before 'written Constitution' to anticipate the critique that the UK already has a written – albeit not a codified – Constitution. For an earlier (pre-devolution and pre-Human Rights Act 1998) attempt to draft a codified constitution see Robert Blackburn, *A Written Constitution for the United Kingdom*, Institute of Public Policy Research (London, Mansell Publishing, 1993). John Macdonald QC drafted a written constitution which was included in the Liberal Democrat Report *We the People: Towards a Written Constitution* (London, Liberal Democrat Policy Unit, 1991). An altogether more radical proposal involving, amongst other things, abolition of the monarchy and House of Lords to be embodied in a Commonwealth of Britain Bill was also advanced by Tony Benn: see Tony Benn and Andrew Hood, *Common Sense – A New Constitution for Britain* (London, Hutchinson, 1993). See the first edition of *Repairing British Politics* (Oxford, Hart Publishing, 2010) by Richard Gordon for the most modern form of constitution.

[5] The expression 'the People of the United Kingdom' means those persons who are entitled to vote in UK parliamentary elections (see Part 14).

PREAMBLE: OBSERVATIONS AND EXPLANATORY NOTES

Nature of a Preamble

The Preamble to a written constitution sets out its main principles and purposes and can sometimes serve as a mission statement or set of values for what follows. The purpose of a Preamble, which precedes the enacting formula, is to state the reasons for and the intended effects of a Bill of great constitutional importance or a Bill to give effect to international conventions.[6] By its very nature, a constitution is of 'great constitutional importance' whether or not it is prefaced by a Bill.[7]

However, there is no necessity for such a statement and there are even some dangers in including one.[8] The risk of stating values in any detail is that other equally important values may be overlooked.[9]

There is also a danger of ambiguity if that which appears in the Preamble does not find its way expressly into the main body of the Constitution and is in tension with it. It is often thought that a Preamable has no legal force. However, in some countries the courts have held that the Preamble operates as a general framework within which the Constitution is to be interpreted.[10]

These dangers are sought to be avoided by keeping the drafting simple, by not stating a set of values other than by reference to certain categories of rights and interests which will be elaborated in the Constitution itself, and by emphasising the need for clear constitutional and democratic principles which are reflected in the Constitution.

Why a Preamble?

There is a scope for disagreement over whether there should be a Preamble at all. The reasons for including one are twofold. Each is related to a premise that fundamental changes are needed; hence the need for a new written Constitution.

First, it was relevant to identify at the outset that the concept that underpins our present constitutional arrangements (parliamentary sovereignty) is no

[6] See *Erskine May: Parliamentary Practice*, 25th edn (London, Lexis Nexis, 2019) para 26.8. See, for example, the Parliament Bill 1911 and the Parliament (No 2) Bill 1969.

[7] A Bill may throw up too many associations linked with the sovereignty of Parliament.

[8] See, of the many examples, the start of David Runciman's article 'Politicians in a Fix', *London Review of Books*, 10 July 2003, where he castigates Valery Giscard d'Estaing for citing Pericles out of context for actually removing democracy from the Athenian people.

[9] Nor is agreeing a statement of values an easy task: see eg 'In Search of British Values', *Prospect*, October 2007.

[10] For example, the courts of South Africa and India rely heavily on the mention of equality in the preambles to their constitutions when adjudicating constitutional questions. But the values set out in the preambles have also been used by the courts to define the spirit or nature of the society they govern (for example, they are used to define the identity of the jurisdiction/society concerned).

longer sufficiently effective as a constitutional principle (see Chapter 1 'Setting the Scene', above). It is certainly true that parliamentary sovereignty – a doctrine that enables Parliament to make and unmake laws as it chooses because it is 'sovereign' – has led to some considerable benefits. It has, for example, inspired trust in the legislature; a trust which the legislature has, not in the main, sought to abuse. It has also been influential in 'shaping' the early constitutions that were set up in many common law jurisdictions such as India, Canada and Australia. However, the development of rights-based cultures and recognition of the dangers of a purely statistical democracy have led to an almost universal principle of constitutionalism in which a perceived need to protect the rights and values entrenched in a codified written constitution places significant legal constraints on the legislature.

Parliamentary sovereignty is thus inconsistent with this type of written constitution[11] because it permits a legislature, unrestrained by a constitution, simply to legislate as it chooses.[12] Since one of the principal reasons for adopting a written constitution in the sense used above is to substitute constitutionalism for sovereignty, there is good reason to foreshadow this in a Preamble.[13]

The second justification for having a Preamble is to make it clear that the social fabric of British society (including the changes wrought by devolution) has altered so much in modern times that a written constitution is necessary to reflect these important developments.

This last factor also encompasses Britain's growing multiculturalism, which is an important root cause of an increasing disaffection with politics. It is perhaps especially important that a post-millennium written constitution is seen to be the common heritage of everyone and not the exclusive preserve of a privileged or indigenous section of society. In the wake of the real prospect of such

[11] In a limited sense the UK already has a written Constitution because it has written laws which are of a constitutional nature. It lacks only a *codified* Constitution. But this distinction ignores the logic underlying parliamentary sovereignty, which is that written laws (whether codified or not) may be unmade at any time and are not in any meaningful sense entrenched. Even if an Act of Parliament contained entrenchment provisions, such provisions could easily be repealed. It is the entrenchment of constitutional provisions that creates the dividing line between a written constitution as envisaged in this book and an organically evolving set of laws that may be written down but can be repealed by a majority (over 50%) vote in Parliament.

[12] A constitution expresses and determines the reality of exercise of public power. The scope of that power is reflected in the language of the Constitution. Some maintain that parliamentary sovereignty is merely a political theory and that it is what Parliament can do in practice that matters. But theory mirrors power. It is the theory of parliamentary sovereignty that is said, for example, to prevent Parliament from being bound by a written constitution and the courts from being able to strike down legislation that violates fundamental rights.

[13] The consequences of parliamentary sovereignty being so powerful are: (i) it entails the conclusion that Parliament has the right to pass, free of legal limitation, any law it chooses; (ii) a corollary of this is that a later statute repeals an earlier statute; (iii) the sovereignty of Parliament means that only Parliament has the right to challenge a law; (iv) Parliament decides the law and judges merely interpret the law. But see Lord Steyn, Lord Hope and Baroness Hale in *Jackson v Attorney-General* [2005] UKSC 56.

growing disaffection it is important at least to consider including explicit recognition of the fact that this Constitution accepts that as a society we have changed and are no longer exclusively Christian. We may or may not be a 'broken society' but our Constitution at least must seek to promote inclusion, not separation.[14]

These social changes pose enormous challenges for the legislature. Much of the symbolism of a state reflects the strength of its component parts.[15] There are dangers of alienating minority values or regions in the choice of (for example) a national flag or anthem, or in the selection of an official language or languages, or in the development of citizenship values. For the most part this draft Constitution does not attempt to deal with the detail of such matters but the strong recognition in the Preamble of the fact of such social change lays a foundation for future development in these areas.

Under the Constitution those who are entitled to vote in UK elections possess sovereignty rights since the expression *the people* includes British citizens and other persons entitled to vote in UK general elections (see Article 2 and Part 14). It should be noted that most of the fundamental protections provided by the Constitution (see generally Part 9) are not confined to such persons but available to all. In principle, this Constitution is intended in terms of its values and protections to be a charter for all the people.

Other Preliminary Questions

The inclusion of a Preamble is but one of numerous threshold issues that arise in attempting to draft a written constitution for the UK. If it is decided that a Preamble should be included, then its contents will include having to address at least some of the following questions, as identified in a paper entitled 'Towards a Codified Constitution':[16]

(i) What should a constitution say about sovereignty?
(ii) Should principles such as separation of powers and independence of the judiciary be explicitly set out in a constitution or merely reflected in its provisions?

[14] How inclusion is to be promoted is a more complex question (and probably one that is more than policy-making for a constitution), although entrenched constitutional protection of minority rights forms part of the picture. Similarly, a constitution must be flexible enough to ensure that group recognition or conferment of minority rights does not subvert democratic values. However, whether or not a concept of citizenship should be developed to seek progressively to integrate cultural minorities into the majority community, or whether an older multicultural model of respecting different cultural and religious identities should prevail, or whether these two models can co-exist, has been the subject of protracted debate. It is thus probably better left to domestic law rather than attempting to set it out in the Constitution, provided that such law is compatible with the Constitution.

[15] Consider, for example, the US flag with its 50 stars representing the 50 states of the US.

[16] Stephen Hockman QC, Professor Vernon Bogdanor et al, 'Towards a Codified Constitution' (2010) 7(1) *Justice* 74. See also Andrew Hindmoor in *Haywire: A Political History of Britain Since 2000* (Allen Lane, 2024) and *The Right to Rule* by Ben Riley-Smith (John Murray, 2023).

(iii) Should a constitution be for the whole of the UK or should there – as in a federal state – be separate documents for its component parts (England, Scotland, Wales and Northern Ireland)?
(iv) How should a constitution reflect the interaction between 'the people' and the various institutions of government?

These are but examples of the issues which drafting a written constitution is likely to involve. Various 'choices' have had to be made in this Constitution, the reasons for which are set out in the Parts of the Constitution that follow.

There is one final but important preliminary drafting question. Many – but no means all – written constitutions have title headings over each article, this being the model adopted in statutory drafting in the UK. Should that method be adopted here?

The argument for title headings is that they are user-friendly. However, as is indicated by the whole approach to producing a final written constitution for the UK, this draft is, necessarily, incomplete. It is introduced as a working document rather than as the product of finely-tuned legislative drafting. It will be subject to considerable revision in subsequent versions if is it not jettisoned altogether. To say the least, the positioning of articles can be expected to change and the content of some of the provisions in one article may well be taken out and placed in another. For these reasons, title headings for each separate constitutional provision do not appear in this draft Constitution.

PREAMBLE: KEY POINTS

The Preamble

- The preamble to a constitution is a summary of the effect of that particular Constitution. Whether to have a preamble at all is a matter for debate: some jurisdictions go straight to the preamble for confirmation of what the words in a constitution actually mean.
- Two things militate in favour of a preamble:
  (i) A preamble can be used to identify principles that will disappear forever if a constitution is established: the effect of this Constitution of is to remove the principle of parliamentary sovereignty, because parliamentary sovereignty (according to Dicey) means that the Government may make and unmake laws as it wishes, which is obviously no longer possible if a Constitution lays down certain inviolable principles.
  (ii) A preamble can recognise the changes in the last fifty years that have revolutionised society. Underpinning all those changes is a growing multiculturalism, which has led to a deep-rooted disaffection with national politics of the sort that is currently practised.

PART 1

THE STATE AND THE CONSTITUTION (ARTS 1–9)

1. The United Kingdom is a sovereign, democratic, secular state consisting of the Nations of England, Scotland, Wales and Northern Ireland. Save as otherwise provided,[17] nothing in this Constitution shall affect the constitutional relationship between the Crown and those territories set out in Schedule 1 to this Constitution[18] which do not part form part of the United Kingdom but which have either historical associations with the United Kingdom, or else are Crown Dependencies or British Overseas Territories.

2. National sovereignty shall vest in the people,[19] who shall exercise that sovereignty through delegation of the powers, as set out in this Constitution, to their representatives and through the other provisions of this Constitution including the establishment of a Citizens' Branch acting in exercise of powers conferred, and subject to obligations imposed, by this Constitution.

3. This Constitution is the supreme law of the state and the exercise of power is only lawful if permitted by this Constitution. In particular, the Bill of Rights Act 1689 is to be read as subject to, and as amended by, the provisions of this Constitution.

4. It shall be the duty of those parties mentioned in this Constitution to comply with its provisions and use their best endeavours within their jurisdiction under the Constitution to secure and to safeguard the rights and interests protected by it. There shall be a general right of challenge

[17] Art 24 should be noted. This provides for Orders in Council (the legislation affecting the Commonwealth of Nations made by the Privy Council in the name of the King) to be brought in as Bills so as to ensure Parliament's involvement.

[18] Schedule 1 is not reproduced, as the detail of the Commonwealth territories that would be included is not, for present purposes, relevant to the drafting of the Constitution. It should, however, be borne in mind that 'the United Kingdom' (see also Part 14) is limited to England, Scotland, Wales and Northern Ireland. However, the reference to 'the people' in Art 2 does, at present, encompass citizens of certain other states provided that they are resident in the UK and/or fulfil other specific conditions that entitle them to vote (see Notes to Part 14). There is a constitutional convention that alterations to the constitutional relationship between the UK and the Commonwealth territories set up by the Statute of Westminster 1931 requires the consent of the Parliaments of those territories. But a convention of that kind would not operate to prevent the proposals envisaged in this Constitution, as they are confined to proposals affecting the UK as defined. It is likely that following the change in the status of the Crown the constitutional relationship between the Crown and Commonwealth territories would require some modification. This is happening in any event, as those countries become progressively detached from their ties to the Crown.

[19] The term 'the people' is defined in Part 14.

to any breach of this Constitution in citizens sought to be protected by it, provided that an identifiable breach of such duty to them is apparent. That apart, the Constitution identifies specific cases where increased rights of challenge are available to particular branches of it.

5. Subject to the provisions of this Part of the Constitution (Part 1), any law that is contrary to this Constitution is invalid but only to the extent of the inconsistency. Where this Constitution is silent as to the method by which particular provisions shall be implemented, laws must provide for the method and detail of implementation and such laws must be compatible with the Constitution.

6. In the interpretation and application of one or more provisions of this Constitution –

(i) each and every provision of this Constitution shall be construed and applied in a manner compatible with the rights and interests protected by this Constitution and, in particular, consistently with the needs of a representative democracy in a modern and developing society including, where appropriate, making use of the benefits of technological developments;
(ii) a construction should be adopted that will promote the purpose or object underlying the provision or provisions, taking into account the spirit of this Constitution as a whole;
(iii) regard must be paid to the context in which this Constitution was drafted, and to the intention that constitutional interpretation place particular emphasis on–
    (a) developments in the understanding of the content of particular rights mentioned in this Constitution; and
    (b) developments in the promotion of those rights;
(iv) regard may be had to the precedents of foreign jurisdictions including comparative materials and international treaties.[20]

[20] There are obvious arguments on both sides of the debate as to whether (and if so, how) courts and other bodies should refer to foreign law in interpreting domestic constitutional provisions. For example, there is the view that domestic constitutional provisions should be interpreted using purely domestic values or norms. This can be contrasted with the view that there is a need to have an organic/global understanding of the content of rights so as to keep in line with international standards (this of course assumes that international standards are higher than domestic standards). These divergent views have fuelled the existential debate over whether or not courts have any power at all to refer foreign law in constitutional adjudication (most notably in the US, as evident in the Scalia-Breyer debate in death penalty cases). There are different degrees to which constitutions can make reference to the courts' powers in using foreign/comparative law. The South African Constitution *requires* courts to make reference to foreign law, whereas the Hong Basic Law simply *permits* it.

7. Laws, whenever made, are to be interpreted and applied consistently with this Constitution and if they cannot be so interpreted and applied must be declared to be unconstitutional by the Supreme Court.[21] Common law principles must be applied consistently with this Constitution. Any principle of the common law which cannot be so applied must be disregarded. But statutes passed and coming into effect prior to the coming into effect of this Constitution shall be presumed to be effective in terms of time and the manner of their passing into law.

8. Laws made after the coming in force of this Constitution shall in particular promote equal access by men and women to elective offices and posts and public appointments as to well to professional and social positions subject to approval on merit.[22]

9. This Constitution may not be wholly or partially suspended or abrogated.

THE STATE AND THE CONSTITUTION: OBSERVATIONS AND EXPLANATORY NOTES

Overview

This Part outlines the structure of the British state and sets out the role of the Constitution in that state. That is what makes a written constitution – in the sense of a codified constitution – different from a constitution built up incrementally, like the UK's current Constitution and one or two others according to the western model – New Zealand and Israel. The first point to note in our

There is obvious scope for debate, but the solution proposed here is to permit such reference to be made. Other provisions in the Constitution contain stricter obligations on the courts in the context of fundamental rights (Part 9) and in the context of treaties that have been ratified but not incorporated into domestic law (Art 6(iv)). This provision is without prejudice to those other constitutional provisions.

[21] A declaration is simply a remedy granted by the court which states what the law is or its legal effects by reference to the court's judgment (acting within its jurisdiction). See also Part 14 for definitions of particular types of declaration created by this Constitution. EU law was an exception to this general rule but that changed following the referendum held in Great Britain and Northern Ireland on 23 June 2016, the result of which was that 51.9% of the votes cast were in favour of Great Britain and Northern Ireland leaving the EU. This result was controversial (Scotland and Northern Ireland voted in favouring of remaining in the EU) but the result (a bare majority) was measured by the percentage of those persons entitled to vote in the referendum. The Brexit referendum, as it came to be known, was responsible for major changes to the existing UK Constitution, and no doubt it will continue to have a significant effect on (amongst other things) devolution in Great Britain and Northern Ireland.

[22] This provision could have been included in Part 9 (fundamental rights) but is positioned here as a distinct positive obligation on the state when applying the Constitution.

Constitution is the description of the new state that is envisaged: a description of the state as 'sovereign, democratic, and secular'. We the people authorise you the Government to act on our behalf. That is what is meant by 'sovereign'; that is what is meant by 'democratic'; that is what is meant by 'secular'. All three words emphasise that what is intended is a constitution that truly represents the people.

The Cabinet Manual

The Cabinet Manual was described as an 'essential guide to our system of government'.[23] It can only be a guide rather than a passport to something new and exciting. That is the essential difference between a written constitution and one hewn out of past struggles. That is why the Government was clear that *The Cabinet Manual* was written '*by* the executive, *for* the executive and did not require endorsement from Parliament, let alone joint ownership'.[24] It is also the reason for the omissions in *The Cabinet Manual*.

Just by way of example, Chapter One of the *Manual* contains a single paragraph on the royal prerogative, and does not make mention of the reserve powers of the monarch. Chapter Two contains an account of the Fixed-term Parliaments Act, subsequently repealed by the Conservatives in 2022, and softened the wording about certain conventions which were contested. Even this description of the first two chapters shows that the constitutional arrangements are so bare as to leave question marks about the decision to have a cabinet manual at all.

The most important thing about *The Cabinet Manual* was, as the name suggests, that it was a manual written so that the executive could be conversant with the things that mattered. This was vital in helping to explain to politicians and the media that the monarch had no discretion, but would appoint as Prime Minister the person most likely to be able to command the confidence of Parliament once the political parties had concluded their negotiations and determined who that person was.

But as a concluded narrative about the process that led us to where we are now, *The Cabinet Manual* sadly makes no sense whatsoever.

[23] *The Cabinet Manual: a Guide to Laws, Conventions and Rules on the Operation of Government* (Cabinet Office, October 2011) Preface by the Cabinet Secretary, Sir Gus O'Donnell. The trouble with such a document is that the UK's Constitution keeps changing: for example, the Fixed-term Parliaments Act 2011 has been repealed.

[24] Robert Hazell and Timothy Foot, *Executive Power* (Oxford, Hart Publishing, 2022) 28; Twelfth Report from the House of Lords Constitution Committee, *The Cabinet Manual* HL 107 (2010–2011) para 39; Cabinet Office, *Government Response to the House of Lords Constitution Committee, Political and Constitutional Reform Committee and Public Administration Select Committee on the Cabinet Manual and Committee Reports of Session 2010–12* Cm 8213 (2011).

Establishing a Secular State (Art 1)

A significant proposed change is the transition from a Christian-based society to a secular one. There is constitutional precedent for the express creation of a secular society (as, for example, in the 1958 French Constitution) but the enormity of the change and its social consequences should not be understated.

Crucially, the change reverses the effect of many hundreds of years of national history both by removing the constitutional relationship between the Crown and religion and, specifically, by effecting the disestablishment of the Church of England, which was created in 1534 when the English monarchy under Henry VIII broke away from the Roman Catholic Church. Creating a secular society reflects the fact the Britain has undergone profound social change in the last 70 years and that its first 'post-Cromwell' written constitution should demonstrate recognition of that change. A written constitution that simply assumed the continued hegemony of a property-based class – either leisured or founded on Protestant ethics – that has been our constitutional stereotype for so long would be still-born in terms of achieving consensus, as it would be subject immediately to the critique that it is out of touch even before it has begun. Reflecting the reality of social change in this way is significant, since a constitution is an important means of forging a national identity.

Transition to a secular society would have a profound impact on the monarchy, although, as will be seen, this Constitution seeks a constitutional monarchy rather than abolition of the monarchy altogether. The Crown still serves a powerful cultural and totemic function in modern Britain and attracts considerable loyalty. In those circumstances abolition would, it is suggested, be a mistake.

However, many changes are likely to be necessary if the approach advocated here is to be adopted. The King is currently Head of the Church of England (ie the State-approved Church for England) and, following the Act of Settlement of 1701, is indissolubly bound to it. This is considered by many to be an historical anachronism.[25] It is argued here that retention of the monarchy as constitutional Head of State carries with it the sensitive and difficult task of unpicking the strongest of ties between the Crown and the Church of England if the Crown is to survive as a credible institution in the modern age. It also requires a number of other changes to bring the monarchy up to date, including – most notably – repeal of the Succession to the Crown Act 2013.[26]

Those who oppose the concept of a secular state should ask themselves what, for the foreseeable future, is the alternative? It cannot be denied that society is

[25] For one thing, there is no equivalent church for the kingdoms of Wales, Northern Ireland or Scotland.

[26] The first edition of this book advocated repeal of the Royal Marriages Act 1772. This was repealed in 2013 by the Succession to the Crown Act 2013. But the successor Act still bars Roman Catholics and those of other faiths from succeeding to the throne.

both multicultural and consists of different denominational faiths (including the belief that there is not a God). If that reality is ignored, we could see the present strains and tensions that plainly exist explode into something far more dangerous.

Operational Rules (Arts 2–9)

Articles 2–9 set out clear and unambiguous ground rules for the operation of the Constitution. Three ideas flow through these provisions. One (see Art 3) is that the Constitution is the supreme law of the land, which includes exercising supremacy over the common law (see Art 7).[27] This supremacy is often left implicit in constitutional provisions but is made explicit in some constitutions (such as the 1970 Fiji Constitution, abrogated by the President in somewhat unfortunate circumstances in 2009). Article 9 makes it clear that the Constitution may not be suspended or abrogated.

Importantly, Art 3 amends even 'constitutional' statutes. Express reference is made to the Bill of Rights 1689 which, amongst other things, limited the rights of the Crown and purported to define the rights of Parliament. Some see the Bill of Rights 1689 as establishing the doctrine of parliamentary sovereignty, though this is less than clear (see Chapter 1 'Setting the Scene' above). The Bill of Rights is regarded as one of the core constitutional documents of the UK's informal Constitution (others include Magna Carta 1215, the Act of Settlement 1701, the Acts of Union 1707, 1800, the Representation of the People Act 1832, the Parliament Acts 1911, 1949, the Human Rights Act 1998 and all the legislation disentangling the UK from the EU)[28] and contains other important provisions, including determining succession to the throne and, by virtue of Article IX, the doctrine of parliamentary privilege. Under this draft Constitution, the Bill of Rights 1689, Article IX will remain in force but will be subject to the Constitution so that it cannot be used to stifle the effect of the Constitution.[29] Any other provision of the Bill of Rights (or any core constitutional document)

[27] The Constitution no longer has the problem of legislating about contrary EU law. See the Notes immediately below.

[28] The European Communities Act 1972 was one of the core constitutional documents but was this repealed following the UK's decision to leave the EU. Key pieces of legislation of the Brexit decision and the events that followed included: the European Union (Withdrawal) Act 2018, the European Union (Withdrawal Agreement) Act 2020, the United Kingdom Internal Market Act 2020, the European Union (Future Relationship) Act 2020, and the Retained EU Law (Revocation and Reform) Act 2023. Other constitutional statutes arise and it must be for a court to pronounce on whether or not individual Acts amount to a constitutional statute. The importance of this controversy is diminished if we have a written constitution.

[29] See 'Free Speech in Parliament is Precious, says Lord Chief Justice', *The Guardian*, 20 October 2009 on the possible dangers of an over-subservient judicial approach to the scope of the privilege attaching to parliamentary proceedings.

that conflicts with the Constitution is similarly amended (or repealed) so as to give effect to the provisions of this Constitution.

The second key idea is that of *interpretation*. Non-lawyers need to be aware that there are two sets of provisions requiring principles as to how they should be interpreted. There is the Constitution itself, and there are all the laws (Acts of Parliament and delegated legislation[30]), whether they were enacted before the present Constitution or come into force after the Constitution. Interpreting both the Constitution and laws must be purposive, that it to say that the strict language used is not the be all and end all of what is meant.

What matters is the spirit of the Constitution and the rights and interests that it is designed to protect. Purposive interpretation is increasingly used in this country as a result of the Human Rights Act 1998 (HRA 1998) and it has been used by the European Courts (especially in human rights and EU law cases) for many years. As explained below, the HRA 1998 respects parliamentary sovereignty so that if an Act of Parliament breaches human rights then such Act still continues in force. That unjust state of affairs is remedied in this Constitution, which makes it clear (see Art 7) that any laws which are incompatible with the Constitution are liable to be held to be unconstitutional by the Supreme Court, with the consequence that they are invalid. By definition, no *constitutional* provision can be invalid and so (see Art 6) the Constitution must be interpreted in a way that is compatible with the rights and interests that it protects.

Importantly, the Constitution is a living instrument. Article 6 makes it clear, amongst other things, that developments since the original Constitution was drafted are to be taken into account in interpreting it. This is intended to avoid the originalist controversy that has dogged constitutional interpretation in the US where some judges – notably Justices Antonin Scalia, Clarence Thomas and Robert Bork – have propounded the idea that the meaning of the US Constitution was fixed at the time that it was drafted so that any developments since then must be the subject of constitutional amendment if they are to become law.

Finally, a key idea underpinning the whole Constitution is that of *representative* democracy. Direct democracy involves direct participation by all citizens in political decision-making. Such a concept is often said to have been practised in ancient Athens.[31] On any view, direct democracy of that kind is not feasible in a modern, pluralistic state and there is obviously a need for representative institutions. The institutions should, it is argued, be truly representative and, for reasons developed more fully in Chapter 1 'Setting the Scene' above, our present political system is not truly representative. Many constitutions use the language of democracy without even mentioning the concept of representation

[30] Delegated legislation (often called secondary or subordinate legislation) is a law (often in the form of regulations) made by the authority of an Act of Parliament and containing details necessary to carry out specific matters relating to the Act.

[31] Whether this is in fact so has not always been accepted: See John Keane, *The Life and Death of Democracy* (London, Simon and Schuster, 2009) esp 42–44.

that it necessarily imports. But Arts 2 and 6 expressly refer to the notion of representation and Art 6(i) makes it clear that the needs of a representative democracy constitute a principle of interpretation which informs the whole Constitution.

The Brexit Decision

'Brexit' is the name given to the UK's decision to leave the EU.[32] In terms of decision-making, in domestic law, it was achieved by repeal of the European Communities Act 1972. The subject is addressed in the following ways in this draft Constitution:

(i) the Brexit decision and its general effects;
(ii) effect on law-making;
(iii) effect on devolution;
(iv) reform of the House of Lords (the Senate);
(v) effect on constitutional conventions;
(vi) effect on referendums.

The decision to leave the EU came as the consequence of a referendum held on 23 June 2016. Although the referendum was not binding it was treated as being decisive of whether or not Britain should remain a member of the EU. In part, this was due to a statement from the then Prime Minister, David Cameron, that the referendum was binding;[33] in part it was due to the constitutional significance of the issue at stake. It is simply inconceivable that the Government could choose not to be bound by the result.[34]

The point to make first is that the result of the referendum was constitutionally significant. It effectively split the UK into two distinct camps. The results were:

(i) England: Leave 53.4%; Remain: 46.6%;
(ii) Northern Ireland: Leave: 44.2%; Remain: 55.8%;
(iii) Scotland: 38%; Remain: 62.0%;
(iv) Wales: 52.5%; Remain: 47.5%.

In general, the effects of Brexit can be divided into two categories: (1) the immediate effects; and (2) longer term effects.

[32] It is a combination of 'British' (or 'Britain') and 'exit'. See an analysis of the Brexit vote by David Goodhart in *The Road to Somewhere* (Hurst, 2017).

[33] Given the content of the Bloomberg speech of 23 January 2013.

[34] Any more than in it could, in reality, have chosen not to be bound by the Scottish independence referendum in 2014 or with respect to the referendum on continued membership of the common market in 1975. Neither of these referendums were triggered by statutes that purported to bind the government as a matter of law.

Immediate Effects of the Brexit Decision

Immediately Brexit was quite tricky for central Government. It led immediately to the resignation of David Cameron as Prime Minister and to his replacement by Theresa May. It plunged Theresa May into a catastrophic general election in 2017, from which she emerged with a minority Government only saved by forging an alliance with the Democratic Unionist Party (DUP) from Northern Ireland. Negotiations then become more complicated and May's Government was defeated on 33 occasions in the House of Commons. May's proposed deal with the EU was finally rejected by the House of Commons on 15 January 2019 (with 432 to 202 votes to reject the deal, making it the largest defeat in history for a sitting Government). Theresa May, following two more failed attempts to have the deal accepted, resigned on 24 May 2019. Her place was taken by Boris Johnson, whose motto 'get Brexit done' chimed brilliantly with the public mood of dissatisfaction with the whole Brexit process.[35]

Longer-term Effects

The longer-term effects of Brexit were, in constitutional terms,[36] worrying. It set off debates in at least five areas of concern: (i) the effect on lawmaking; (ii) the effect in terms of devolution; (iii) reform of the House of Lords (renamed as the Senate in this Constitution); (iv) the effect on constitutional conventions; and (v) the effect on referendums. Each of these aspects is addressed in turn in this book and in this Constitution. What follows is a summary of the key points.

Lawmaking

Lawmaking in the post-Brexit world was affected in two ways:

(i) The judges became political because the work that they had to cover was increasingly concerned with politics in the sense of the possibility of conflict with major government policy.[37] This led to the allegation by the

[35] The general election that followed (12 December 2019) was a triumph for Boris Johnson. Great Britain left the EU on 31 January 2020. The EU and the UK set out the terms of their deal in three agreements: (i) the Trade and Cooperation Agreement; (ii) the Information Security Agreement; and (iii) the Nuclear Cooperation Agreement. The detail of the negotiations is irrelevant for the most part for present purposes but the Prime Minister's faltering attempts to keep control of the House of Commons is relevant and is addressed in Part 2.

[36] For an analysis of this aspect of Theresa May and Boris Johnson's regimes see Michael Gordon, *Ministerial Irresponsibility in UK Government: Constitutional Accountability after Theresa May and Boris Johnson* (published Public Law July 2024, Sweet and Maxwell).

[37] The most notable Brexit, or post-Brexit, decisions were: *R (Miller) v Secretary of State for Exiting the European Union* [2017] UKSC 5; *R (Miller) v The Prime Minister* [2019] UKSC 41; *the UK Withdrawal from the European Union (Legal Continuity) (Scotland) Bill A Reference by the Attorney General and the Advocate General for Scotland* [2018] UKSC 64; *Reference by the Lord Advocate of devolution issues under paragraph 34 of Schedule 6 to the Scotland Act 1998* [2022] UKSC 31; *In the matter of an application by James Hugh Allister and Others for Judicial Review (Appellants) (Northern Ireland)* [2023] UKSC 5; *R (on the application of AAA and Others) v The Secretary of State of the Home Department* [2023] UKSC 42.

Conservative party, in particular, that judges were allowing their traditional task of adjudicating on law to turn into a bid for a democratic mandate to interfere with major government decision-making.[38] This in turn led to constitutional uncertainty as to how the Government intended to resolve this perceived threatened inroad by the judges.

(ii) Lawmaking became difficult, given the amount of 'heavy lifting' that EU law had done pre-Brexit. There was such a quantity of EU law to replace that it was not easy to see how it could be done except by the use of Henry VIII clauses, which enabled both primary and secondary legislation to be repealed, or amended, by order of the appropriate Secretary of State. The difference between using a Henry VIII clause on accession[39] and the position post-Brexit was that judgments on which parts of EU law to retain and which to remove would not, in the real world, be made by Parliament, but only by a Government Minister.[40]

Devolution

The results also threatened the stability of the UK. In terms of devolution, the devolution statutes, prior to Brexit, contained prohibitions on the devolved Parliaments' jurisdiction from legislating outside EU law. Thus, s 29(2)(d) of the Scotland Act 1998 stipulated that Acts of the Scottish Parliament that were incompatible with EU law were outside the legislative competence of the Scottish Parliament. In similar vein, s 108(6) of the Government of Wales Act 2006 provided that any act of the Welsh Assembly that was incompatible with EU law, fell outside its legislative competence. Section 24 of the Northern Ireland Act 1998 operated to prohibit any legislation that was contrary to EU law. Each of these statutory provisions has now been repealed. But the result, which affects countries that voted to remain in the EU (ie Scotland and Northern Ireland), has led to concern in those countries: they voted to prevent revocation of membership, and nonetheless EU membership has been revoked. The effect on devolution is obvious.

Scotland began, through its majority party the Scottish National Party (SNP), to ask for a referendum to claim the right to demand independence as soon as the Brexit result appeared.[41] Although the UK Government has so far resisted these requests, it is doubtful whether it will continue to resist them successfully.

[38] See, for example, Owen Bowcott 'What is Judicial Review and Why Doesn't the Government Like It?', *The Guardian*, 11 February 2020.

[39] This was achieved by s 2(2) of the 1972 Act, now repealed.

[40] The details of scrutiny in Parliament are addressed in Part 2.

[41] Nicola Sturgeon, then leader of the SNP, gained the approval of the Scottish Parliament in 2017 to seek a section 30 order under the Scotland Act 1998 to hold an independence referendum 'when the shape of the UK's Brexit deal will become clear'.

All the more so as the Conservative Government told Scotland, during the 2014 Scottish independence referendum, that they were in the Union and that this was, rather than independence, the best way of achieving the desired result of staying in the EU.[42]

Northern Ireland has a statute, the Northern Ireland 1998, which provides that Northern Ireland will remain within the UK unless a majority of the people of Northern Ireland vote to form part of a united Ireland. A 2021 census of Northern Ireland showed that, for the first time, Catholics outnumber Protestants (45.7 per cent to 43.48 per cent) and in the May 2022 elections Sinn Fein, under leader Michelle O'Neill, overtook the DUP as Northern Ireland's biggest party, making O'Neill eligible to become first Minister, which she did on 3 February 2024.[43] The future of Northern Ireland, like that of Scotland, remains unclear but the results of the Brexit referendum in Northern Ireland shows that there was a majority of Catholics supporting remaining in the EU.

Reforming the House of Lords

Reforming the House of Lords has clear links too with the devolution issue.[44] Government policy has shifted continuously but the one common thread has been the need to ensure that all the regions of the UK are fully represented. One idea which came from the Government following the December 2019 election was that of a 'second chamber of the nations and regions'. That, it was thought, might assist to 'cement the union'. More recently, the Brown Commission in December 2022 unveiled a series of constitutional reforms aimed at '[reducing] this over-centralisation of power which poisons almost every aspect of our political system'. First on the list was devolution:

> [i]t bedevils the relationships between central government and the devolved institutions of Scotland, Wales and Northern Ireland, with Whitehall seemingly unable to respect their separate authority or work coherently to improve co-operation in areas of shared interest … It allows nationalist parties like the SNP to weaponise grievances, helping them in their campaign to break up the country.[45]

[42] For example, during the referendum the 'Better Together' website said: 'Scotland enjoys membership of the EU because of our membership of the UK and if we are no longer members of the UK then it follows that we are no longer part of the EU'.

[43] Unfortunately the DUP, for political reasons largely connected to the Northern Ireland Protocol, opted out of the formation of a new government from February 2022 (Paul Givan resigned) until February 2024. Michelle O'Neil (Sinn Fein) became the First Minister, thus ending the deadlock, which had been caused by the lack of a Minister with First Minister status in February 2024.

[44] Reform of the House of Lords goes much wider than devolution, of course. An outline of the main issues is considered in Part 4 of the draft constitution.

[45] Brown Commission Report, *A New Britain: Renewing our Economy and Rebuilding our Democracy* (6 December 2022) Ch 3, at 37. One of the proposals was for an Assembly of the Nations and Regions. Another was the set of recommendations dealing specifically with Scotland, Wales and Northern Ireland, giving the people of those countries the opportunity to pursue faster change within a reformed UK.

It may be too late now for proposals such as these to get anywhere, especially as those wishing to achieve separation from England may have little sympathy for a House of Lords with new powers and greater legitimacy.

Constitutional Conventions

Brexit was also responsible for the disfavour into which constitutional conventions were placed as the result of the decision of the Supreme Court in *R (Miller) v Secretary of State for Exiting the European Union*.[46] The Supreme Court said this about the Sewel Convention (at para 151):

> … we do not underestimate the importance of constitutional conventions, some of which play a fundamental role in facilitating harmonious relationships between the UK Parliament and the devolved legislatures. But the policing of its scope and the manner of its operation does not lie within the constitutional remit of the judiciary, which is to protect the rule of law.

It was believed, by many, that if the entire purpose of the convention under scrutiny was to facilitate important relationships then this should have been synonymous with the task of the judiciary.

Law in Relation to Referendums

The last area of debate about the Brexit decision is the impetus it gave to reform of the law about referendums and especially of constitutional referendums such as the Brexit referendum itself. The problem with the 2016 Brexit referendum was that there was no way out for the loser if the choice was to exit. In an interesting article David Runciman, in the *London Review of Books*,[47] points out that there is nothing wrong with the idea of two stages for a referendum but those two stages would have to be written into the referendum at the start. The problem is that the legal regime for referendums is basically uniform with the decision as to the content of the referendum, ie left to the Prime Minister or other principal arranger of the referendum.

THE STATE AND THE CONSTITUTION: KEY POINTS

The Current UK Constitution

- **The executive** enacts laws;
- **Parliament** (usually) rubber-stamps the laws that are created;
- **The judiciary** interpret the laws.

[46] See n 37.

[47] See David Runciman, 'Too Few To Mention', 40(9) *London Review of Books*, 10 May 2018. David Runciman also observes that there are other flaws in the Brexit referendum.

The State and the Constitution

- Listed above is, roughly, the state of the UK Constitution as it is lived now. The real danger is twofold: (i) where the executive is strong and doesn't worry about the Constitution except for reasons of policy; or (ii) where the executive is weak and doesn't have time to consider the Constitution. Parliament is weak and does (roughly) what the executive expects; the judiciary cannot expect to prevail unless the executive desires it (and the executive never does).
- All this is changed in a constitution of that type that is provided in this book – the Constitution represents the highest law; inferior laws can (and must) be annulled by the UK Supreme Court – parliamentary sovereignty is jettisoned.
- The Constitution drafted here is a vast improvement on earlier attempts at drawing up a constitution. *The Cabinet Manual* (2011) was written as a guide for the executive and therefore did not require endorsement from Parliament. It omitted several points of substance and is inadequate as a guide to where we are now (let alone what we have a right to expect).
- The Church of England must be set aside as a State Church. The transition from a Christian-based society to a secular society reflects the fact that the UK has undergone profound social change in the last 70 years. Certainly this change would have a totemic impact on the monarchy and would require the monarch to cease to be the head of the Church. It would require the country fully to take into account the implications of its multiculturalism.
- Three ideas flow though the operational rules. The first is the idea that the Constitution is supreme and overrides the common law when the common law is conflict with it. The second is the idea of interpretation – that which matters is the Constitution and the rights and interests that it is designed to protect. The third is the idea of representative democracy – the institutions must be truly representative; representative democracy is an important principle which informs the whole Constitution.
- The Brexit decision was effectively made when the referendum of 23 June 2016 gave a positive decision that the UK must leave the EU. The referendum was constitutionally significant. It effectively split the UK into two camps: (i) England and Wales, who voted to leave the EU; and (ii) Scotland and Northern Ireland (who voted to remain in the Union). Immediately the Brexit decision was catastrophic for the Tory Government which, under Theresa May, suffered the worst defeat in Parliamentary history. She resigned on 24 May 2019 and Boris Johnson took over. There were longer-term consequences for the Constitution: (1) the effect on lawmaking; (2) the effect on devolution in Scotland and Northern Ireland; (3) the reform of the House of Lords; (4) the effect on constitutional conventions; and (5) the effect on referendums.

PART 2
LAWMAKING (ARTS 10–31)

Parliamentary Primary Legislation (Acts of the Westminster Parliament)

10. There shall be a Parliament sitting at Westminster (or such other place as appears appropriate taking account of the wishes of the MPs in the House of Representatives) consisting of the Head of State (previously known as the King/Queen), the House of Representatives (previously known as the House of Commons), and the Senate (previously known as the House of Lords). The number of members of the House of Representatives shall if possible approximate to that of the Senate. The House of Representatives and the Senate are to be known collectively as the Houses of Parliament and, save as set out in this Constitution and subject to this Constitution or by separate law consistent with this Constitution, the internal parliamentary procedures previously obtaining for the conduct of enacting parliamentary primary legislation shall be unaltered but may themselves be subject to change as determined by either or both of the Houses of the Parliament in accordance with this Constitution.

11. The power to make Parliamentary primary legislation[48] under Part 2 vests, subject to the other provisions of this Constitution, in the Houses. Primary legislation is created through the enactment of Bills passed by both Houses of the Parliament and assented to by the Head of State under this Constitution whereupon they become Acts of Parliament.

12. The Head of State is not empowered to refuse to assent to a Bill duly presented for his or her assent save where the Supreme Court has, before assent, declared the Bill to be incompatible with this Constitution. In such a case the Head of State must refuse to assent to the Bill.

13. The House of Representatives is to be elected under free, fair and equal elections based on the principle of universal suffrage for a fixed term of four years in accordance with the election procedure set out for the House of Representatives in Part 3 of this Constitution but subject to those laws to which Part 3 refers. The House of Representatives may only be dissolved before the end of that fixed term, but must then

[48] This term is defined in Part 14.

immediately be dissolved by the Head of State and a general election called, if –

(i) the Government is defeated on the floor of the House of Representatives on a vote of no confidence and the Prime Minister (as he is then required to) resigns; and
(ii) in such circumstances the Head of State having received the resignation of the Prime Minister is unable, after appropriate consultation, either to find a person best able in the opinion of the Head of State to form a new Government or such person has been found and has been appointed interim Prime Minister by the Head of State but cannot secure approval from the House of Representatives for that Government within three weeks of the resignation of the Prime Minister; or
(iii) the Constitution or laws consistent with the Constitution stipulate that a general election can be (or must be) called.

14. The Senate is, as to fifty per cent of its composition, to be elected under free, fair and equal elections based on the principle of universal suffrage at the same time as elections for the House of Representatives for a fixed term of four years (subject to the qualification expressed in Article 13) in accordance with the voting procedure set out for the Senate in Part 4 of this Constitution. The elected part of the Senate is to be known as the elected body of the Senate.

15. The Senate is as to fifty per cent of its composition to be appointed by an elected Senate Appointments Commission in accordance with the appointments procedure set out for the Senate in Part 4 of this Constitution. The appointed part of the Senate is to be known as the appointed body of the Senate and the term of office of an appointed member is to be in accordance with Part 4 of this Constitution.

16. The rules relating to dissolution of the House of Representatives under Article 13 shall, once applicable, also require dissolution of the Senate.

17. Bills, other than Money Bills (which originate in the House of Representatives) may originate in either the House of Representatives or the Senate and do not require either the consent of the Head of State or the consent of the Government before they may be proceeded with.[49]

[49] Crown consent is currently required if a Bill affects Crown prerogative or the interests of the Crown, the Duchy of Lancaster or the Duchy of Cornwall. The primary rationale for this requirement logically falls away under this Constitution, given the transfer of effective prerogative power to the executive (see Part 5).

18. Following passage of a Bill in either House, the Bill is sent to the other House.

19. Either House may pass a Bill that has been sent to it or may amend or reject it.

20. Where a Bill originates in the Senate and is then brought from the Senate to the House of Representatives the decision of the House of Representatives as to whether the Bill shall be passed or amended or rejected shall be final (subject to the procedure itemised below being followed with the necessary modifications).

21. Where a Bill that has originated in the House of Representatives is brought to the Senate and is amended by the Senate, the House of Representatives may agree to the amendment, reject it or agreed to it in an amended form.

22. If the House of Representatives does not accept the amendment made by the Senate, or if the Bill has been rejected by the Senate, the Bill is returned to the Senate in the form in which it has again been passed by the House of Representatives.

23. If the House of Representatives passes a Bill (other than a Money Bill) in two successive sessions and an interval of at least six months elapses between its passage on each occasion and on each occasion the Senate rejects it or amends it in a manner not agreed by the House of Representatives, then the Bill may be presented to the Head of State for assent. Money Bills certified as such by the Speaker of the House of Representatives, which are not passed by the Senate without amendment within one month after they are received, may be presented for assent to the Head of State.

Legislation Other than Parliamentary Legislation of the Westminster Parliament

24. Instruments previously made by Order in Council and which are legislative in character shall henceforth be brought in as Bills.[50]

25. Otherwise, nothing in the arrangements set out in this Constitution for the enactment of primary legislation under Part 2 shall affect, subject to this Constitution, arrangements for the passing of secondary legislation.[51]

[50] Orders in Council are currently formally made in the name of the Crown by the Privy Council.
[51] This term is defined in Part 14.

26. Similarly, nothing in the arrangements set out in this Constitution for the enactment of primary legislation by the Westminster Parliament shall, subject to this Constitution, affect the passing of legislation (whether primary or secondary as the case may be) by the devolved governments of Scotland, Wales and Northern Ireland.

Federalism[52]

27. There shall be a referendum in Scotland, Wales and Northern Ireland (which area shall include for the purposes of this referendum the republic of Northern Ireland) binding as to the intended result to be achieved, to establish whether there are any circumstances in which the country in question is willing as a matter of principle to be bound by the Federal part of this Constitution. The referendum is binding in favour of the change if 60 per cent of the population of the registered electorate for the area in question vote for the change in status, provided that 20 per cent of the population entitled to vote actually do vote in this first referendum. If the vote is against the referendum committing the said population to accept the Federal part of the Constitution then the Federal part of this Constitution does not arise as against the electorate in question and the binding referendum referred to in Article 28 does not occur.

28. There shall be a referendum in Scotland, Wales and Northern Ireland when the information is to hand (the same stipulations occur in defining the area in question as occurred in the case of Northern Ireland in the preceding Article) by the Federal part of this Constitution. The referendum is binding if 60 per cent of the population of the area in question vote in favour of the alteration in status, provided that 20 per cent of the population actually vote. In the case of Northern Ireland the vote is only binding if 60 per cent of the population in question of both the areas of Northern Ireland and the Republic of Ireland vote in favour of the change in status and provided that 20 per cent of both areas actually do vote in this second referendum. If the result the second referendum is not binding there shall be a third referendum leaving out for the purposes of the third referendum the option which obtained the fewest votes in the second referendum.

[52] See Michael Kenny's *Politics, Sovereignty and the Fight to Save the UK* (Hurst & Co, 2024), where a subtly different interpretation is adopted.

29. There shall then be a third referendum conducted on exactly the same terms as to participation and result, namely whether Scotland, Wales and/or Northern Ireland shall be bound by the Federal terms of this Constitution or be independent or be subject to all the terms apart from the remainder of this Part.

30. If the result of the second or third referendums is that each of the parts of the United Kingdom wants independence or to be subject to all the terms of this Constitution save the Federal provisions then Federalism properly so-called in the United Kingdom from the point of view of this part of the Constitution does not arise. But one or more of the countries voting to be bound by the Constitutional provisions (apart from England) means that Federalism can take place between England and that country or countries. Only if 60 per cent of the people voting in the third referendum vote positively for devolution or independence can those options be chosen.

31. Laws shall be made following consultation to establish the best way in which England is to be developed to create the conditions under which a more transparent and coherent system of government could be constructed. The major parties should pledge to complete the federal map (ie to include England) within five years of the entry into force of this Constitution.

LAWMAKING: OBSERVATIONS AND EXPLANATORY NOTES

Overview

This cluster of articles addresses the subject of lawmaking under the Constitution. There are a number of traps that might surprise the unwary when seeking to formulate an acceptable structure setting out how laws are passed in the UK. Some of the problems, at least, are attempted to be resolved in this Constitution.

The Absence of EU Law in Our Constitution

It is the absence of EU law in our constitutional arrangements that causes most concern. Just as devolution was getting off the ground (taking a notable example) it was given the shock of the UK's break with the EU. Obviously, the shock of Brexit is not limited to the devolved territories. It has had wider constitutional effects.

The UK is no longer part of the EU. The first dramatic change is that now, for the first time for almost 40 years, there has been a drastic alteration of the law. Getting out of the EU is so much more complex than getting into it.

Brexit occurred on 31 January 2020 and, from 31 December 2020, all EU law became part of domestic legislation. The Withdrawal Agreement between the EU and the UK set out the arrangements for the UK's withdrawal from the EU at 11.00pm on 31 January 2020 (exit day). EU legislation which included a transition or implementation period during which EU law continued to apply in the UK is treated separately from the point of view of the Withdrawal Agreement. The implementation period expired at 11.00pm on 31 December 2020 (IP completion day) as set out in the European (Withdrawal Agreement) Act 2020. EU legislation which applied directly or indirectly to the UK before 11.00pm on 31 December 2020 has been retained in UK law as a form of domestic legislation known as 'retained EU law' (also known as REUL). Section 4 of the European Union (Withdrawal Act) 2018 ensures that any remaining EU rights and obligations, including directly effective rights within EU treaties, continue to be recognised and available in domestic law after exit. The European Union (Future Relationship) Act 2020 implements the arrangements for the relationship between the EU and the UK after the end of the implementation period, as agreed on 24 December 2020.

But, the Retained EU Law (Revocation and Reform) Act 2023 changes the constitutional balance in the ways considered in the Notes below. For further detail see also the Retained EU Law (Revocation and Reform) Bill 2022–2023[53] and Retained EU Law (Revocation and Reform) Act 2023.[54]

Primary and Delegated Legislation

There is the initial difficulty that laws come in different shapes and sizes. The most basic division is that between primary and secondary legislation. Parliamentary primary legislation in the sense used in this Part of the Constitution consists of Acts of Parliament made by the Westminster Parliament. Secondary (or delegated) legislation consists of laws that are passed otherwise than by such Act of Parliament but under authority conferred by an enabling Act. Secondary legislation may take a variety of forms. The main form of secondary legislation used in the UK is the statutory instrument, which is subject to certain controls by the Westminster Parliament.

Primary legislation is subject under the current law to an absence of judicial restriction in view of the doctrine of parliamentary sovereignty. But there is

[53] House of Commons Library, 17 October 2022.
[54] House of Commons Library, 28 July 2023.

parliamentary scrutiny.[55] Secondary legislation is subject to judicial review and the High Court is empowered to grant a quashing order or any of the reliefs in judicial review proceedings to render the statutory instrument void.[56]

Problems of Lack of Parliamentary Scrutiny Over Secondary Legislation[57]

This issue is dealt with directly in the House of Lords' Select Committee on the Constitution Report[58] titled 'The Legislative Process: The Delegation of Powers'.[59] There are three broad issues with the delegation of powers to Ministers in Acts.[60] Each of them requires that more accountability be granted to Parliament:

(i) The powers granted to Ministers to make delegated legislation are frequently too broad (paras 41–50). The Constitution Committee thought that 'it is incumbent on the Government to provide Parliament with a full explanation of, and justification for the delegated power it seeks.' Even then, the scope for parliamentary scrutiny is limited.

(ii) Too many Acts are now 'skeleton' Acts that contain a host of powers rather than policy (paras 51–58). The Constitution Committee thought that 'Skeleton bills inhibit parliamentary scrutiny and we find it difficult to envisage any circumstances in which their use is acceptable.'[61]

[55] For interesting articles on the degree of scrutiny offered see Kate Dewnip, 'The Purpose of Legislative Scrutiny', *The Constitution Society*, 21 April 2023, and Professor Meg Russell and Lisa James, 'Parliamentary Scrutiny: What Is It and Why Does It Matter?', *The Constitution Unit Blog*, 12 September 2023.

[56] See Jack Simson Caird, 'What is the Aim of Parliamentary Scrutiny of Delegated Legislation?', *Hansard Society Blog*, 28 April 2020, and Thomas G Fleming, 'Parliamentary Scrutiny of Delegated Legislation: Lessons from Comparative Experience', *Wiley's Online Library*, 6 July 2023.

[57] This has existed for many years; see eg Lord Hewart of Bury, *The New Despotism* (London, Ernest Benn, 1929).

[58] There are two committees principally concerned with this issue. One of them, the Joint Committee on Statutory Instruments, looks at legal, technical or non-merits grounds. The other, the Secondary Legislation Scrutiny Committee, is a permanent committee based in the House of Lords which examines the policy effects of instruments subject to proceedings in Parliament. Other committees look occasionally at related issues, for example the Constitution Committees.

[59] HL Paper 225, 16th Report of Session 2017–19, 20 November 2018. See also the voices of concern raised by Delegated Powers and Regulatory Reform Committee, *Democracy Denied? The Urgent Need to Rebalance Power between Parliament and the Executive* (2021–22, HL 106); Secondary Legislation Scrutiny Committee, *Government by Diktat: A Call to Return Power to Parliament* (2021–22, HL 105); Joint Committee on Statutory Instruments, *Rule of Law: Themes from COVID-19 Regulations* (2021–22, 57, HC 600). The Hansard Society undertook a review of delegated legislation and the final results are expectedly shortly.

[60] Parliament has virtually no power of amendment and the risk of a SI being rejected is remote (as of 2018 only 16 had been rejected: para 107). The only effective procedure is the enhanced scrutiny procedure but this is only available if Parliament choses in include it in the parent Act.

[61] But having said that, the Committee then said 'the Government must provide an exceptional justification for them'.

(iii) The so-called 'Henry VIII powers', which enable Ministers to amend or repeal primary legislation by statutory instrument, are problematic (paras 59–67). Henry VIII powers constitute a departure from constitutional principles and in the opinion of the Constitution Committee '[w]idely drawn delegations of legislative authority cannot be justified solely by the need for speed and flexibility'.

The problems inherent in delegating powers to Ministers can only intensify as a result of the decision to exit from the EU. This is because of the difficulty of Parliament having to debate each of the very voluminous areas of EU law, and the problems associated with it all being left to Ministers for decision. The original Act was a broadly conservative piece of legislation called the European Union (Withdrawal Act) 2018 (which came into force on 26 June 2018). It gave Ministers sweeping powers to get rid of unwanted pieces of retained EU law (which it called REUL), but broadly speaking it left things as they were.

However, by the time of the passing of the Retained EU Law (Revocation and Reform) Act 2023, things had become more complicated. In simple terms, REUL (to be renamed as 'assimilated' once the new Act is fully effective) is a category of domestic law created at the end of the transition period (11 pm on 31 December 2020). It is made up of certain EU laws that were 'copied or pasted' or preserved in the UK statute book in order to minimise disruption on exiting the EU and avoid gaps in important areas such as employment law and the environment. The 2023 Act radically alters the 2018 status of REUL, broadly empowering Ministers to restate, revoke or replace REUL with only limited parliamentary scrutiny. Although the Government switched its approach from abolishing much of REUL to sun-setting a far more limited schedule (600 pieces of REUL), the 2023 Act still makes important alterations to the status, content and operation of REUL and contains broad Ministerial powers that could be used to achieve post-Brexit deregulation.[62]

There are three problems (at least) with the Retained EU Law (Revocation and Reform) Act 2023:

(i) acceptance of the automatic expiry of REUL will be an abdication of Parliament's scrutiny and oversight role;
(ii) the broad and ambiguous wording of powers will confer excessive discretion on Ministers. The scope of Henry VIII powers is, for example, actually increased by including the power to amend REUL;

[62] In brief, the Retained EU Law (Revocation and Reform) Act 2023 provides for the following: (i) the repeal of that legislation contained in Sch 1 in 2023 (provided that Ministers or devolved legislatures had opted to do so by 31 October 2023); (ii) the repeal of directly effective retained EU rights and obligations at the end of 2023; (iii) the end of the supremacy of EU law in UK law at the end of 2023; (iv) the abolition of the general principles of EU law in UK law at the end of 2023; (v) the conferral of broad powers of Ministers to restate, revoke and replace secondary REUL and assimilated law; (vi) the facilitation of the future departure from retained case law by domestic courts.

(iii) there are potentially serious implications for devolution and the future of the Union. The difficulty is that there is the potential for UK Ministers and Ministers in the devolved administrations to become involved in using the same powers. The Act is, for example, completely silent about what should happen if a Minister in the UK chooses to legislate in areas of devolved competence.

The Devolved Legislatures

The devolved legislatures also have the power to make primary legislation and secondary legislation. Devolution is addressed in the section with the heading 'Federalism/Devolution'. But the important difference, so far as lawmaking is concerned, is that Scotland, Wales and Northern Ireland have powers devolved to them from the Westminster Parliament and so the courts are empowered to address by judicial review not just secondary but also primary legislation.

The test for whether or not the court is in a position to grant any relief in such primary legislation cases was well set out by Lord Hope in *AXA General Insurance Ltd and Others (Appellants) v The Lord Advocate and Others (Respondents) (Scotland)*[63] (at para 52):

> … that acts of the Scottish Parliament are not subject to judicial review at common law on the grounds of irrationality, unreasonabless or arbitrariness. This is not needed, as there is already a statutory limit on the Parliament's legislative competence if a provision is incompatible with any of the Convention rights: section 29(2)(d) of the Scotland Act 1998. But it would also be quite wrong for the judges to substitute their views on these issues for the considered judgment of a democratically elected legislature unless authorised to do so ….

The only circumstance in which Lord Hope would have granted relief would have been '… if a government which has power may seek to use it to abolish judicial review or to diminish the role of the courts in protecting the interests of the individual' (see para 51).

Terminology

In creating a structure for the primary lawmaking powers of the Westminster Parliament, terminology is of some importance. In choosing the names of the institutions that currently comprise the Westminster Parliament a deliberate

[63] *AXA General Insurance Ltd and Others (Appellants) v The Lord Advocate and Others (Respondents) (Scotland)* [2011] UKSC 46. The UK Supreme Court unanimously approved Lord Hope's approach: per Lord Brown at para 84, Lord Reed at para 85, and Lord Kerr, Clarke and Dyson at para 177.

change was thought to be necessary for the new Constitution. If, as is argued, class distinction and feudal privilege have a played a major part in a top-down allocation of authority, nowhere is this more evident than in the names we currently give to our lawmaking institutions. 'House of Commons' and 'House of Lords' perpetuate a 'gentleman versus player' kind of mentality that has no place in the modern world.

The term 'House of Representatives' gives emphasis to the underlying idea of democratic representation that is intended to be embodied in both Houses of the Parliament. The term 'Senate' is one that is usually used in a bicameral parliamentary system to denote the upper house. There is, of course, no magic in these names and it is possible that more creative imaginations may come up with something a little more exciting.

Relationship between the House of Representatives and the Senate (Arts 10–23)

These articles set out the framework for the legislative relationship between the House of Representatives and the Senate.

There have been many criticisms of the ways in which parliamentary legislative business has been conducted, especially in relation to the lack of genuine scope for debate. Article 11 is essentially neutral and makes it clear that unless the Constitution provides otherwise, Parliament is free to conduct its own procedures.

The current relationship between the House of Commons and the House of Lords is a delicate one. The Commons is an elected body whereas the House of Lords is not. Reform of the House of Lords has begun but is, as yet, incomplete. It is thought by many that if the House of Lords were to become a wholly elected body, it would claim equal legitimacy with the Commons and that this could cause constitutional difficulty. On the other hand, an appointed second chamber appears to lack all democratic legitimacy. Devolution, too, plays an important part in arriving at a sensible way forward (see the Notes on federalism/devolution below).

The solution adopted in this Constitution is to make the Senate part elected and part appointed. Considerations of legitimacy play a part in this process. But far from being the greater part (in the first edition of this book it was), since the purpose of the present Constitution is to ensure better scrutiny of proposed legislation and to ensure balance and lack of domination by the House of Representatives, a different solution has been found. Now, appointments to the Senate comprise 50% of its composition, with free and fair elections constituting the other 50%. The appointments process is carried out by a democratically elected Senate Appointments Commission. The elections process has a built-in approach to federalisation in the sense that this is the best attempt so far at incorporation of the units that make it a union.

It is hoped that a balance of this type will enable the House of Representatives still to claim primary legitimacy; the constitutional relationship between that House and the Senate is predicated on that basis. With a few small changes, the Constitution preserves the essential dominance of the House of Representatives (formerly House of Commons), with removal of the Senate's (formerly House of Lords) absolute legislative veto by the Parliament Acts of 1911 and 1949 (see Arts 17–23).

Role of the Monarchy (Art 12)

One consequence of having a constitutional monarchy (using that term in its strictest sense) is that the monarch is subject to the terms of the Constitution. This is reflected in Art 12, which stipulates the circumstances in which the Head of State is required to grant assent to a parliamentary Bill. As a matter of constitutional theory, the monarch (currently) has the power to withhold assent and this power was exercised frequently in the past. Nonetheless, as a matter of constitutional convention, the monarch is bound to accept the advice of the Prime Minister and now Royal Assent to a Bill is a formality.

Article 12 also stipulates one circumstance in which the monarch must *refuse* assent. This is where the Supreme Court has declared a Bill to be incompatible with the Constitution. This is entirely new, because the doctrine of parliamentary sovereignty formerly immunised parliamentary Bills against the jurisdiction of the courts.[64] What is proposed here is that a new power be given to the Supreme Court to declare proposed statutes (as well as actual statutes) to be in breach of the Constitution before enactment. This power is discussed more fully in the section on the judiciary in Part 8 of the constitution.

Fixed-term Parliament (Art 13)

An idea which is supported by many – that of a fixed-term Parliament (of four years) – is included in Article 13. We already have fixed terms for the devolved bodies, local councils and, subject to carefully drafted specified exceptions (also included in Art 13), there seems to be no sensible reason for leaving the calling of a general election to the strategic wiles of the incumbent Prime Minister.

The Fixed-term Parliaments Act 2011 (FTPA 2011) was an Act of Parliament that for the first time set in legislation a default fixed election date for a general election to the Westminster Parliament. Under the FTPA 2011 the next general

[64] Except in HRA 1998 cases, which were subject to the jurisdiction of the Courts but in a way which allowed for the doctrine of parliamentary supremacy to surface because it was recognised in the HRA 1998 itself that Parliament is free to legislate as it chooses. EU law, while it lasted, was the one species of law which trumped parliamentary supremacy.

election was automatically scheduled for the first Thursday in May of the fifth year after the previous general election, or the fourth year if the date of the previous election was before the first Thursday in May. However, the FTPA 2011 also specified two exceptions. One was in the case of a Commons vote of no-confidence in the Government. The other was a vote explicitly in favour of an earlier election that required a vote of a majority of two-thirds of the House of Commons. The first election under the FTPA was held on 7 May 2015. An early election was held in 2017 after the then Prime Minister Theresa May received approval to call it by a two-thirds majority.

Under the FTPA 2011 the next general election was scheduled for 2022. However, the Early Parliamentary General Election Act 2019, passed with Opposition support, circumvented the FTPA 2011, providing for an election on 12 December 2019 while otherwise leaving the FTPA 2011 in place. After winning the election the Conservative Party committed to repealing the FTPA 2011. The legislation to do so was the Dissolution and Calling of Parliament Act, which was granted assent on 24 March 2022.[65] We are back to square one as far as reform is concerned.

There is also a case to be made for adopting the US practice whereby an incumbent Government is eased in over a transitional period, although this is not included here as a constitutional requirement.

Dissolution Matters (Art 16)

With a part-elected Senate (see below), dissolution of both the House of Representatives and the elected part (and appointment part) of the Senate happens at the same time. The present proposal avoids the impasse created by the US system of electing a President separately from Congress[66] (and with Congressional elections themselves occurring at different times for the House of Representatives and the Senate) with the consequent polarisation of interests that can occur as a result of altered electoral views.

Federalism/Devolution (Arts 27–31)

Devolution is probably the only topic in this Constitution that is, at this stage, incapable of resolution. This is because the devolution process started off

[65] The Dissolution and Calling of Parliament Act 2022 has its own host of legal issues. First is the scope and extent of the non-justiciability of the revived prerogative powers clause in s 3. Second is whether there is any restriction on Parliament being the determiner of revived prerogative powers.

[66] The US Congress is the analogue to the UK Parliament. It is the bicameral legislature of the federal government of the US and consists of the Senate and the House of Representatives.

badly, with no consistent aim in sight. The three statutes started (the Scotland Act 1998, the Government of Wales Act 1998 and the Northern Ireland Act 1998) with different objectives, though all combined to make the headline of devolution.

The statutes were necessarily asymmetric as between the different devolved territories. This would not have mattered if there is had been a consistent objective beyond the headline aim of granting more power to the devolved adminstrations. The development of the initial devolution settlements was strongly driven by a path of dependency: for Northern Ireland the previous devolution arrangements under the Government of Ireland 1920; in Scotland and Wales the scope of administrative devolution under the old Scottish and Wales offices in Whitehall. Subsequent changes to devolved competences have been reactive. Also, England was not included in devolution, which is a major error.

Unless devolution is admitted to be a flawed process and incapable of being run except by a constitutional fiat (the alternative being dissolution of the Union either by a declaration of independence or a by disorganised run-down of the present power-grabbing situation) the present problems will continue.

A very brief history of devolution would make the following points:

(i) Devolution is the name given to describe the process of transferring power from central government to the nations and regions of the UK. The legislative framework (and asymmetric frameworks at the start of this process) for this were laid down in the three Acts – the Scotland Act 1998, the Government of Wales Act 1998, and the Northern Ireland Act 1998. The devolved administrations now have legislative and executive powers.

(ii) The three devolved administrations can only pass primary and secondary legislation in their own devolved areas (or 'transferred' in the case of Northern Ireland) with 'reserved matters' being reserved for the Westminster Parliament.

(iii) Metro Mayors in parts of England and the Mayor of London have only executive powers. Combined authorities and the London Assembly scrutinise executive decisions but cannot legislate in the manner of the devolved administrations.

(iv) There is also a non-legislative framework of agreements concluded between Government departments and the devolved institutions which assist in trying to resolve some of the disputes between central government and devolved government. The current Memorandum of Understanding between the Government and the devolved administrations of Scotland, Wales and Northern Ireland was first agreed in 1999 and most recently in 2013. It sets out principles that support relations between all four administrations.

(v) The four issues that have been repeatedly raised in relation to the devolution settlements that have been arrived at are: (1) the West Lothian question; (2) uneven/asymmetrical devolution; (3) the power of the UK Parliament over the devolved bodies; and (4) calls for independence from the United Kingdom.

(vi) Tam Dalyell, then the MP for West Lothian, asked the question (in 1977) '… for how long will English constituencies and English Honourable Members tolerate … exercising important, often decisive, effect on English politics while they themselves have no say in the same matters in Scotland, Wales and Northern Ireland'. The Conservative Government introduced (in 2015) the 'English Votes for English Laws' procedure, which was attacked on both sides of the House and was scrapped in July 2021. So far the answer to a question posed nearly 50 years ago has not been answered. It is suspected that the answer lies in the Government's failure to address the one country in respect of which no devolution proposal has been considered (England).

(vii) The complaint about the uneven quality of much of the early devolution laws is not about the unevenness per se but about the aims of British policy. The policy was about divestment of power but without thought for the consequences of such divestment. Had thought been given to the consequences of divesting power, it is inconceivable that England would not have been in the mix. If England had been in the mix it is less likely than Scotland would be straining as hard as it currently is to escape the supposed bonds of the Union because England would be just one of the several powers making up the Union.

(viii) One issue that frequently arises is the ability of the central institutions to carry decisions that override devolved bodies. Under the doctrine of parliamentary sovereignty, even devolution could be overridden by Parliament just passing another law cancelling out the whole devolution settlement. This gives devolution a weaker basis than, for instance, the territorial systems of Germany or the US when federal and state powers are defined and secured by constitutional law that cannot so easily be overridden.

(ix) To legally secede from the Union would require legislation at the UK level.[67] At the time of writing, no Conservative party or Labour party Prime Minister has agreed to facilitate holding a second referendum on Scottish independence (the first one was held in 2014). This highlights that there is no agreed mechanism by which Scotland could leave the Union. Even in the case of Northern Ireland – where there is provision for this in the Belfast/Good Friday Agreement – there is uncertainty subsisting as to the point at which a referendum on unification might be held.

[67] *Reference by the Lord Advocate of devolution issues under paragraph 34 of Schedule 6 to the Scotland Act* [1998] UKSC 31.

To this turmoil of issues this Constitution seeks to resolve the situation as follows:

(i) a binding referendum to be held in Scotland, Wales[68] and Northern Ireland (which includes the Republic) of the peoples of the respective areas, asking whether they want to bound by a constitution or be free (free includes both independence or being free to continue as at present);

(ii) the second referendum in each area (if it comes) comes only after completion of the negotiations which are equally binding on each of the nations; only if one or more of these areas wish to be bound by the Constitution should one consider the various ways in which the Constitution might actually bind the areas which have agreed to the Constitution binding them in terms of its devolution proposals. This leads up the second referendum;

(iii) a third referendum (if process reaches such a stage) is the final choice of the devolved administrations to say whether they really want to be free or be bound into the federal part of the Constitution, or (which is the consequence of failing to vote to the standard required) whether they want to remain in their current position.

Obviously, if the result is that the devolved administrations do not wish to be bound by the Constitution in the area of federalism, the area in question reverts to being free (either in the sense of being independent or not being subject to the federalism provisions).

The two stages of federalism that then follow if the vote is positive are: (i) to make England the relevant party of a federal set of arrangements; and (ii) to make the other countries equal partners.

LAWMAKING: KEY POINTS

- **Type of lawmaking and brief description of its aims:** In the UK there are currently three types of lawmaking. These are: (i) parliamentary legislation (the conventional Acts of Parliament); (ii) laws passed by (usually) the Secretary of State, generally in the form of statutory instruments or rules given to them under Acts of Parliament; (iii) laws made by the devolved administrations.

[68] The Independent Commission on the Constitutional Future of Wales has published its Final Report in January 2024. In it the Independent Commission made ten recommendations but neither the Conservative nor Labour party has signalled any wish to countenance significant change. One of the Independent Commission recommendations was to introduce a citizens' based process for creating constitutional principles for Wales.

- **The absence of EU law:** An inevitable result of Brexit is the absence of EU law. Brexit took place on 31 January 2020 and all retained EU law became, from 31 December 2020, part of domestic legislation. The EU Law (Revocation and Reform) Act 2023 alters the constitutional balance in a number of important respects, which means that what was formerly EU law is given scant respect by Parliament.
- **Primary and delegated legislation:** Primary legislation is the name given to Acts of Parliament. Because of the doctrine of parliamentary sovereignty laws passed by Parliament cannot be reviewed by the courts. Secondary legislation can be the subject of judicial review (including Acts of the three administrations which are the subject of devolution provisions created by the Westminster Parliament).
- **Problems of lack of parliamentary scrutiny of delegated legislation:** There are three main problems relating to parliamentary scrutiny: (i) the powers granted to Ministers are too broad; (ii) too many Acts are now 'skeleton' in nature; (iii) the so-called Henry VIII powers, which involve the Ministers being able to amend or repeal primary legislation by statutory instrument.
- **Devolution:** Devolution is the name given to the transfer of powers from central government to the three devolved administrations of Scotland, Wales, and Northern Ireland. Four issues are key: (i) the West Lothian question (the question about how long English members of the House of Commons will tolerate the situation of English MPs having no say of what happens in Scotland, Wales and Northern Ireland, when the MPs of the devolved administrations have a say in what happens in England); (ii) the aims of creating asymmetric devolution systems; (iii) the logic of Parliament creating a devolution system that could be swept away by a different Parliament; (iv) for Scotland, the absence of an agreed mechanism for deciding the question of independence.
- **Relationship between the House of Representatives and the Senate:** The relationship between the House of Representatives (currently the House of Commons) and the Senate (currently the House of Lords) is a delicate one, perhaps especially as regards the current bid for independence in Scotland. The Constitution proposes a 50% elected and a 50% appointed membership of the Senate.
- **Role of the monarchy:** The Head of State is governed by the Constitution. All the powers of the monarch are purely symbolic.
- **Fixed-term Parliaments:** Fixed-term Parliaments are included in Article 13 of the new Constitution. There seems to be no logical reasons for leaving the decision on when to hold an election to the Prime Minister.

PART 3
THE HOUSE OF REPRESENTATIVES (ARTS 32–56)

The Work of the Commission for the Houses of Parliament

32. A Commission shall be created called the Houses of Parliament Commission, which shall be an elected body. Laws shall be made which deal with all matters relevant to the working of the Commission no later than six months after the coming into force of the Constitution.

33. The Commission is charged first with the tasking of reviewing the arrangements specified in the Constitution for the new methodology for selection by election to the House of Representatives and the Senate. Its recommendations shall be carefully considered by each House of Parliament. If the Commission recommends that any changes need to be made to the procedures relevant to the House of Representatives, two-thirds of the House of Representatives must vote to negate the Commission's recommendations. The voting by the House of Representatives shall be either for or against the recommendations. This Constitution shall prevail if the House of Representatives vote against the Commission's recommendations. If the Commission's recommendation replaces the Constitution, it shall be noted as the First Amendment.

34. The Commission shall consist of a Chairman and 14 other Commissioners. Those standing for election as Chairman and Commissioners must fulfil the eligibility qualifications.

35. The Commissioners shall be elected by a postal vote of registered electors throughout the United Kingdom from a list of eligible candidates to be drawn up by an independent statutory body. An initial list shall, however, be drawn up by current members of the Judicial Appointments Commission, and subsequent lists by the body mentioned in the statute. The list of eligible candidates shall comprise only citizens who have or have had a distinguished career in any aspect of national or international life, whether in the public or private sector.

36. The 15 candidates who receive the highest number of votes in the election shall be elected as Commissioners, and the candidate receiving the highest number of votes overall shall be selected as Chairman of the Commission.

37. Subject to the Constitution and, in particular, to the voting in the House of Representatives on the recommendations of the Commission to be set up for the purposes of making such recommendations to Parliament, the composition of the House of Representatives shall be as set out in Articles 38–42, and the method of election shall be as set out in Articles 43–46.

Composition

38. In order to be elected to the House of Representatives, a person must be a citizen of one of the nations that comprise the United Kingdom, have civil and political rights, have attained the age of eighteen, be legally resident in the United Kingdom and not be disqualified from occupying a seat in the House of Representatives by reason of one or more the matters set out in this Constitution which are, where relevant, applied by this Article to the period preceding election or the taking up of office as they are to the period following election. There are no disqualifications from election or from continued membership of the House of Representatives save as set out in or incorporated into this Constitution.

39. A member of the House of Representatives may not at the same time be a member of the Senate, the Scottish Parliament, the Welsh Assembly or the Northern Ireland Assembly.

40. The House of Representatives shall initially consist of the same members of those constituencies as comprised the House of Commons immediately before the coming into force of this Constitution.[69]

41. Following all elections (including by-elections but only by-elections after the first general election) after the coming into force of this Constitution, and in accordance with the procedure by which those elections take place, as provided for in this Constitution, the number of Members of Parliament shall be 350 as provided for by the first-past-the-post system of elections and 100 as provided for by elections to multi-member constituencies.[70]

42. The boundaries of the constituencies for election to the House of Representatives shall be determined by regular reviews of the appropriate Boundary Commission in accordance with law.[71] Changes may be made by the appropriate Boundary Commission to the location of the constituencies but no changes may be made to the number of constituencies either by the first-past-the-post elections or the multi-member constituencies save as set out in this Constitution.

[69] At the last general election, in July 2024, there were 650 MPs elected.

[70] See below under 'Elections' for the difference between first-past-the-post and the multi-member constituency processes.

[71] See Part 14 for the definition of 'appropriate Boundary Commission'. Revised constituency boundaries require the consent of Parliament before they may be implemented. Parliamentary consent is, of course, subject to this Constitution.

Elections

43. The House of Representatives shall be elected by election of one member on a first-past-the-post electoral system. The number of seats under this Constitution comes to 350. The remainder of the seats are addressed to multi-member constituencies of which there are 20 consisting of five members for each constituency.

44. Multi-member constituencies[72] are chosen as to represent the United Kingdom with regard being paid to the need to reflect more accurately than with simple majority voting the number of votes cast for each party. The method of election shall include a method of proportional presentation[73] to be set out in laws to be made and to have effect at the same time as the coming into force of this Constitution.

45. Subject to this Constitution, rules relating to the timing and conduct of general elections,[74] the prescribed date by which (other than in a case to which another article of this Constitution applies) newly elected members shall replace the existing Members of the Houses of Parliament (before which time Parliament shall continue in existence and shall not be dissolved)[75] and the procedure to be applied to general elections including eligibility to vote shall be set out in laws to be made and to have effect at the same time as the coming into force of this Constitution. However, laws may not stipulate the age at which a person is to be entitled to vote as being older than 18 or younger than 16.

46. Save for any registered persons aged under 18 at the time of a general election, every person registered as a voter whose right to registration has not ceased must, as prescribed by law, and subject to such exceptions as are laid down by law, vote in every election in the constituencies in respect of which he or she is enrolled. Provision may be made by law for revocation of the right to vote for a stipulated period for repeated breach of this obligation. No law shall make it a breach of this obligation to fail to vote provided that there is a reasonable excuse for failing to do so.

[72] See Part 14 for the definitions of 'constituency' and 'multi-member constituency'.

[73] As to the meaning of 'proportional representation' see the notes below marked 'Proportional Representation'.

[74] The present system with, for example, an Electoral Commission supervising elections, would be encompassed in such laws.

[75] This provision is designed to ensure that Members of the House of Parliament are ordinarily not replaced until a prescribed date. This is achieved by Parliament not being dissolved so that MPs simply continue to hold office until they are replaced by the newly-elected MPs. The position is different in the situation set out in Art 13(i)–(ii) where Parliament must be dissolved.

Conduct and Vacation of Place as Member

47. Members of the House of Representatives shall be remunerated from public funds. Such remuneration, including allowances and other expenses, shall be determined by an independent authority established by law.

48. Laws (which include for the purposes of this article codes of practice and standing orders) shall make provision for the registration of interests and such other benefits as members of the House of Representatives are permitted to hold as well as for the supervision of such register, and for the declaration of interests and other benefits that members are not permitted to hold.

49. Laws (which include for the purposes of this article codes of practice and standing orders) shall make provision for the standards of conduct to be observed by members of the House of Representatives.

50. The place of a member of the House of Representatives shall, subject to this Constitution, automatically become vacant and a by-election shall be held if that member ceases to be qualified (or never was qualified) to sit in the House of Representatives under Article 38 or Article 39 or –

(i) dies;
(ii) is removed from office by being recalled by the voters within his or her constituency under this Constitution;
(iii) is criminally convicted of an offence punishable by imprisonment;
(iv) is criminally convicted of an illegal election practice;
(v) resigns by giving the Speaker a signed resignation;
(vi) ceases to have a right to be registered as a voter in an election to the House of Representatives;
(vii) has any interest being an interest of a kind prescribed by law as an interest that must not be held by a member of the House of Representatives;
(viii) holds or occupies any office, employment or position of a kind prescribed by this Constitution or by law[76] as one that must not be held by a member of the House of Representatives;

[76] Currently, holders of a number of offices and other positions are currently prevented from becoming MPs under, amongst other provisions, the House of Commons Disqualification Act 1975 (see Sch 1 to that Act). The list is quite detailed and subject to change. It includes full-time police officers, civil servants and members of the regular armed forces. Hereditary peers who are not elected to sit in the House of Lords may, however, be members of the House of Commons (see the House of Lords Act 1999).

(ix) resigns from or otherwise ceases (save by unlawful expulsion) to be a member of the political party for which he or she was a candidate at the time he or she was elected to the House of Representatives.[77]

51. The law may not prescribe other circumstances in which the place of a member of the House of Representatives shall or may become vacant except that it may prescribe bankruptcy as an automatic disqualification or may prescribe conditions under which bankruptcy will result in disqualification.[78]

52. A number of voters in a constituency representing at least ten per cent of the registered voters may petition the Speaker of the House of Representatives to recall the mandate of the elected representative for that constituency. The procedure for the holding of the petition and if successful for the Speaker of the House of Representatives to hold a by-election (or general election) shall be subject to law and no law may operate to deprive the affected MP of a chance to offer himself or herself for election in the by-election (or general election).

Business

53. All questions proposed for decision in the House of Representatives shall, subject to this Constitution, be decided by a majority vote.[79] There is no casting vote and the question concerned shall be deemed to be lost unless there is a majority vote. The House of Representatives may act despite a vacancy in its membership and the presence of or the participation in its proceedings of a person not entitled to be a member does not invalidate the proceedings.

54. Subject to this Constitution the House of Representatives shall –

(i) decide its procedure;
(ii) elect its Speaker by such method as it shall decide (whether or not the method of election decided upon is by majority vote).

[77] This last category imports potential difficulties. As drafted, it would catch those moving from a specific party allegiance to becoming an independent. It would catch those such as Dick Taverne, who moved from Labour to Democratic Labour (albeit after a by-election) and it would catch an emergent party such as the Social Democratic Party, whose claim – at least initially – was that it was the true inheritor of the Labour tradition and that it was the Labour Party that had deviated. Despite these difficulties, there seems to be principled reason for requiring a by-election where the electorate has voted not necessarily merely for a candidate but also for the policy of the party to which that candidate belonged when elected to Parliament.

[78] The former law on bankruptcy, being automatic disqualification on being elected on sitting as an MP, was changed by the Enterprise Act 2002 and is now qualified in a number of respects.

[79] See Part 14 for a definition of the term 'majority vote'.

Powers of the House of Representatives

55. The powers of the House of Representatives are derived from this Constitution. Apart from anything else in this Constitution the House of Representatives cannot pass legislation calculated to facilitate a breach of public international law and must correct any legislation which is found by a court, including a judgment of the International Court of Justice, to have breached public international law.

56. Apart from its other powers conferred by this Constitution and subject to this Constitution, the House of Representatives shall have power to do those things which are calculated to facilitate or are conducive or incidental to the discharge of its functions under this Constitution.

THE HOUSE OF REPRESENTATIVES: OBSERVATIONS AND EXPLANATORY NOTES

Composition of the House of Representatives (Arts 38–42)

Although the age requirement for eligibility to sit as an MP is still 18 (see Art 38; it was reduced from 21 in 2006), more stringent requirements are laid down, in terms of MPs' conduct, as to their continued eligibility to sit in Parliament. The opportunity has also been taken to make it clear that a Westminster MP may no longer sit simultaneously in a devolved legislature (Art 39). This was one of the recommendations set out in the Kelly Report,[80] which has not, at the time of writing, been implemented.

More Women in Parliament (Art 8)

Important changes were proposed in the previous version of this Constitution. The broad effect of the changes that were proposed in the first edition would have seen a radical change to the number of women MPs. Since then, however, things have markedly improved. There are now (a result of the general election on 4 July 2024) 263 women elected to the House of Commons. This is an all-time high amounting to some 40 per cent. The results are a growing trajectory for the number of woman MPs: the figures for the 2019 general election were 220 women were elected to Parliament, the results of the figures for the 2017

[80] Committee on Standards in Public Life, *MP's Expenses and Allowances – Supporting the Taxpayer* Cm 7724 (November 2009) Recommendation 40.

general election were 208 women and in 2015 191 women were elected to the House of Commons. Moreover, two out of the last four Prime Ministers from the Conservative Party (Theresa May and Elizabeth Truss) were women and were selected as leader of the Conservative Party in 2016 and 2022 and (because the Conservative Party was the governing party) as Prime Minister.

Things are getting better and it is not just the House of Commons that has benefited from the strong increase in female representation. Over time, the proportion of members of the UK's parliaments and assemblies who are female has risen. As of 2022 the London Assembly has the highest number of female members at 52 per cent. And the most recent data shows, for example, that 45 per cent of public appointments were women, as were 54 per cent of civil servants and 34 per cent of judges.

The present position, then, is that the best thing to do so far as the Constitution is concerned is to step away from the difficulties of the affirmative action that was suggested in the previous edition. Three things have led to this conclusion:

(i) The first thing to note is that the number of MPs would have increased dramatically if the solution proposed in the previous edition for implementation (a two-member constituency in a second-past the-post system of government or an equal number of men and women in multi-member constituencies) had actually been implemented.
(ii) A temporary experiment such as women-only shortlists has been at risk of being declared unlawful. Labour, the party with the most consistent record of using all-female shortlists dropped such shortlists after it received legal advice that continuing to use them when women had a majority of MPs in the House of Commons was unlawful. But, there is a wider argument that using such shortlists is discriminatory because it ignores the fact that merit is the only proper division between men and women.[81]
(iii) Persuasion rather than force is the best method of achieving compliance with what is self-evidently a desirable outcome.

The situation is still far from ideal. Most of the junior appointments, it has to be admitted, go to women. Moreover, the numbers are, on the whole, far from balanced. Resolution of these difficulties, however, is a matter of policy rather than constitutional requirement.

Proportional Representation (Arts 43–44)

A major constitutional reform is that proposed for the system of electing members of the House of Representatives. This is quite a complicated and

[81] But the Equality Act 2010, s 104 makes it lawful, provided the statutory criteria are followed, to have all-women shortlists. Section 105(3) extends the deadline to 2030.

somewhat technical topic.[82] The Constitution puts in place a first stage of electoral reform, namely the structural transition from a simple first-past-the-post system to one of fairer representation, if not necessarily proportional representation in the strictest sense.

It is, however, a requirement of the Constitution that the final detail of whichever electoral system is chosen is to be set out in laws and by recommendations from a review Commission to be specially set up, and Parliament has to vote on the recommendations. If Parliament chooses to reject any (or indeed all) of the recommendations, it needs a majority of two-thirds before it can do so, and the Constitution prevails unless the proposed amendments can be severed. The detail will need to be very carefully considered and is likely to require much empirical research, including comparative research.

For that reason, the form of proportional representation (if any) has yet to be determined and what follows is an outline of the key provisions of the main forms of voting. It should be noted, however, that a referendum was held in 2011 (the United Kingdom Alternative Vote referendum). It operated under the provisions of the Parliamentary Voting System and Constituencies Act 2011 and was the first national referendum to be conducted under provisions laid out in the Political Parties, Elections and Referendum Act 2000. The proposal to introduce the alternative vote system was decisively rejected by 67.9 per cent of voters.

Proportional representation, or PR (in the extended sense used here, which includes the alternative vote and comparable electoral systems: see below) is to be contrasted with the first-past-the-post (FPTP) system currently in operation for election to the House of Commons. FPTP is a winner-takes-all-system for single-member constituencies in which victory by a single vote is all that is required to secure a parliamentary seat. The Constitution currently proposes the FPTP system be retained (350 seats), alongside a scheme of 20 new constituencies with five members each (making an additional total of 100 new MPs), all to be chosen by a PR system. In this fashion it is hoped that a degree of fairness will be incorporated into a system otherwise known for its rigidity.

The random unfairness of our present electoral system has been extensively documented. Although FPTP is often said to produce strong government,[83] the reality is that it produces arbitrary government in that the party with the highest number of constituencies wins, whatever its share of the national vote. Since the Second World War every election has produced a winning party that has polled less than 50 per cent of the vote. One advantage of the FPTP system is that it guarantees a link between that constituency and the MP selected.

[82] For a sceptical view addressing the merits of the FPTP system (which is currently in use in central government) see Jasper Miles, 'Accountability and Electoral Reform' in Richard Johnson and Yuan Yi Zhu, *Sceptical Perspectives on the Changing Constitution of the United Kingdom* (Oxford, Hart Publishing, 2023) 189–205.

[83] For a useful corrective to the perceived necessity for 'strong' government, see *Making Minority Government Work* (Institute for Government, 3 December 2009), which draws on experience from effective minority governments in New Zealand, Canada and Scotland.

This can lead, though, to serious injustices. For example, in the 2005 general election the Liberal Democrats secured 22 per cent of the national vote but gained only 10 per cent of the seats in the House of Commons. In the 1983 general election the combined vote share of the two major parties was 70 per cent, which enabled them to gain 93 per cent of the seats. On two occasions the majority party has even received fewer votes than its main rival (1951 and February 1974).

By contrast, PR in its strictest form aims to approximate the percentage of votes cast to the percentage of seats gained. It is the system used for elections in Scotland, Wales, Northern Ireland and London but has never been applied to Westminster elections.

There are many different types of PR, as well as particular voting systems which are arguably less unfair.

The main PR system, AV,[84] permits voters to cast votes for the various candidates in order of preference. The candidate who receives an outright straight majority of first preference votes (that is, more votes than the other candidates combined) is elected. If there is no such candidate, then the second preference votes of the candidate finishing last are redistributed and this process is repeated until a candidate emerges who has received more first preference votes than the others combined. One advantage of AV is that it can easily be used in the single-member constituencies that we currently have. Another advantage is that it preserves a constituency link, thus ensuring that voters are casting their vote for specific candidates linked to the particular constituency.

However, AV might be even more out of line with the overall cast for each party than FPTP. This was the conclusion following research conducted by Democratic Audit in 1997.

Alternative vote plus (AV+) was the system of (quasi-) PR invented and chosen by the Jenkins Commission, a body set up in 1997 to consider reform of the voting system following the general election that first voted New Labour into power. Under this system most MPs would be directly elected by AV (see above). There would then be a relatively small number (perhaps 15–20 per cent) of additional members elected from regional top-up lists. Whilst still retaining a considerable electoral advantage for the two main parties, AV+ introduces an element of PR which could produce a fairer electoral system than the present one. Thus, AV+ enjoys quite a wide measure of support because it is thought to combine the potential for strong government with greater equity between all competing political parties.

As to PR in its fullest sense, one system is the party list. This is a system of PR by which the parties provide candidate lists which are then matched to the

[84] Another possible method entailing the notion of an absolute majority is the 'second ballot' method by which all candidates except the last candidates (usually two) go through to a second and final round.

percentage of votes cast. Thus, if the Liberal Democrats obtain 30 per cent of the national vote, they are allocated 30 per cent of the seats. The list may be a closed list, where voters have no influence over the identity of the candidates on the party lists. Alternatively, the list may be open, meaning that voters have varying degrees of influence over the identity of the candidates that receive seats. It would appear to be difficult to match this with the necessity for strong government or to the need to match this with the present constituency linkage. But it does provide a fairer system.

Another well-known variant of PR is the single transferable vote (STV) system, which is used in Australia and Ireland, amongst other countries. It is suitable for multi-member constituencies. In STV the single votes cast may be transferred to different candidates (the number of candidates depending on the size of the constituency) but votes cast for candidates who are not successful (or which are not necessary to secure election) are then re-allocated to the other candidates according to voters' express preferences until all are eliminated but the most successful candidates.

Party list systems and STV would in fact give a considerable advantage to the Liberal Democrats, who have been under-represented in Parliament for a great many years. However, for that reason amongst others, neither system of PR is likely to receive support from the two main political parties.

The key choice to be made is between simple FPTP[85] and PR (including AV and similar systems) and this Constitution comes down firmly in favour of a mix between FPTP and the limited quantity of AV with the detail to be worked out in separate laws following a period of empirical research. This was essentially the conclusion of the Power Inquiry (2006), which was concerned that FPTP compounded the problem of voter apathy because under FPTP so many votes were wasted, in the sense that they had no prospect of affecting the electoral outcome in particular constituencies. But the Power Inquiry had no effective answer to the problem of how to implement such a plan, and reached a tentative solution which is not the one proposed in this Constitution.

Care needs to be taken in relation to the electoral system chosen because the nature of that system may have an effect on other aspects of the Constitution, such as by-elections and the recall of MPs.

Compulsory Voting (Art 46)

A change proposed in this Part of the Constitution is the introduction of compulsory voting, although there are strong arguments for not stigmatising it

[85] Or, as in the present constitutional suggestion, a hybrid mixture of simple FPTP (with, or without, additional votes by a sort of PR) and PR. A possible variant of simple FPTP would be second-past-the-post, namely the election of the first two candidates with the highest votes. It would be interesting to ascertain what changes in party representation at Westminster this might produce.

by way of criminal or even civil penalty. The sanction proposed for not voting is loss of entitlement to vote for a stipulated period. However, if the voting age were reduced to below 18 for being able to vote in a general election (see Art 46, which envisages that such a law could be introduced), there would be no duty to vote on those below the age of 18.

Compulsory voting has a respectable heritage, having been used in ancient Athens where red-stained ropes were used to herd recalcitrant voters into the assembly place and identify those who were trying to shirk their duty. Some countries, such as Australia and Belgium, now provide for compulsory voting. Some impose penalties for failing to vote; others do not enforce the requirement. The model adopted here is similar to that used in Belgium, where repeated failure to vote may result in disenfranchisement.

There are many good reasons to consider the imposition of compulsory voting for persons over 18 years of age. It reflects the idea that voting is a civic duty and, arguably, confers greater legitimacy on the party forming the Government by the far higher turnout of voters that is likely to result. Although there are objections to imposing a requirement to do that which, it may be said, is an entitlement rather than a duty, the underlying justification behind proposing compulsory voting is the argument that, with other changes, it is likely to increase citizen engagement. Turnout in general elections since 1997 has fallen.[86] Baroness Kennedy's inquiry into democracy concluded that voters are not alienated from politics as such, but feel that they have no active influence under the present electoral and party political system. Compulsory voting, without more, is unlikely to produce real change. However, if the wider electoral changes and alterations to the current party political system proposed by this Constitution are adopted, voters will have more influence. Compulsory voting is a logical component of a representative democratic society. In such a society, citizens have a real influence in shaping decision-making and are expected, as part of their civic responsibilities, to exercise that influence. This is consistent with a developing concept of citizenship which, as seems to be common ground between the parties, should be encouraged.

MPs' Interests and Conduct (Arts 47–52)

Public anger over the expenses scandal in 2009 compelled legislative reform and this led to the inquiry by Sir Christopher Kelly[87] and the perhaps over-hasty

[86] See Elise Uberoi, *Turnout at Elections* (House of Commons Library Briefing Paper, 10 January 2023): 'In 2001, turnout fell to 59.4%, its lowest level since 1918 and down 12 percentage points compared with 1997. Although turnout rose again between 2005 and 2007, before declining again slightly in 2019, it remained below its 1997 level.'

[87] Sir Christopher Kelly's report, *MPs' Expenses and Allowances* (n 79), was published on 4 November 2009.

passing of the Parliamentary Standards Act 2009, which is directed towards the House of Commons. That creates an Independent Parliamentary Standards Authority (IPSA) and an officer known as the Commissioner for Parliamentary Investigations. The IPSA is responsible for drawing up schemes of members' allowances and for paying the salaries of MPs. The 2009 Act provides that the Commissioner will investigate lapses in MPs' conduct, including breaches of that Code. The making of false claims against MPs is a criminal offence punishable by up to 12 months' imprisonment.

There is also the select Committee on Standards which was created on 13 December 2012 because, following the expenses scandal, it was considered desirable for lay members to provide oversight of standards of conduct of MPs but not for breaches of parliamentary privilege. The former Select Committee on Standards and Privileges was therefore split in two. In the wake of the Owen Patterson affair in November 2021, the Conservative Government proposed removing the lay members entirely but the 'reform' was abandoned following widespread criticism including from Conservative MPs. The Select Committee on Standards is appointed by the House of Commons to oversee the work of the Parliamentary Commissioner for Standards.[88] A revised code of conduct for MPs was published, effective from 1 March 2023.[89]

These and other standards as they have evolved over the years are welcome. But it should not obscure the fact that much stronger and entrenched reform will be needed to restore trust to the House of Commons and, as importantly, the House of Lords.

This Constitution therefore proposes entrenched provisions for independent control over MPs expenses and allowances (Art 47), registration of permitted interests with declaration of non-permitted interests (Art 48), and standards of conduct (Art 49). These provisions build a little on the current legislation and, as importantly, place external constitutional restraints on MPs' interests and conduct which possess additional, symbolic force.

The blatant cynicism displayed by some MPs over expenses claims has engendered interest in the constituents being able to force them out of office. In response to the expenses crisis the Conservative and Liberal Democratic coalition Government enacted the Recall of MPs Act on 26 March 2015.[90] Essentially, this Act envisages three scenarios whereby MPs can be recalled: (i) a custodial prison sentence including a suspended sentence; (ii) suspension from the House of Commons of at least 10 sitting days or 14 calendar days following a report by the Committee on Standards; and (iii) a conviction for providing false or

[88] There is a similar system for the House of Lords. The current House of Lords Commissioners are Martin Jelley and Akbar Khan.

[89] See House of Commons Library, *Reviewing the Code of Conduct for MPs* (Briefing Paper, 28 February 2023). The House of Commons Standard Committee, *The House of Commons standards landscape: how MPs' standards and conduct are regulated* (Third Report of Session 2023–24. 23 May 2024).

[90] See the House of Commons Library briefing paper, *Recall Elections* (21 October 2022); section 9 covers international comparisons.

misleading expenses claims.[91] There then follows a mandatory procedure, which requires approval by 10 per cent of the registered voters in the MP's constituency (in the first edition of this book, it was suggested that 20 per cent was an appropriate figure), triggering the loss of the MPs seat and a by-election. The affected MPs is allowed to stand in the by-election.

The Recall of MPs Act 2015 has been used on six occasions[92] and only one of those met the 20 per cent figure canvassed in this book's previous edition. In the 2015 Act, the figure is 10 per cent and the consequence is a by-election at which the affected MP is allowed to stand. The three scenarios envisaged in the Act have not appeared in this Constitution and the matter is left in the hands of the registered voters.

The positive outcome of a recall referendum is but one of a number of ways in which, under this Constitution, MP are, or become, automatically disqualified from sitting in the House of Representatives.

Article 50 lays down a number of eligibility requirements for continued membership of the House of Representatives beyond those of age and citizenship. New provisions (other than recall) include: (i) a criminal conviction for an offence punishable by imprisonment (the Representation of the People Act 1981 current only disqualifies MPs from sitting if they are detained for any offence for more than a year or detained indefinitely); (ii) the holding of an interest proscribed by law (there is no current automatic disqualification for interests that may compromise or may reasonably be thought to compromise their independence when voting for particular proposals which might conflict with those interests; and (iii) ceasing to be a member of the political party for which he or she was elected (currently, an MP may in exceptional circumstances be rejected by his or her party or may simply disagree with its policies and resign but still remain in office).[93]

Nothing in the Constitution diminishes the effect of the Parliamentary Standards Act 2009 but, as can be seen, the reforms suggested in the Constitution's provision go rather further.

[91] Suspensions imposed by the Independent Expert Panel (established 2020) originally could not trigger recall. However, amendments were made to the Standing Orders of the House of Commons and the Committee on Standards must recommend suspension if asked to do so by the Panel.

[92] The Act was used to trigger the recall of Fiona Onasanya (27.6% signed the petition), Christopher Davies (18.9% signed the petition), Margaret Ferrier (15% per cent signed the petition); Peter Bone (13.2% signed the petition) and Scott Benton (petition terminated because of resignation of the MP). The petition signing was unsuccessful in the case of Ian Paisley JR (only 9.4% signed the petition). A recall petition was not triggered in the case of Rob Robert's six-week suspension from the House of Commons, as this was judged by the Independent Expert Panel before the amendment to the rules. Owen Paterson and Boris Johnson resigned before a vote could be taken in a proposal to suspend them for 30 days for breaching the lobbying rules (in the case of Owen Paterson) and 90 days for lying to Parliament and making the document public prior before the intended date of publication (Boris Johnson). Keith Vaz, Chris Matheson and Chris Pincher also all resigned before a vote could be taken on their conduct.

[93] In the latter case a by-election would be triggered and the MP in question could stand as an independent candidate.

Other Matters (Arts 55–56)

Articles 55–56 deal with the procedure of the House of Representatives which comes from the Constitution. Finally, Part 3 of the Constitution ends (see Art 55) with a reminder – implicit in the very existence of a written constitution – that the lawmaking and other powers of the House of Representatives are derived from the Constitution (and, therefore, not from parliamentary sovereignty).

Article 55 also contains a prohibition against legislation designed to facilitate a breach of public international law. It is at first sight surprising that this is considered to be a necessary part of the Constitution. Lord Bingham, in his rule of law book, categorised this as the last principle of his eight-fold classification of well-known aspects of the rule of law ('the rule of law requires compliance by the state with its obligations in international law as in national law').[94] Lord Bingham was the last but one lead judge in the House of Lords before it handed over to the Supreme Court on 1 October 2009.

The House of Lords Constitution Committee referred to this extract in its 6th report *The Office of Lord Chancellor*[95] and stated (at para 21) that 'these are the most recent and widely accepted articulation of it'. On 18 January 2023 the House of Commons Constitution Committee again referred to this definition and (at para 39) observed that '[t]he law itself must conform with a fundamental concept of justice'.[96] Since the revised oath of the Lord Chancellor's requires him to 'respect the law of law'[97] that might be thought to be that.

But the courts have got themselves into a twist over this. In *Miller v Secretary of State for the European Union*[98] it said, 'the general rule is that the power to make or unmake treaties is exercisable without legislative authority and that the exercise of that power is not reviewable by the courts'. But the rule of law is a fundamental constitutional principle and at the very least the courts should be able to intervene where the state breaks one of those cardinal principles. In any case, with the abolition of parliamentary sovereignty the way is now clear for the courts to be in a position to intervene should the state threaten to introduce a Bill that violates a treaty.

It should also be noted that new powers, including a parliamentary veto over the exercise of former prerogative powers by both the House of Representatives and the Senate are contained in this Constitution.

[94] Tom Bingham, *The Rule of Law* (Penguin, 2010) p 110.

[95] The Office of Lord Chancellor, 11 July 2007. Those views were, for example, shared by the two former Attorneys-Generals, the Rt Hon Dominic Grieve KC, MP and the Rt Hon The Baroness Scotland of Asthal KC and by the former Lord Chancellor Mr Jack Straw (see, again, para 21 Chapter 2).

[96] *The Role of the Lord Chancellor and the Law Officers*, 9th Report of Session 2022–2023, HL Paper 118, 18 January 2023. It is clear from other sections of the Report that the Constitution Committee thought that including international law was a 'fundamental concept of justice' (see eg paras 41–59).

[97] Constitutional Reform Act 2005, s 17.

[98] [2017] UKSC 5.

THE HOUSE OF REPRESENTATIVES: KEY POINTS

- **Overview:** This section focus upon the House of Representatives from the point of view of: (i) the composition of the House of Representatives; (ii) more women in Parliament – the present position; (iii) the system of proportional representation; (iv) compulsory voting; (v) MPs' interests and conduct; (vi) other matters.
- **Composition of the House of Representatives:** Age requirement is still 18. But more stringent requirements have been laid down in terms of MPs' conduct as to their continued eligibility to sit in Parliament. The requirements in terms of election are set out in the section on proportional representation.
- **More women in Parliament:** There are now more women in Parliament – the data figures are given in the Notes. Affirmative action to increase numbers further is not recommended, for the reasons given in the Notes.
- **Proportional representation:** Proportional representation in national general elections is a major reform of the present first-past-the-post (FPTP) system, in which victory by a single vote suffices to gain a seat in Parliament for the successful candidate. The present Constitution suggests a halfway house in which FPTP is retained for most of the seats (350) but an additional 20 new constituencies are created, with five MPs accorded to each of them, making a total of 100 new MPs all selected via a PR system. The detail on PR is set out in the Notes above and the detail is to be decided by a review commission subject to parliamentary approval.
- **Compulsory voting:** A change in the Constitution is compulsory voting. The sanction proposed for not voting is loss of the civic entitlement to vote (save in respect of citizens under 18).
- **MPs' interests and conduct:** The conduct of MPs is currently regulated by a raft of provisions. There is tighter regulation brought in by the creation of IPSA and the Committee on Standards as well as the Commissioner for Parliamentary Investigations. There is also the Select Committee on Standards. But the draft Constitution goes further and proposes new articles on independent control of MPs' expenses and allowances, registration of permitted interests together with a declaration of a non-permitted interests and standards of conduct. There are automatic disqualifications from sitting in the House of Representatives (House of Commons), which include the recall of MPs, the criminal recording of an offence punishable by imprisonment, the holding of an interest prescribed by law or ceasing to be a member of a party for which the MP was elected.
- **Other matters:** This section of the Constitution ends with an assortment of things but the most important point is that the Government must do nothing which would constitute a breach of international law, being a constituent element of the rule of law. This definition appears in the book *The Rule of Law* written by Lord Bingham and has been approved by the constitution committees of both the House of Commons and the House of Lords.

PART 4
THE SENATE (ARTS 57–87)

The Work of the Commission for the Houses of Parliament

57. The Commission for the Houses of Parliament in the Constitution shall have, so far as Articles 32–37 of the Constitution are concerned, equal application to the Senate except that in Article 37 references to the constitution of the Senate be references to the Senate as described in Part 4 of the Constitution.

Composition

58. The composition of the Senate shall initially consist of the same members as comprised the House of Lords immediately before the coming into force of this Constitution.[99]

Composition and Standards for the Elected Body of the Senate

59. The elected body of the Senate is to be established by elections to be held at the first general election following the coming into force of this Constitution and, except where a seat is vacated, members of the elected body will hold office for the same period as members of the House of Representatives.

60. Only citizens, who have civil and political rights, of one of the nations that comprise the United Kingdom, who have attained the age of forty, are legally resident in the United Kingdom, and are not disqualified from occupying a seat in the Senate, may be elected to the elected body of the Senate.

61. The number of members of the elected body of the Senate shall be fifty per cent of the total number of members of the Senate, which makes a total of 225 members of the elected body of the Senate.

62. The provisions of Articles 47–52 of this Constitution shall apply, with the necessary modifications, to members of the elected body of the Senate.

[99] At present the House of Lords has around 800 members who are eligible to take part in the work of the House of Lords. The majority are life peers. The three types of peer are: (i) hereditary peers; (ii) spiritual peers; and (iii) life peers. Of the life peers, most are awarded by the Prime Minister from his or party and the remainder awarded by the other parties. A few are appointed by the House of Lords Appointments Commission (the people's peers).

63. In particular, the circumstances in which a seat in the elected body of the Senate shall automatically become vacant or, as the case may be and as applicable, shall not become available to be occupied by a person shall, with the necessary modifications, be the same as those applicable to the House of Representatives as specified in Articles 39–40 of this Constitution and the references in those articles to the House of Representatives shall be references to the elected body and the references to constituency shall be references to the large, regional constituencies represented by members of the elected body (which shall be known as the larger regional constituencies)[100] and not to the constituencies represented by members of the House of Representatives. There are no disqualifications from election save as expressly set out in this Constitution.

64. A member of the elected body may not be a member of the House of Representatives, the Scottish Parliament, the Welsh Assembly, the Northern Ireland Assembly, or the appointed body of the Senate at the same time.

65. The boundaries of the larger regional constituencies of the elected body shall be determined by the appropriate Boundary Commission[101] in accordance with law and, thereafter, monitored by regular reviews by the appropriate Boundary Commission. Their number shall reflect the eligible number of members of the elected body but the number of available constituencies must conform to the following scheme: (i) England [...], (ii) Wales [...], (iii) Scotland [...], (iv) Northern Ireland [...].

66. All elections (including by-elections) shall be put into effect after the coming into force of this Constitution, and in accordance with the rules for those elections as set out in this Constitution. Laws giving effect to this Constitution shall apply.

Elections to the Elected Body of the Senate

67. Articles 43–46 of this Constitution shall, with the necessary modifications, apply to elections to the elected body of the Senate as they apply to elections to the House of Representatives.

68. The method of election to the elected body of the Senate shall give priority to the need for a fair balance in relation to the votes cast as between political parties seeking election of their members to the elected body.

[100] See Part 14 for the definition of 'larger regional constituencies'.
[101] See Part 14 for the definition of 'appropriate Boundary Commission'.

The Appointed Body of the Senate

69. The appointed body is to be established by appointments, following open competition, made by a body known as the Senate Appointments Commission after the coming into force of this Constitution and before the first general election after its coming into force. The appointments shall take effect at the same time as the date on which the members of the elected body of the Senate take up their seats in accordance with law.

70. Only citizens who have civil and political rights of one of the nations that comprise the United Kingdom, who have attained the age of forty, are legally resident in the United Kingdom, and are not disqualified from occupying a seat in the Senate may be appointed to the appointed body the Senate. There are no disqualifications from appointment or continued membership of the appointed body of the Senate save as set out in or incorporated in this Constitution.

71. Subject to this Constitution, the number of members of the appointed body shall be fifty per cent of the number of members of the Senate. That makes a sum of not greater than 225 members of the appointed part of the Senate.

72. The provisions of this Constitution shall apply, with the necessary modifications, to a member of the appointed body of the Senate.[102]

73. The term of office of a member of the appointed body of the Senate shall be the same as that of a member of the elected body of the Senate who is elected at a general election. Appointment is for the same period or periods, with the appointment taking effect at the same time as the date on which the members of the elected body are elected.

74. Where a seat on the appointed body of the Senate become vacant there shall be a competition for appointment. However, no competition for appointment is to be held where the seat becomes vacant less than six months before the date of the next general election, when the whole of the appointed body becomes eligible for reappointment when the general election is held.

75. In appointing the initial candidates to the appointed body of the Senate or the appointment of new candidates, the Senate Appointments Commission shall, subject to this Constitution, have regard amongst

[102] Formerly a peer could not resign. This was changed by the House of Lords Reform Act 2014. See Notes immediately below.

other factors to the importance of some continuity of appointment of existing members of the Senate at the time of coming into force of this Constitution, to the need to ensure an overall balance in terms of independence, representation of men and women, as well as regional representation, to the extent to which candidates have contributed towards society and the likelihood of their contribution to public service in the Senate, and to the need for outstanding personal qualities including integrity and independence, as well as to the overall representation of national interests consistent with this Constitution that will be served by the election of individual candidates and by the list of appointed candidates as a whole.

76. In deciding whether to renew appointments to the appointed body of the Senate, the Senate Appointments Commission shall, subject to this Constitution, have particular regard to the record of attendance and quality of attendance of the candidate seeking renewal of his or her appointment.

The Senate Appointments Commission

77. There shall be a body corporate called the Senate Appointments Commission, which shall be an elected body responsible for making all appointments to the appointed body of the Senate. Laws shall be made which provide separately for matters relating to the election of the Senate Appointments Commission, ensuring, amongst other things, that the electorate is informed as to the merits of the eligible candidates for election to the Commission, for the funding of elections, for the spending limits (if any spending is to be allowed) to be applied to such elections, and for the remuneration of those elected to the Commission. Laws may also make further provision relating to the work of the Senate Appointments Commission.

78. The Commission shall consist of a Chairman and fourteen other Commissioners. Those standing for election as Chairman and Commissioners must fulfil the eligibility qualifications.

79. The Commissioners shall be elected by a postal vote of registered electors throughout the United Kingdom from a list of eligible candidates to be drawn up by an independent statutory body. The first such list shall be drawn up by current members of the Judicial Appointments Commission. The list of eligible candidates shall comprise only citizens who have or

have had a distinguished career in any aspect of national or international life, whether in the public or private sector.

80. Subject to this Constitution, subsequent lists shall be drawn up from time to time, by other independent bodies, as determined by law.

81. Those candidates receiving the highest number of votes in the election shall be elected as Commissioners and the candidate receiving the overall highest number of votes shall be selected as Chairman. If a vacancy arises for the office of Commissioner the candidate receiving the next highest vote in the original postal vote shall be eligible for office. Where the office of Chairman becomes vacant, the Commissioner receiving the next highest vote in the original postal ballot shall be eligible for office.

82. Commissioners shall serve for the same term as that of the appointed body, but shall serve only once.

Business

83. All questions proposed for decision in the Senate shall, subject to this Constitution, be decided by a majority vote. There is no casting vote and the question concerned shall be deemed to be lost unless there is a majority vote.

84. The Senate may act despite a vacancy in its membership and the presence of or participation in its proceedings of a person not entitled to be a member does not invalidate the proceedings.

85. Subject to this Constitution the Senate shall –

(i) decide its procedure;
(ii) elect its Lord Speaker by such method as it shall decide (whether or not the method of election decided upon is by majority vote).

Powers of the Senate

86. The powers of the Senate are derived from this Constitution.

87. The Senate shall have power to do those things which are calculated to facilitate or which are conducive or incidental to the discharge of its functions.

THE SENATE: OBSERVATIONS AND EXPLANATORY NOTES

Background to House of Lords Reform

The idea of reforming the House of Lords has probably caused more recent and heated debate than any other aspect of constitutional reform, largely because of the strength of the competing arguments.[103]

The 1997 Labour manifesto contained the following promise: 'The House of Lords must be reformed. As an initial self-contained reform, not dependent on further reform in the future, the right of hereditary peers to sit and vote in the House of Lords will be ended by statute.' This was partially achieved by the House of Lords Act 1999 which left a rump of 92 hereditary peers pending further reform. But further reform (apart from two Acts in 2014 and 2015 which achieved no structural reform, see below) has not yet happened. More than 20 years ago a respected peer observed: 'to seek to reform the House by first abolishing the hereditary peers without deciding the final constitution and form of the second chamber seems to be dangerous and irresponsible folly'.[104] Thus far at least, it might be thought that Baroness James has been proved right.

Unsurprisingly, there has not been a consensus as to how to achieve reform. As long ago as the Parliament Act 1911, the need to modernise the House of Lords was apparent. The entitlement of hereditary peers to participate in government merely by virtue of their birthright had long been seen as indefensible, but lassitude followed because of the obstacles to comprehensive reform that were perceived to exist. The Preamble to the 1911 Act stated prophetically: '... it is intended to substitute for the House of Lords as it at present exists a Second Chamber constituted on a popular instead of hereditary basis, but such substitution cannot be immediately brought into operation'.

There are powerful arguments for retaining the status quo, at least in the form of a wholly appointed (as opposed to elected) second chamber. The danger of a predominantly elected second chamber is that it will largely be composed of professional, full-time career politicians (or those who have had their careers and want to retire to the second chamber to 'put their feet up'). There is much to be said for the current arrangement or something similar, composed of men and women with experience and expertise in diverse fields.

True it is that the House of Lords, as currently constituted, is something of an anomaly. In a literal sense it can hardly be said to be a representative (and hence democratic) institution. On the other hand, the system works and the House of Lords has often proved to be a more independent body than the

[103] Apart from numbers. There seems to be consensus that the House of Lords is currently too big. It currently has about 800 sitting members.

[104] PD James, *Time to be in Earnest – A Fragment of Autobiography* (London, Faber and Faber, 1999). PD James died on 27 November 2014.

House of Commons, especially when executive-driven legislation is being forced through Parliament. The composition of the current House of Lords (in which, as a matter of deliberate policy, no party has overall majority) also provides a counterbalance to the House of Commons in an electoral first-past-the-post system in which the governing party now almost invariably has much less than 50 per cent of the popular vote. It may also be said that an elected second chamber has the demerit of giving that chamber added legitimacy, thereby creating tension with the House of Commons which is, in reality, the chamber designed to wield final legislative authority.

There are equally compelling arguments for an elected second chamber. The 'added legitimacy' argument is, properly analysed, a reason for having a mainly elected House. Whatever reforms are undertaken, it can always be made clear (and is made clear in this Constitution) that the first chamber (the House of Representatives) wields the superior legislative authority. In the present climate of distrust, what is arguably needed is a *more* rather than *less* legitimate second chamber in which the executive is made more accountable to parliamentary scrutiny and in which the public has confidence. This is more likely to be achieved in an elected rather than an appointed second chamber.

And, of course, there is devolution. Only in an elected second chamber could one have any hope of being able to separate the different component parts of what is often referred to as a 'Union'. The Brown Commission proposed an elected second chamber, which it said should be smaller than the current House of Lords and should be more representative of the nations and regions of the UK.[105]

The history of House of Lords 'reform' has for the most part consisted of the struggle for primacy of the House of Commons over the Lords and the removal of the historical power of the latter to veto any legislation. This resulted in the Parliament Acts of 1911 and 1949. The power of the Lords to veto legislation was curtailed in the 1911 Act by removing their power to veto money bills and by giving the Commons power to trump the Lords' veto over other legislation after three parliamentary sessions. The 1949 Act allowed the Commons to overrule the Lords' veto after only two parliamentary sessions.

Another important restriction on the former powers of the House of Lords came in the form of a constitutional convention called the Salisbury Convention. This convention, which developed during the twentieth century, was introduced by the fifth Marquess of Salisbury and operates to prevent the House of from opposing (in the second or third reading) any Government legislation that has been advanced in its election manifesto.

There were also piecemeal reforms to the system of hereditary peerages in the sense that life peerages were introduced by the Life Peerages Act 1958.

[105] Brown Commission Report (n 45).

Virtually all peerages since then have been life peerages rather than hereditary peerages.[106] The system of hereditary peerages was further weakened by the Peerage Act 1963, which allowed hereditary peers to disclaim their peerage and (if so minded) stand for election in the Commons.[107]

There matters stood until Labour took office in 1997. In 1999 it enacted the House of Lords Act in which membership of the Lords effectively removed the hereditary element, apart from 92 hereditary peers.[108]

Meanwhile, a Royal Commission set up to examine reform issues in 1999 (under the chairmanship of Lord Wakeham) and its Report in 2000 recommended a largely appointed House of Lords but with approximately one fifth or one third of members being elected. The concern was to modernise the second chamber (for example, peerage would no longer be a requirement of membership) but, at the same time, avoid it being filled with professional politicians.

The Government accepted the Commission's recommendations and even went so far as to announce the members of a non-statutory appointments commission. However, cross-party discussions failed. It became increasingly clear that the media and public response to reform was that there was a need for many more elected members. After further protracted and inconclusive debate a 2003 vote in the Commons and the Lords resulted in the Commons failing to vote for any single reform proposal, while the Lords voted strongly in favour of an all-appointed House.

However, the tide has been turning strongly in favour of a largely elected second chamber. A 2007 White Paper proposed a 50/50 elected/appointed House. But a vote in the Commons later in 2007 on the proposals in that White Paper resulted in a strong majority for an 80 per cent or all-elected upper House (with the Lords, perhaps predictably, still voting for all-appointed House). This led to the publication of a 2008 White Paper[109] setting out proposals based on the result of the Commons' vote (and proposed abolition of the remaining hereditary peers) as well as proposals addressing the options for electoral systems for an elected House.

For the present, that is all the reform that there has been to the House of Lords. There has been nothing, effectively, since the Parliament Act 1911 to shake the foundations of the House of Lords' authority and influence.[110]

[106] One exception since then was William Whitelaw, who was created as the 1st Viscount Whitelaw by Margaret Thatcher in 1983. But the 1st Viscount Whitelaw was regarded as too old to become a father and the hereditary title disappeared with his death on 1 July 1999 (Whitelaw's four daughters were unable to inherit the peerage).

[107] The Peerages Act 1963 was designed to give Anthony Wedgwood-Benn the opportunity to stand for Parliament by disclaiming the title of the 2nd Viscount Stansgate.

[108] And in 2005 Labour passed the Constitutional Reform Act, which set up the Supreme Court and abolished the appellate jurisdiction of the House of Lords.

[109] *An Elected Second Chamber: Further Reform of the House of Lords*, Cm 7438 (July 2008).

[110] After an attempt at reform (Nick Clegg's House of Lords Reform Bill 2012 was abandoned later that year), the only moves towards reform were the House of Lords Reform Act 2014, which allowed

The most recent proposal for reform of the House of Lords involves the former Prime Minister Gordon Brown. He was tasked by Sir Keir Starmer in 2020 to produce plans 'to settle the future of the Union' and to devolve 'power, wealth and opportunity' throughout the nation. Brown established a commission which made wide-ranging suggestions for reform to the whole Constitution, including the House of Lords.[111] As far as reforms to the structure of the House of Lords are concerned the Brown proposals appear late in his report after various proposals to devolution and were intended to tie the whole system together.

But how many of Brown's proposals will be enacted now that Starmer is our Prime Minister? Sir Keir Starmer is noted for his cautious approach to political issues. But he has said in pre-election broadcasts that his party would abolish the House of Lords and replace it with a democratically elected second chamber, presumably along the lines of Gordon Brown's legacy for reform in his report. It is not necessarily easy to see how he will achieve this, given the degree of opposition in his own party as well as in the Conservative party. Now that he has been elected, it is too early to saywhether his original plan will be pursued.

This Constitution contains proposals for a mixture of elected representatives and appointed representatives. In recommending this, the Constitution takes into account the following important factors:

(i) Devolution. It seems that we are at a most precarious time and that unless there is total engagement in the devolution process, that process – if left unchecked (in the sense of being allowed to follow the devo-max line to Scotland alone – will add further fuel to the independence case. Put bluntly, either England creates a federation or else the rest of the UK is likely to seek independence. The first stage is to reform the House of Lords by having elected representatives for each of the regions.

(ii) It would be unfortunate to lose the expertise of distinguished people from a great variety of areas, for example, police, arts, education, business, which are not found in the House of Commons/House of Representatives which has increasingly become filled with career politicians who become political advisers after university and have never experienced life outside politics.[112]

peers to resign or retire permanently, and the House of Lords (Expulsion and Suspension) Act 2015, which allowed the House to expel or suspend members. There have been other Acts and attempts at reform of the structure but the main ones have been dealt with in this Note.

[111] These proposals were criticised most helpfully by Meg Russell in *House of Lords Reform: Navigating the Obstacles* (Bennett Institute for Public Policy, March 2023); see also 'The Brown Commission's Proposals on Reform of the House of Lords, *The Constitution Unit Blog*, 1 March 2023. Note also Philip Rycroft, *Not by Design: The Erratic Evolution of the British Constitution since 1997* (Bennett Institute for Public Policy, November 2022). The Labour Government announced in the King's Speech that at its first parliamentary session it will remove the right of hereditary peers to sit in the House of Lords.

[112] See the Report of the Lord Speaker's committee on the size of the House of Lords, 19 November 2018.

To convert the House of Lords into the Senate, from a wholly appointed body to a mixture of elected and appointed members, may seem a surprising result. It is, therefore, proposed, that when the Constitution comes into force the membership of the old House of Lords remains the same so that the changes to make it into a fully functioning Senate can be synchronised as between what will be new and different parts of the Upper Chamber.

Composition of, and Standards for, the Elected Body of the Senate (Arts 59–66)

There is some danger of the party political machine taking over an elected second chamber, and the proposals in this Constitution are designed to reduce that risk. One such proposal is that there be a ceiling for elected members – only fifty per cent of members may put themselves up for election and the number of members must match those of the House of Representatives (making a total of 225 members).

Another proposal (also suggested by the Power Inquiry) is to place an age-related eligibility requirement of 40 on membership of the Senate (Art 60). As the Power Inquiry observes, such a requirement makes it less likely that career politicians will seek membership, since their trajectory commonly involves a seamless transition from politics student to researcher for an MP to policy adviser, before entering Parliament at a young age. Moreover, an age-related requirement of this kind is likely to encourage women to seek membership (whether by election or by appointment); by 40 they have may have had children and be ready to seek new challenges. Despite this, it may be argued that a difference in age eligibility will not produce significantly different types of persons running for election to the two Houses and that a much longer – possibly even non-renewable – term of office for elected senators is what is needed so that they become very much more independent of party.

Consistent with the aim of achieving simplicity where possible, this Constitution does not in fact propose (as did the 2008 White Paper, the Power Inquiry and the 2005 cross-bench reform package) three finite and non-extendable parliamentary terms (currently between 12 and 15 years) for elected members or (as the 2008 White Paper suggested) three similar electoral cycles for appointed members.[113] What is proposed instead is the same electoral and appointed terms of office in the Senate as in the House of Representatives (Art 59). In the case of elected members, they may seek re-election (subject to other provisions of this Constitution relating to political parties), and appointed members may seek

[113] There is an argument that having electoral cycles injects more variety into the Senate. However, the eligibility requirements and appointment procedures have been designed to maintain an eclectic mix.

reappointment (though they will not be automatically entitled to reappointment: Arts 75–76). A key principle of the 2008 White Paper was that members of the Senate should serve a long term of office. However, this Constitution suggests a less rigid approach, namely that members of the Senate *may* serve a long term of office but there is no necessity that they should do so.

It is also proposed (see, too, Notes above) that the total number of members of the Senate should match that of the House of Representatives (Arts 61 and 71). The constituencies for the elected body of the Senate are likely to be somewhat larger than those of the House of Representatives and they are here called larger regional constituencies (Artis 63 and 65). Larger regional constituencies for elected members of the Senate are consistent with the aims of the 2008 White Paper.

The provisions relating to conduct standards and registration of relevant interests that apply to the House of Representatives also apply, by Art 62, to the elected body of the Senate.

Elections to the Elected Body of the Senate (Arts 67–68)

Many of the other provisions relating to elected members of the Senate (and more generally relating to business and powers of the Senate) are parallel provisions (with minor consequential changes) to those relating to members of the House of Representatives, and reference should be made to those provisions in the Notes to Part 3 on the House of Representatives.

However, a slightly different provision is that in choosing the method of PR for elections to the elected body of the Senate, priority be given to the need for balance in relation to votes cast as between parties (see Art 68). The purpose of this is to make it easier to break the constituency link in elections to the elected body of the Senate where a relationship between an MP and constituents does not have the significance than it has in elections to the House of Representatives. The detail of which form of voting system (see also Notes to Part 3 of the Constitution) is the most appropriate for an elected second chamber may require more consideration. What is needed is a system that will facilitate the best balance amongst the political parties in the Senate.

The single transferable vote (STV) may well be the best method of PR for the reasons set out in the 2008 White Paper, which, whilst suggesting a variety of possible voting methods, observed of STV that (in common with a list system) it would help to produce a greater balance between parties in the second chamber than other forms of voting. While STV is, as the White Paper points out, more complicated than a list system, it would seem that in principle any form of list system would be likely to weaken the prospects of independent candidacies and candidates who were not from the main parties. For that reason, STV may be preferred as the method of PR for electing the elected body of the Senate.

Provisions Relating to the Appointed Body of the Senate (Arts 69–76)

Appointments to the appointed body of the Senate, provisions dealing with standards of conduct, the interests to be registered, composition of the appointed body of the Senate and vacation of office for misconduct etc mirror, with, necessary modifications, the parallel provisions relating to the elected body.

It is necessarily implicit in the qualification requirements for appointment (or indeed election) to the Senate that holding a peerage is not a requirement. There no proposals in this Constitution to abolish either hereditary or life peerages. This is a matter of Government policy.

With reference to making appointments to the Senate, some general criteria are set out (see Arts 69–76). For the most part they include those suggested in the 2008 White Paper; they also include the need to exercise quality control over the list of appointed candidates as a whole so that the list is truly representative. In this fashion, it is likely that many existing members of the House of Lords would be appointed under the new system. Since the process for selecting members of the Senate Appointments Commission is itself designed to elicit the highest possible quality of Commissioners making appointments to the Senate, the criteria in Arts 69–76 are not overly prescriptive and are couched in general terms. No specific bar has been imposed on past politicians or past office-holders being appointed. It may be counter-productive to do so if they satisfy the test of merit. However, by imposing criteria which compel consideration of an overall balance in terms of, amongst other things, independence, the aim is that the danger of partisanship is reduced.

An important concluding provision in respect of Senate appointees is Art 76. Under this article it is clear that appointments may be renewed, but the Commission is required, when considering renewal, to examine the attendance record and quality of attendance of the appointee in question. Because of this requirement it is neither possible nor desirable to guarantee an equal number of men and women, though the general criteria for selection include the need to have regard to the overall balance in terms of the representation of men and women (see Art 75).

Senate Appointments Commission (Arts 77–82)

These provisions deal with the mechanism for making appointments to the Senate. An elected Senate Appointments Commission is envisaged in order to enhance the legitimacy of appointments made by the Commission. This is significant in circumstances in which the persons appointed to the Senate are being appointed to be completely independent. Articles 77–82 set out a scheme of election to the Commission which involves a list being drawn up from an independent appointed body (which will differ from general election to general election) by reference to identified characteristics. It is proposed (Art 82) that Commissioners should serve only once and for the term of the Parliament.

Other Matters (Arts 83–87)

These provisions, which concern procedure in, and the powers of, the Senate, mirror the articles addressing such issues in the House of Representatives (Arts 53–56).

THE SENATE: KEY POINTS

- **Background to House of Lords reform:** There are equally compelling arguments for an elected as opposed to an appointed body. The 1997 Labour prospectus promised significant reform but in the end only the House of Lords Act 1999 (which left a rump of 92 hereditary peers pending further reforms) was all that Labour could achieve. Most of the discussion since then have been a division of opinion being adopted between the present system with a few tweaks (see the Lord Wakeham report in 2000) and a major reversion to the elected system (2007 vote in the Commons, 2008 White Paper, Gordon Brown's Report of December 2022). The history of the relationship between the Houses has been the struggle for primacy of the House of Commons over the Lords.
- **Composition and standards:** One proposal is that there shall be an age limit of 40 for membership of the Senate. That is consistent with the aim of including more women and consistent too with the aim attracting more members who are not professional politicians. Moreover, the Constitution does not propose three finite and non-extendable parliamentary terms. Instead, it proposes the possibility of re-election or reappointment. Finally, the Constitution proposes that the total number of members of the Senate should replicate the number of members of the House of Representatives and that the position should be identical in the Senate as regards the standards applicable to the Senate and as regards the timing of the elections.
- **Election to the elected body of the Senate:** Many provisions mirror the same provisions for the House of Representatives (although the actual numbers do not match: 225 is the ceiling). However, a change is probably needed for the method of PR that is necessary to facilitate the best balance among the political parties in the Senate and there is no need for a constituency link.
- **The appointed body of the Senate:** With regard to new appointments to the Senate the list of criteria is not overly prescriptive (see Arts 69–70). The overall criterion is merit. There is, though, a predominant criterion of achieving a fair balance. With regard to the re-election of old members there is an important concluding criterion (see Art 70), requiring the Appointments Commission to take into account the attendance record and quality of attendance of the particular member. Holding a peerage is not a constitutional requirement. Apart from these requirements, the rest of this part mirrors the constitutional requirements for the House of Representatives.

- **The Senate Appointments Commission:** The Senate Appointments Commission must be independent. That is the rationale for the mechanism in the Constitution (see Arts 71–76).
- **Other matters:** These provisions mirror the provisions for the House of Representatives.

PART 5

EXECUTIVE GOVERNMENT (ARTS 88–118)[114]

Appointment and Responsibilities of Ministers and Advisers

88. The Head of State symbolises the unity of the State and, in that capacity, possesses executive authority. However, the Head of State has no power outside this Constitution and, except as provided for under this Constitution, must act where is power to act only on the advice of the Prime Minister acting through Cabinet as provided for by this Constitution.

89. The Head of State has power to summon, prorogue and dissolve Parliament but this is a function exercised solely on the advice of the Prime Minister acting through Cabinet.

90. There shall be a Prime Minister who shall be appointed by the Head of State. The Prime Minister shall be a member of the House of Representatives who, in the Head of State's opinion,[115] will be able to form a Government that has the confidence of a majority of the House of Representatives. The Prime Minister shall have power to appoint and dismiss members of the Cabinet.[116]

91. Subject to this Constitution, executive power shall be vested in the Prime Minister, acting through Cabinet.[117] However, nothing in the conferment of that power limits provisions in this Constitution, or laws compatible with this Constitution, from conferring on specified persons or bodies specific executive or other functions or powers, including freedom from direction or control by any person or authority in relation to the performance of their functions or exercise of their power.

[114] This section poses particularly difficult questions of definition. *Towards a Codified Constitution* (the article referred to in the Notes to the Preamble) identifies no fewer than 21 institutions and a number of terms such as 'the executive' which could be given constitutional status or definition.

[115] If the Head of State acted in bad faith or otherwise unlawfully in forming a judgement this would be a breach of the Constitution and would be enforceable by the courts.

[116] See Part 14 for a definition of 'Cabinet'.

[117] The maximum number is 25 Ministers other than the Prime Minister (see Part 14). It is the Prime Minister who exercises the task of deciding the offices of State.

92. To be eligible for appointment to the Cabinet, a Minister must be a member of the House of Representatives or of the elected body of the Senate.

93. The Cabinet is collectively responsible to the Houses of the Parliament for the governance of the State.

94. Subject to this Constitution the Prime Minister may make Ministerial appointments outside the Cabinet and may also appoint persons to advise the Cabinet who are not members of the House of Representatives or of the elected body of the Senate. However, except where the holder of such appointment is a member of the House of Representatives or the elected body of the Senate, their appointment must be confirmed by the House of Representatives, by a process to be determined by the House of Representatives, and such persons must be accountable to the House of Representatives through select committees as provided for by the House of Representatives.

95. All Ministers are also individually responsible to the Houses of Parliament for all acts done by or under the authority of the Minister in the execution of his or her office. They shall have such individual responsibilities as the Prime Minister shall determine from time to time according to law. The Prime Minister shall also have individual responsibility to the Houses of Parliament for any part of the business of the Government not assigned by him to a Minister or Ministers.

96. Before taking office the Prime Minister, Cabinet Ministers, other Ministers and advisers must swear an oath of allegiance to this Constitution as set out in Schedule [...][118] and in the manner there prescribed.

97. If a Minister's appointment (including that of the Prime Minister) ceases by virtue of the expiry or dissolution of the House of Representatives he or she shall continue in office until the appointment of a new Prime Minister and shall continue until the new Prime Minister makes a contrary appointment.

The Executive Powers of Ministers

98. Laws may confer specific executive and other powers on a Minister. In particular, the raising by the Government of revenue or money, whether

[118] No form of oath is included here or elsewhere in the Constitution.

through the imposition of taxation or otherwise, must be authorised by or under the enactment of a Bill passed by the Houses of the Parliament under Article 11.

99. Except as otherwise provided by this Constitution, but subject to this Constitution, the powers formerly exercised under Crown prerogative shall be abolished, but shall become constitutional powers exercisable by the Prime Minister, acting through Cabinet. However, the express powers set out in Article 100 shall not be exercised without the prior approval of the House of Representatives and exercised by majority vote.

100. The exercise of such powers of the Prime Minister acting through Cabinet shall include power –

(i) to make and unmake treaties;
(ii) to declare war (save in emergency situations);
(iii) to make peace;
(iv) to deploy the armed forces on operations overseas;
(v) to withhold a passport;
(vi) to grant honours;
(vii) to grant a free or a conditional pardon.

The Head of State

101. The Head of State derives his or her authority and powers from this Constitution. Lest there be any doubt about it, the Crown is always advised by the Prime Minister about the exercise of any function otherwise left to the monarch.

102. The Sovereign reigning at the time of the coming into force of this Constitution and all future Sovereigns shall, provided that they swear an oath of allegiance to this Constitution as set out in Schedule [...] and in the manner there prescribed, become Head of State. The civil list[119] shall be established by law.

103. The Sovereign and his or her successors shall no longer be Head of the Church of England and that Church shall henceforth be disestablished. The former powers of the Crown over the Church of England and any other powers exercised over that Church by Parliament or by third parties are transferred to the General Synod of the Church of England and shall be exercised in accordance with any rules laid down by that body.

[119] The term 'civil list' is defined in Part 14.

104. The rules determining the line of succession to the throne, including rules for the appointment of a Regent in case of the Sovereign's incapacity or minority, shall be determined by a law which shall come into effect at the time of coming into force of this Constitution but which shall be subject to this Constitution.

105. In determining the line of succession to the throne, any rights, privileges and dignities belonging thereto as provided for in this Constitution or by law, no account shall be taken of gender or religion notwithstanding any previous custom or rule of law to the contrary. Nor shall royal consent be required for any marriage. Nor shall the Sovereign be required to be a Protestant, nor to declare allegiance to the Protestant faith. The Royal Acts[120] shall, to the extent that they are inconsistent with this Constitution, have no continuing legal effect.

106. The Head of State has the right to be informed by the Prime Minister on all matters relating to the governance of the United Kingdom.

107. The former powers exercised under Crown prerogative shall no longer be exercisable by the Head of State save for the express powers referred to in this Article. The Head of State shall have the powers and duties conferred or imposed elsewhere in this Constitution subject in all cases to the constraints imposed by this Constitution. Subject to those constraints the Head of State shall have the following express powers –

(i) to summon, prorogue and dissolve Parliament;
(ii) to exercise the prerogative of mercy;
(iii) to grant honours;
(iv) to create corporations by Charter;
(v) to receive diplomats.

Role of the Attorney-General

108. The Attorney-General shall be the chief legal adviser to the Government but shall not henceforth be entitled to exercise any functions of a political nature whether for and on behalf of the Government or otherwise.

109. A person shall not be eligible to be appointed as Attorney-General unless he or she is qualified to practise as a barrister or solicitor in the United Kingdom and has been so qualified for at least ten years.

[120] The term 'Royal Acts' is defined in Part 14.

110. The Attorney-General shall not be eligible for appointment as a Minister or for membership of the House of Representatives or the Senate and all devolved legislatures and must resign any such position as a condition of holding office as Attorney-General.

111. The Attorney-General may exercise any other function as provided for by law subject to the fact that it is compatible with this Constitution, and subject to, this Constitution.

Relationship between the Executive and Parliament

112. The exercise of executive power shall be accountable to the Houses of the Parliament.

113. Select committees of the House of Representatives and the Senate and of Joint Committees of the Houses of the Parliament shall be composed of members of each of the Houses of the Parliament chosen from time to time by means of a free and independent secret voting system in a manner determined by each House.[121]

114. There shall also, without prejudice to the generality of the foregoing, be established by means of such independent voting system a select committee of the House of Representatives which shall have the remit of scrutinising the activities of the executive in supranational bodies and multinational negotiations.

115. Select committees of the House of Representatives and of the Senate shall have the power to subpoena and examine witnesses in proceedings before such committees on oath and to compel the disclosure of documents including from departments of Government.

116. Select committees of the House of Representatives and of the Senate shall have the power to co-opt members with specialist expertise (whether or not a member of either House) to assist them in their deliberations if it is considered expedient to do so.

117. A select committee of the House of Representatives shall have the power to require such persons as have been appointed by the Prime

[121] A number of detailed recommendations, including recommendations for strengthening the work of the select committees, were made by the Reform of the House of Commons Committee under the chairmanship of Tony Wright. It reported on 12 November 2009 and made a number of recommendations in a document entitled *Rebuilding the House*. However not all of Mr Wright's reforms were implemented.

Minister under this Constitution (whether Ministers or special advisers), but who are not members of the House of Representatives or of the elected body of the Senate and whose appointment has been confirmed by the House of Representatives, to provide a report from time to time of the manner in which they have exercised their functions and to appear at such times before that select committee as the committee, in its discretion, determine to account for the manner in which the relevant functions have been exercised.

118. The House of Representatives and the Senate shall have such power to initiate legislation and public inquiries in certain circumstances as may be provided for by law.

EXECUTIVE GOVERNMENT: OBSERVATIONS AND EXPLANATORY NOTES

Executive Power and Executive Authority

In this Constitution executive power and the executive authority of the state are distinguished. Executive *power* refers to the governmental authority and responsibility that, in the UK, is exercised by the Prime Minister through the system of Cabinet government. The executive *authority* of the state has traditionally been vested in the monarch. Executive authority is now largely symbolic, but executive power – unless carefully supervised – can quickly spiral into dictatorship. Nazism's original source of authority was democratic but Hitler used the institutions of the state to make laws which were the very antithesis of democracy.

Questions Raised by the Need to Control Executive Power

The exercise of executive power and the means of regulating and controlling it give rise to a number of constitutional issues that, in any democratic constitution, need to be carefully addressed.

Two questions are of particular importance and resonance in modern Britain. First is the question of how best practical effect is to be given to the doctrine of separation of powers in order to guard against the dangers to democracy of an over-mighty executive (or judiciary). Second, how best in a representative democracy can the institutions of government be made directly accountable to the voters? Resolving these two questions is the leitmotif of any modern constitution for the UK and they are closely related. It is the theme of this book that the democratic future points to egalitarian democracy rather than liberal democracy as the gateway to future reform.[122]

Fusion not Separation of Powers

The traditional constitutional doctrine of separation of powers is that in a democracy power that is exercised by the executive, the legislature and the judiciary should be separated so that each provides a check on the other. One of the main complaints about the British system of government is that separation of powers is not really working. Parliament (the legislature) has, it is argued, become the tool of the executive, so that in reality Parliament is not exercising proper legislative scrutiny over the wielding of executive power. In a different and potentially contradictory sense it is also often contended (especially in the field of human rights) that the judges are interfering with laws in such a way in such a way as to reduce the effectiveness of Parliament's (in reality executive Government's) intentions when passing the law in question.

In Britain we do not, strictly, have separation of powers between the executive and Parliament. Nor until the creation of the Supreme Court from October 2009 did we enjoy separation of powers as between the legislature and the judiciary, because judges at the then highest level of court – the House of Lords – were also members of that House and entitled to vote on legislation. This was an historical anomaly in an age when, for example, EU law could require House of Lords judges to hear challenges to legislation which they may have voted on as members of the House of Lords.

In this respect, what we currently have in Britain is not so much a *separation* of powers as a *fusion* of powers. Government Ministers must by convention be selected from Parliament, and the Prime Minister and Chancellor of the Exchequer must be selected from the House of Commons. Separation of powers would operate to *prevent* a Minister from being a member of either House. Indeed, under the Act of Settlement of 1701 there was a clause (clause 111) that included a stipulation that 'no person who has an office or Place of Profit under the King ... shall be capable of serving as a Member of the House of Commons'. In the eighteenth century a person having an office or place of profit under the King was the equivalent of a Minister today. Had this clause survived (it was repealed in 1705) it would have set Britain on a somewhat different constitutional course, leading perhaps to a true separation of powers.[123]

It is probably unrealistic to consider a change from fused to separated powers. That being so, what are needed are changes: (i) to the electoral system by reducing the dominance of the two-party system (through PR); to the party system

[122] See Colin Crouch's work on post-democracy, eg *Post-Democracy* (Polity Press, 2020), where the arguments for an egalitarian system are further explored.

[123] For a large part of the last century, an MP who was made a Minister had to stand for re-election.

(by reducing the influence of the whips), by increasing the legitimacy and powers of the Senate (where currently no party has a clear majority but where the House of Lords is wholly unelected), and (the key area for reform) by increasing the independence of Parliament (but especially the House of Representatives) vis-à-vis the executive.

Danger of an Over-mighty Executive

The significance of having a fusion of powers is that it makes the relationship between the executive and Parliament a delicate one; great care is needed to ensure that the executive is not given unfettered influence to pass whatever laws it wishes.[124]

The real risk of an over-mighty executive stems from at least six factors. These are: (i) the FPTP system; (ii) the control of time; (iii) the system of whips; (iv) the increased use of special advisers; (v) the passing of laws where there is so little examination of Bills in the Commons that it might as well not happen at all; and (vi) the system of delegated legislation.[125]

Dealing with these briefly, first is the FPTP system. That is best described as the winner-takes-all electoral system. The party achieving an electoral majority is usually able to dominate the House of Commons – and in practice (because of the legislative primacy of the House of Commons) the second chamber as well. The result is a form of tyranny, as the Rwanda refugee policy demonstrates. The Supreme Court held in November 2023 that the Tory Government's Rwanda policy was unlawful because genuine refugees sent there would be at risk of being returned to their own countries – in other words a breach of Art 3 of the European Convention on Human Rights. The new Labour Government has not gone ahead with the Rwanda refugee policy, though the previous Prime Minister, Rishi Sunak, would have proceeded.

[124] Bagehot considered that a fusion of powers was superior to a separation of powers and that there was a distinction to be drawn between *efficient* and *dignified* parts of the Constitution – the latter being typically exemplified by the Crown. This may have been true in the nineteenth century when the UK Constitution was more balanced, with a strong House of Lords. But the Constitution has become less balanced with the weakening of the House of Lords in the Parliament Acts of 1911 and 1949 and the growth of the modern party system. These points are well made in The Hon Mr Justice Beatson's (as he then was) 'Reforming an Unwritten Constitution' 31st Blackstone Lecture (2010) 126 *Law Quarterly Review* 48.

[125] There is an interesting report from a commission chaired by the former Attorney-General Dominic Grieve published on 1 February 2024, entitled *Governance Project: Proposals for Reform* published by the UK Governance Project. The members of the project team consisted of Dominc Grieve, the Right Honourable Margaret Hodge, Professor David Howarth, Sir Jonathan Jones, Helen MacNamara, Professor Anand Menon, the Right Honourable the Lord Neuberger of Abbotsbury and the Right Honourable Baroness Pashar. Whilst the report suggests partial reform, the crucial thing is that the report offers only a temporary solution, as the power is still held by the executive.

Second is the control of time. Standing Order No 14 is arguably the most important of all the rules in the British Parliament because it ended the operation of the House of Commons as an independent body. By clause 14(1) '[s]ave as provided in this order, Government business shall have precedence at every sitting'. True it is that there are exceptions, such as the space for private members bills (which do not have a chance of being converted to law unless the Government approves) and confers on the Opposition 20 days a session to hold debates. But, the basic reality is ultimately is the same today as when the rule was introduced in 1902.[126] The House of Commons is told what it is going to do and for how long it is going to do it.

Third is the system of whips. It should be borne in mind that the dangers of unchecked executive power are reinforced by the Government whips, who wield considerable power. The Chief Whip (who has a seat in Cabinet) of the governing party in the House of Commons is in overall charge of the whipping system by which members of the party, on pain of sanction, are compelled to attend the House and vote as the Government dictates.[127] Such a system has the effect of creating a career hierarchy in which pleasing the whips can take priority over independent judgement.[128]

Fourth is the increasing use of special advisers. In recent times, Prime Ministers (and increasingly many Cabinet Ministers too) appoint special advisers who have no connection with either House of Parliament or the civil service yet who hold power that can, at least in some cases, rival that of Cabinet Ministers. This trend, started by Margaret Thatcher (1979–90), has been continued by successive Prime Ministers including Boris Johnson, who appointed Dominic Cummings from 24 July 2019 to 13 November 2020.

Fifth is the scrutiny of Bills in the House of Commons (the Lords is materially the same).[129] The Bill enters the Chamber via the first reading, which is a purely formal process. The report stage is the time for debate on the Bill's content, but debate is generally limited to one day or two days or, very occasionally, three days.[130] The use of the word 'day' is something of a euphemism, as the day begins after the end of Ministerial statements, urgent questions and whatever else happens that morning. And it must end an hour before the 'moment of

[126] Many bodies possess independent decision-making processes. For a proposal for reform see Meg Russell and Daniel Govers, *Taking Back Control: Why the House of Commons Should Govern its Own Time* (The Constitution Unit UCL, January 2021).

[127] A three-line whip is very serious and could result of a whip being withdrawn; that means effective expulsion from the party unless the whip is restored.

[128] House of Commons Library research briefing, *The Whip's Office* (10 October 2008).

[129] All of the progress through the Chamber ignores the start of the whole process, which is seriously flawed. For a good recent description see Ian Dunt, *How Westminster Works … and Why It Doesn't* (Weidenfeld & Nicholson, 2023) 281–89.

[130] One day is the usual time for stage 2. If the Bill is a major piece of legislation, it is allowed two days, and on a very few occasions three days. In the decade 2000–2010 only three times was a Bill's report stage given three days.

interruption' – the code word for the end to the parliamentary day.[131] After the Bill is introduced at the end of the second reading it is unamendable, except when a supplementary programme motion is added before report stage. The Bill then enters a third reading, which is usually a valedictory affair and usually lasts an hour.

In the words of Ian Dunt, no real scrutiny of Bills took place at any time during the process in the House of Commons in Parliament or earlier:[132]

> It did not take place at the PBL committee. It did not take place through the needlessly rushed writing process at the Office the Parliamentary Counsel. It did not place at first reading, which is a formality. It did not take place at second reading, which was a general debate. It did not take place at committee, which was purposefully structured to prevent meaningful assessment or improvement. It did not take place at report stage, which was stitched up between opposition and government to prioritise theatrics over substance. And it most certainly did not take place at third reading, which acted as if the preceding stages had been more meaningful than they really were.

Sixth is the system of delegated legislation which makes it unnecessary to consult Parliament at all. Delegated (or secondary) legislation is so called because Parliament is delegating its lawmaking power to someone else. Statutory instruments were formalised in the Statutory Instruments Act 1946 and were meant to satisfy two main issues: (i) to allow Ministers to get on with innocuous technical adjustments; and (ii) to provide law with the flexibility to make inevitable changes in circumstances. Sadly, those instruments have been misused. The story of how the power to make delegated legislation was misused is a long one and its essence is summarised under the heading 'Problems of Lack of Scrutiny over Secondary Legislation'.

Of course, Parliament is also an active body and one would expect some reaction from them. There has been a form of reaction and it has come from three events: (i) the origins of the select committee system; (ii) the Wright reforms; and (iii) the changes introduced by John Bercow, when he was Speaker of the House of Commons. None of them, however, has altered the power balance in Westminster.

The select committee system is by far the most significant of the reforms engineered from within Parliament. Norman St John-Stevas did something remarkable; he created the modern select committee system. Select committees stay in place, only re-forming after an election. A select committee of the House of Commons has a general responsibility for overseeing the work of the government departments and agencies.

[131] For an extended version of the report stage see Ian Dunt (n 129) 296–306.

[132] Ian Dunt (n 129) 306–307. Once the Bill reached the House of Lords the scrutiny was different and much more penetrating; but of course the Second Chamber has less legitimacy than the House of Commons.

Then were the Wright reforms. These came in 2009. Dr Tony Wright made a number of recommendations which were aimed at restoring the Commons' authority over its own affairs and improving backbench MPs' ability to scrutinise legislation effectively. The most important of all the reforms that were implemented were: (i) election of members and chairs of select committees by secret ballot; and (ii) the establishment of a Backbench Business Committee. The Backbench Business Committee is not able to control what happens with Government business but it is allowed an awful lot of time (27 days) for MPs to debate whatever they want. Unfortunately, this has not been successful, in that most of the debates have been trivial. Professor Meg Russell has blamed the politics.[133]

The third of the Parliament's counter-reaction came with the election of John Bercow as Speaker in 2009. Mr Bercow's approach to the task of interpreting the standing orders was, first, to interpret them in the most liberal way possible (thus he interpreted Standing Order 33 as permitting three amendments, rather than two as the rule clearly stated). Second, he rediscovered two powers that had rarely been used – the emergency debate and the urgent question.

Who Wields Executive Power (Arts 88–107)

The starting point for regulating executive power more effectively is to identify who wields it and then to circumscribe the nature of the powers that may be exercised. The British monarch becomes entitled to exercise prerogative power on a hereditary basis. In strict theory, the monarch may exercise largely unchecked prerogative power. The fact that as a matter of constitutional convention the advice of the Prime Minister, which the King or Queen must accept, determines how prerogative power is exercised does not alter the theoretical constitutional position of the monarch.

This Constitution recognises the constitutional reality that the King/Queen exercises no effective powers but nonetheless has an important symbolic role to play in society. It therefore identifies the monarch's role as being of executive authority as opposed to executive power (see Art 88).

The Exercise of Executive Power (Arts 90, 91 and 98–107)

Articles 94, 98, and 99–100 set out the main ways in which executive power may be exercised under the Constitution. There are, broadly, three proposed categories: (i) the power of the Prime Minister to appoint Ministers and special advisers

[133] 'But they're not doing what it was for. There have been big, important topics that MP's complain government isn't scheduling for debate, which they've then failed to schedule themselves. Unfortunately somehow the politics is not enabling it to be used': Meg Russell in an interview with Ian Dunt.

(see Art 94); (ii) the conferment of executive functions by law (see Art 98); and (iii) the executive power of the Prime Minister in respect of prerogative power not currently controlled by laws (see Arts 99–100).[134]

As to appointments under the Constitution, Ministerial appointments remain for the most part under the effective control of the Prime Minister (other than his/her own appointment, which continues to be made by the Head of State). Some have proposed that Parliament should have the power to veto key appointments, but confirmation hearings (such as those that take place in the US, where hearings are held by the US Senate to gather information in order to decide whether to approve or reject candidates for high federal office who are nominated by the President) would slow the process of appointing Ministers and would, it is suggested, unnecessarily and detrimentally hamper the process of executive Government.

However, this should not be at the expense of accountability. Minsters appointed from the House of Representatives or from the elected body of the Senate will, by definition, have to account to the electorate. They will also be accountable to their respective elected House.

This does not apply to special advisers, who are almost invariably not members of either House and have never been elected. In addition, there is some merit in appointing Ministers who have special expertise despite the fact that they have not been elected and are not members of either House. In practice, this is not currently permitted. The risk of allowing such persons to be appointed to influential posts with the prospect of exercising or affecting the exercise of governmental powers is that of lack of accountability. The risk of not doing so is the consequent loss of talent and expertise.

There are, no doubt, many ways in which these difficulties could be tackled. However, if it is accepted that some appointments of such persons outside Parliament are in principle justified, there seems little merit in banning special advisers at the highest level[135] or retaining the convention that requires all Ministers to belong to one or other of the two Houses (especially when the current House of Lords is non-elected).

This Constitution envisages that the appointment of special advisers should continue and that the convention whereby Ministers must belong to one of the two Houses will cease except at Cabinet level. But the appointment of special advisers and Ministers who are not members of a relevant elected body must be endorsed by the House of Representatives (see Art 94) and such appointees are required to provide regular progress reports to a special committee of that House.

[134] By Arts 99–100 only the most important powers require the authority of the House of Commons. The remainder are attributable to the Prime Minister acting alone.

[135] Ministers (other than the Prime Minister) would, by virtue of this Constitution, be banned from appointing special advisers.

These constitutional reforms in respect of special advisers do not affect the reforms contained in the Constitutional Reform and Governance Act 2010, which will run in parallel.

As to conferring executive functions by law, this is the most common source of such functions, and it is in substance the statutory source of power that renders the exercise of executive subject to judicial review. However, to be clear, any laws that are enacted which confer such functions must be compatible with the Constitution.

The third method of exercising executive power permitted by the Constitution is the transfer of prerogative power to executive Government under Arts 99 and 107. This is considered immediately below.

Transferring Prerogative Power (Arts 99 and 107)

The transfer of most prerogative power from the monarch under Articles 99 and 107 forms part of a scheme of profound constitutional change as regards the Crown.

In practice, and as a matter of constitutional convention, prerogative powers are exercised by the Prime Minister on (theoretical) behalf of the King/Queen. Many former prerogative powers were qualified during the Commonwealth and in the so-called Glorious Revolution of 1688. Others have, over the centuries, been restricted by statute. But some important powers remain. Of these, there are powers which are (in the words of the House of Commons Public Administration Select Committee) 'sweeping, but little understood'. They allow governments (amongst other things) to ratify international treaties, go to war, issue passports and grant honours. However, none of them requires parliamentary approval and not all of them are even reviewable in the courts.

A chance for change came with the enactment of the Constitutional Reform and Governance Act 2010 but in the end the only major reform of the prerogative was the decision to make management of the civil service the responsibility of the Civil Services Commission. However, by no means all prerogative powers will be subject to fundamental change. In particular, neither a decision to go to war nor treaty ratifications are subject to absolute parliamentary veto. The 2010 Act created executive discretion to bypass parliamentary scrutiny in making or unmaking treaties[136] and there is only a governmental assurance that Parliament would, in practice, be consulted before a decision was made to go to war. Nothing in terms of a parliamentary veto is proposed to be enshrined in legislation.

[136] In *R (Miller) v Secretary of State for Exiting the European Union* [2017] UKSC 5 the Supreme Court upheld Gina Miller's appeal against the decision of the Government refusing to refer to Parliament its decision to unmake the Treaty of Rome, partly on the grounds that the 1972 Act was an 'overriding source of domestic law'.

This Constitution seeks to entrench this category of executive power by abolishing Crown prerogative altogether and making all pre-existing prerogative power constitutional in nature (and so accountable to the courts). Thus, a number of prerogative powers currently exercised by the Crown (though in reality always exercised consistently with advice tendered by the Prime Minister) are formally transferred to the Prime Minister (see Art 107) but subject to the control of the Constitution.

Whether exercised by the Crown or the Prime Minister, it is strongly arguable that there should be tighter, not fewer, controls on the exercise of such powers and that immense powers of this kind should be subject to parliamentary veto. Many have thought, in relation to a declaration of war, that a convention existed. The problem lies in defining it. The Cameron Government stated in the *Cabinet Manual* (2011) that a convention had developed in Parliament that before troops were committed the House of Commons should have the chance to debate the matter. The real problem, apart from the generality of this wording, is in matching policy to practice.

The Government clearly wanted Parliament to back the war against Syria (2013) in 2014 but the motion in Parliament was defeated. David Cameron again consulted Parliament, this time for air strikes against Iraq. The motion was carried by a landslide. However, in August 2015 the UK and US carried out drone strikes without consulting Parliament. By the time Teresa May entered in Downing Street the convention had been destabilised to such an extent that its very existence was under threat. On 14 April 2018 the UK, in conjunction with France and the US, executed coordinated attacks on Syria's chemical weapons facilities but no prior authorisation from the Commons was forthcoming. By 11 January 2024 Parliament was permitted to debate rather to decide the issue. The most recent parliamentary report into the war powers convention was published by the House of Commons Public Administration and Constitutional Affairs Committee, which concluded unsatisfactorily that the instability of the content of the convention was undermining the Government's accountability to Parliament.

Moving away from the power to declare war, was the decision to withdraw from the Treaty of Rome without even consulting Parliament, an error corrected by the Supreme Court in *R (Miller) v Secretary of State for Exiting the European Union*.[137] In *Miller (2)*[138] the Supreme Court again intervened to quash an order to prorogue Parliament for what the court considered to be an unreasonable period.

The Constitution provides, at least in most cases, for a parliamentary veto by majority vote in such cases by the House of Representatives (see Arts 99–100).

[137] See n 136.

[138] *R (on the application of Miller) v The Prime Minister* [2019] UKSC 41.

The Monarchy (Arts 101–107)

The issues surrounding changes to the constitutional position of the monarchy are likely to be controversial and will warrant the most careful consideration.[139] Monarchy has, for hundreds of years, been tightly regulated by law and two of the areas of law affecting the role of the monarch have been concerned with his/her constitutional position. The first area concerns the rules of succession and the second the three oaths.

As long ago as The Act of Settlement 1701 (which laid down that the monarch had to be someone other than a Roman Catholic and could not marry someone who was a Roman Catholic[140]) and the three religious oaths (the oldest of which dated to 1689) cemented the requirement that the King/Queen take oath as a practising Protestant. The two Acts placed a practical restriction on the King/Queen being anything other than a Protestant, and one prepared to devote time to safeguarding the true faith. Quite apart from the fact that this reflected the values of a different era, it also reflects the fact that the monarchy was indissolubly bound up with the requirements of a religion now practised by under 50% of the population.

Abolition of the monarchy has often been proposed by a minority. But the shape and size of that minority has shifted. According to a YouGov poll undertaken just before the coronation of King Charles III, young Britons (aged 18–24) are far less likely to support keeping the royals than their elders. In fact, while backing for the Crown stands at 79 per cent among the over-65s, with only 15 per cent preferring an elected head of state, younger Britons are split. Only 36 per cent want to keep the monarchy, compared to 40 per cent who want to have an elected head of state. The factors leading to this point are various but the most important three are probably: (i) the recent death of the Queen; (ii) the stepping back from royal duties of Prince Harry and the Duchess of Sussex; and (iii) Prince Andrew and his association with Jeffrey Epstein.

But the break with centuries-old tradition that this would entail is not currently, at least, considered to be in the national interest (see also Chapter 1 'Setting the Scene' above, where the virtues of the monarchy are discussed). One of the difficulties with halfhearted House of Lords reform is that tradition has been violated without any corresponding improvement in the vices that bedevil a wholly unelected body. Indeed, one of the many curiosities of the current House of Lords is that it is solely the hereditary peers who elect which of their dwindling number outside the Lords will replace those current members who

[139] Graham Smith in his *Abolish the Monarchy* (Torva Books, 2013) sets out the position very well from a republican standpoint.

[140] The requirement that the spouse of the monarch must be a Protestant was abandoned in 2013, as was the requirement that priority must be given to male heirs: see the Succession to the Crown Act 2013.

die. Even where breaking with tradition is necessary, it does not follow that the symbolic nature of that tradition should be destroyed.

However, a hereditary system of monarchy can only sensibly be defended if the monarch's authority is purely symbolic. That is precisely what is envisaged in Arts 101–107. These provisions accept the principle of a hereditary monarch but set out procedures to be followed before the successor to the throne can become Head of State.

The change of substance is that the Head of State (whether monarch or president) is subservient to the Constitution. This is the position in nearly all democracies with a written constitution and it would be the position if the UK had a true constitutional monarchy. That is why Article 102 mandates (as does the Belgian Constitution) the monarch's taking of an oath of allegiance to the Constitution before constitutional powers may be assumed.

Retaining the monarch as Head of State with essentially symbolic authority does not necessarily entail disestablishing the Church of England (of which the King is the supreme head). However, separating Church from state is a necessary precondition of a modern, secular constitution in which multiculturalism is an important foundation (see the Preamble and Notes thereto). Moreover, adherence to a hereditary monarchy and state church has impeded reform of the House of Lords. Both the hereditary principle and the asserted need for bishops and archbishops in the House of Lords have been said to be important. If they were replaced by an elected House, they would, it has been argued, be a threat to the continuation of the monarchy itself. But this Constitution envisages that, amongst other things, the Church of England will be disestablished (see Article 103) and that inconsistent statutes (Article 107) will no longer have effect, and that elections will take place for the elected body of the Senate (225 members). It also outlines a proper appointments system for the appointed body of the Senate (also 225 members) (see, especially, Articles 59–66 for the elected body of the Senate and Articles 69–76 for the appointed body of the Senate).

The powers retained by the Head of State are contained in symbolic powers. First, the Head of State must assent to all Bills presented save where the Supreme Court has, under new powers, held that such legislation would be incompatible with the Constitution. Second, the Head of State derives all power from the Constitution and any powers conferred are subject to the constraints imposed by the Constitution. Third, the Head of State wields executive authority, which symbolises the unity of the state. Fourth, the Head of State appoints the Prime Minister but is constrained by the constitutional requirement that this must be the person best able to enjoy the confidence of Parliament. This essentially replicates the present position where, in substance, the Prime Minister is the head of the political party in power. As explained below, all breaches of the Constitution are potentially actionable in the courts and it follows that the monarch as Head of State (who according to current constitutional theory can do no wrong) could be subject to judicial review if the constitutional power to appoint the Prime Minister were abused. Finally, the Head of State has the express powers referred to in Article 107, which are more symbolic than substantive in nature.

The changes envisaged here have the benefit of both retaining and modernising the Crown as an institution.[141] Modernisation is achieved by repeal of those statutes the effect of which has primarily been to require the monarch to be a Protestant. It seems a generation ago (but in fact it was only changed by the Succession to the Crown Act 2013) that the monarch was required to marry a Protestant and succession to the throne was through the male line.

The Attorney-General (Arts 108–111)

The Attorney-General is the chief law officer of the Crown in England and Wales and provides legal advice and, where appropriate, legal representation in court (often in sensitive criminal prosecutions) on behalf of the Crown and departments of state. Yet the Attorney-General is also supposed to serve as a key Government Minister. There is a clear conflict of interest here, as was evidenced by the embarrassment over Lord Goldsmith, as Attorney-General, having to advise objectively on the legality of the Iraq War yet also having to defend the war as a Government Minister.[142] Similarly, the criminal investigation undertaken by the Serious Fraud Office into allegations of unlawful arms deals between BAE Systems and Saudi Arabia was dropped after Tony Blair wrote to the Attorney-General, pointing out that prosecutions could endanger national security.[143]

Difficulties of this kind would not arise if the Attorney-General's role were confined to law rather than embracing both law and politics. The Government originally proposed reforms to the office of Attorney-General in the Green Paper leading up to the introduction of what became the Constitutional Reform and Governance Act 2010. However, those proposals were dropped.

An argument often used against reform is that the Attorney-General's dual role provides a necessary wide perspective when providing legal advice and

[141] There have been suggestions that constitutional changes of this kind might require the consent of the Commonwealth under the Statute of Westminster 1931. However, this is not considered by many commentators to be an obstacle in practice and the effect of a written constitution would be that the former Royal statutes would no longer have legal effect.

[142] The Chilcot Inquiry was a British public inquiry. On 6 July 2016 Sir John Chilcot announced the report's publication. The report stated that at the time of the invasion of Iraq in 2003 Saddam Hussein did not pose an urgent threat to British interests, that intelligence regarding weapons of mass destruction was presented with unwarranted certainty, that peaceful alternatives to war had not been exhausted, the UK and the US had undermined the authority of the United Nations Security Council, that the process of identifying the legal basis of the invasion was 'far from satisfactory' and that a war was unnecessary.

[143] See Tom Clark, 'A New Politics: One Law for All', *The Guardian*, 20 May 2009.

representation. However, such an argument could be said to be just as relevant to judicial membership of the House of Lords, which, it is now accepted, is a violation of the principle of separation of powers (see Notes on the Supreme Court below).

In February 2022 the House of Lords Constitution Committee opened an inquiry into the role of the Law Officers; it published its report on 18 January 2023. The Committee came to the conclusion that, essentially, the Attorney-General's functions should not be changed.

This Constitution (see Articles 110 and 111) does not, despite the view of the House of Lords Constitution Committee, allow the Attorney-General to exercise functions of a political nature or to be a member of either House of Parliament, and requires the holder of such an office to resign membership of the Houses of the Parliament as a condition of appointment.

The Executive and Parliament (Arts 112–118)

Alongside the significant strengthening of parliamentary control over former prerogative powers (see above), there is a widely recognised need to strengthen the power of Parliament against the executive more generally. This is largely sought to be achieved by enhancing the select committee system that is currently increasingly relied upon in both the House of Commons and the House of Lords.

Select committees are committees that deal with specific fields or issues. They comprise a small number of members of the relevant House, chosen ostensibly for their expertise in those areas rather for any party adherence. This gives them a degree of legitimacy and authority. Select committees of the House of Commons generally mirror the work of Government departments and agencies, whereas those in the House of Lords are concerned with wider issues such as constitutional reform. Some select committees are joint committees of both Houses, such as the Joint Committee on Human Rights, which currently consists of six MPs and six members of the House of Lords. There was generally a positive response to the proposal that there should be a secret ballot across the whole of the House of Commons for the person who was going to chair the joint committee and for a secret ballot to choose that person (though certain select committees still have the problem of the whips).[144] There is, however, one significant practical difficulty. It is that select committees have no real power. The executive generally can do anything it wishes and often responds to select committee inquiries with a bland and inconsequential response.

[144] The select committees themselves are allocated a fixed quota that, at least, generally approximates to the party strength in the House of Commons. Elections take place on a secret basis that differs according to the party concerned.

In a report published in May 2021[145] the Privileges Committee published the latest in a long series of proposals trying to find a way to make the penalties for committing a breach of parliamentary rules real and potentially effective. The approach of the Privileges Committee was to suggest that the matter be the subject of a statutory regime.

The resolution that this Constitution has arrived at improves the efficacy of select committees, at least to some extent. What is first proposed is the emasculation of the party whips at least in relation to select committees (Art 113). Second, the powers of the relevant committees should be enhanced in a number of ways, including conferring the power (currently lacking) to subpoena and examine witnesses (Art 115), to co-opt members with specialist expertise (Art 116) and – in the case of a relevant select committee of the House of Representatives – to ensure the parliamentary accountability of certain Prime Ministerial appointments of un-elected persons (Art 117). A recommendation of the Power Inquiry was that an overarching select committee should be established to scrutinise how the executive acts on the international level.

Article 118 provides that both Houses of the Parliament have power to initiate legislation and public inquiries as provided for by law. The need for consideration of such a power by the relevant committee with expertise in this area was recommended by the Power Inquiry, which was chaired by Baroness Kennedy. At present, Parliament has no such power. If Parliament had such a power it would, in conjunction with stronger select committee, go some way to weakening the executive's control over what legislation is introduced. It would also make it more difficult for the executive to resist exposure in areas that central government would rather not be subjected to public scrutiny. But the conditions of the exercise of such power require careful consideration.

EXECUTIVE GOVERNMENT: KEY POINTS

- **Executive power and executive authority:** Executive *power* is the governmental authority and responsibility of the Prime Minister acting through Cabinet. The executive *authority* is vested in the monarch and is now largely symbolic.

[145] Paper published by the Privileges Committee. It was entitled *Select committees and contempts: clarifying and strengthening powers to call for persons, papers and records* 1st Report Session 2019–2021 HL 350, published on 27 April 2021. The inquiry followed two cases of persons admonished in one of the cases lying to the DCMS (two witnesses having lied about their knowledge of illegal phone hacking) and in the other (the Director of Vote Leave, Mr. Dominic Cummings) Mr. Cummings having refused an Order of the House of Commons that he attend the hearing of the DCMS (the predecessor committee before the Privileges Committee). RJF Gordon and Amy Street also produced a paper entitled *Select Committees and Coercive Powers – Clarity or Confusion* published by the Constitution Society in 2012.

- **Questions raised by the need to control executive power:** There are two basic questions: (i) how best is practical effect to be given to the separation of powers, since otherwise an over-mighty executive or judiciary could swerve out of control? (ii) how best in a representative democracy can the institutions of government be directly accountable to the people?
- **Fusion not separation of powers:** It is probably too late for a true separation of powers to exist. But what is certainly necessary is a change to the electoral system to reduce the dominance of the two-party system, plus increasing the independence of Parliament so that Parliament exercises greater control of the legislative system.
- **Danger of an over-mighty executive:** The real danger of the executive is that left unchecked it can pass whatever laws it chooses. Six factors are important: (i) the FTPT system; (ii) control of parliamentary time is left in the Government's hands; (iii) the whips; (iv) the increased use of special advisers; (v) the passing of laws with no effective scrutiny in Parliament; and (vi) the system of delegated legislation.
- **Who wields executive power:** The Prime Minister acting through Cabinet exercises power. The monarch exercises a power which is to all intents and purposes symbolic (see Arts 101–107).
- **The exercise of executive power:** There are broadly three categories of constitutional functions: (i) the power of the Prime Minister to appoint Ministers and special advisers (Art 94), (ii) the conferment of executive functions by law (Art 98); (iii) the executive power of the Prime Minister in respect of prerogative power not currently controlled by law (Arts 99–100).
- **Transferring prerogative power:** The transfer of prerogative power from the monarch to effectively the Prime Minister forms part of a scheme of constitutional control over a system that has lasted (with amendment) for centuries. Even so there remained a number of gaping holes for central government without further amendment from the Constitution. For example, the ratification of international treaties, going to war, the issuing of passports and grant of honours. The Constitution provides for a Parliamentary veto by the House of Representatives for these and other functions.
- **The monarchy:** The hereditary system of monarchy can only sensibly be defended if the authority of the monarch is purely symbolic. That is precisely what is envisaged in Articles 101–107 of the Constitution, where the monarch is retained as subservient to the Constitution. Retaining the monarch as Head of State is possible without disestablishing the Church of England. However, separating Church from State is a necessary pre-condition of a modern secular constitution.
- **The Attorney-General:** The Constitution (see Arts 108 and 110) does not propose to allow the Attorney-General to exercise functions of a political nature or to be associated with either House of Parliament (this view is

contrary to the view of the House of Lords Constitution Committee, which reported on this issue on 18 January 2023).

- **The executive and Parliament:** The Constitution has a raft of provisions including emasculation of the whips (Art 113), enhancing the powers of the select committees in a number of ways (Arts 115, 116 and 117) and the power to initiate public inquiries and legislation (Art 118).

PART 6
EMERGENCY POWERS (ARTS 119–127)

119. Emergency laws or regulations enacted by Parliament, which shall be decided by the Supreme Court in cases of doubt, shall be subject to the provisions of, and effects provided for, by this Part of the Constitution and they may only be made in accordance with this Part of the Constitution. No emergency law or regulation may derogate from a fundamental provision of this Constitution as defined in Part 14, and any person or body having a sufficient interest in the matter may bring legal proceedings in the appropriate court or tribunal concerning such alleged breach by an emergency law or regulation or any other alleged breach of an emergency law under this part of the Constitution to the extent permitted by this Constitution.

120. No provision of this Constitution may be invoked, interpreted or applied so as to invalidate or seek to invalidate any law or regulation enacted by Parliament which is enacted in time of war or armed rebellion and which is expressed to be for the purpose of securing the public safety and the preservation of the State in time of war or armed rebellion, or to nullify any act done or purporting to be done in time of war or armed rebellion in pursuance of any such law, and the right of challenge under Article 4 in respect of such challenge shall be limited accordingly but not limited in the sense that no emergency law can derogate from the fundamental provisions of the Constitution.

121. Subject to this Part of the Constitution the Prime Minister may, acting or his or her own judgement, make emergency regulations if there is a serious threat to human welfare or the environment, or in case of war, armed rebellion or terrorism. Such emergency regulations will expire after seven days unless they are confirmed by Parliament.

122. Parliament may at any time enact law under this Part of the Constitution conferring power on the Prime Minister acting alone or through Cabinet to proclaim a state of emergency in such circumstances and in such manner as the law permits. The law may include provisions

conferring on the Prime Minister acting alone or through Cabinet the power to make regulations relating to the state of emergency and for such regulations to have effect for part or all of the period of the state of emergency. However, the law may not permit such regulations to remain in force after the state of emergency has expired in accordance with this Constitution.

123. A measure authorised by regulation or law referred to in Articles 120, 121 and 122 (including measures taken under laws permitting such measures to be taken) may derogate from the rights and freedoms set out in this Constitution but only in accordance with this Constitution, only if the right or freedom in question is one which may be derogated from under this Constitution and only if the regulation or law or measure in question specifies in express terms that it is intended to derogate from specified rights and freedoms.

124. Upon a state of emergency being proclaimed in accordance with this Constitution the Head of State must, acting on the advice of the Prime Minister, summon a meeting of the Houses of the Parliament.

125. If the House of Representatives has been dissolved in accordance with this Constitution, the members of the Houses of the Parliament at the time when the House of Representatives was dissolved shall be summoned and those members shall have capacity to exercise all powers conferred on the Houses of the Parliament had the House of Representatives not been dissolved.

126. Once the state of emergency has expired in accordance with this Constitution the provisions of this Constitution shall re-engage as if a state of emergency had not been proclaimed. Time periods stipulated in this Constitution shall, even during a state of emergency, be complied with so far as is possible.

127. The Houses of the Parliament may at any time disallow the continuation of a state of emergency, or disallow or amend any regulations made by the Prime Minister under Article 121.

EMERGENCY POWERS: OBSERVATIONS AND EXPLANATORY NOTES

Overview: Constitutional Control of Emergency Powers

The term 'emergency powers' refers to Government powers to respond rapidly to a public emergency by: (i) making regulations without an authorising act, the necessary authority being given in this case by the Constitution; (ii) acting in a way inconsistent with statutory duties that the Government would ordinarily be bound to observe; and (iii) taking actions that it would not be permissible to take absent the emergency.

Most modern states rely on highly specific constitutional provisions that deal with what should happen in an emergency. This is because there is an ever-present danger that even the most liberal and well-intentioned executive will abuse its power when events can plausibly be argued to threaten the existence of the state itself. The legislative responses of both the US Government (Guatanamo) and the British Government (detention without trial and the recent pandemic) provide illustrative examples of the dangers that lurk below the surface of ostensibly stable democracies.

Whatever the legitimacy of extreme measures such as these, unless they are carefully controlled by a law enforceable by the courts and higher than those generated by a possibly over-reactive executive, the citizen's only 'right' will be to look to a law that fails adequately to protect him.

It has sometimes been suggested that there is a *paradox of constitutionalism*[146] which is that the people who are supposed to confer power on Government are never, in fact, sovereign because the institutions and mechanisms through which power is exercised are in reality established and maintained by a dynamic series of processes in which – whatever a particular Constitution may say – power is simply not capable of being exercised on a 'popular' basis.

The difficulties thrown by this 'paradox' may in practice be reduced, though never eliminated, by a precisely-drafted Constitution in which the people have a clear and recurrent constitutional role. That is one of the purposes of Part 10, which includes provisions for a Citizens' Branch embodied in a Citizens' Council through which a real constituent power is retained by the people which entitles them to place substantive constraints on the exercise of governmental power.

However, in the context of the exercise of *emergency* powers the problem is more acute. The rationale behind such powers is that the ordinary conditions under which law operates do not pertain in certain circumstances. Whatever legal constraints are placed upon the executive, there may be circumstances, which are impossible to predict, in which extra-legal power not only *may* but *must* be assumed in order to preserve the rule of law embodied in the Constitution for the future. If that logic is correct, it would seem to follow that no constitutional provisions can operate to prevent executive Government taking whatever measures it sees fit in a real emergency.[147]

[146] See Martin Loughlin and Neil Walker (eds), *The Paradox of Constitutionalism* (Oxford, Oxford University Press, 2007).

[147] See eg Viscount Radcliffe in *Burmah Oil Co v Lord Advocate* [1965] AC 75, who observed that the essence of emergency prerogative power is 'to act for the public good, where there is no law, or even to dispense with or override the law where the ultimate preservation of society is in question'.

This, however, would be the real paradox of constitutionalism. Under a constitution the power of the executive might be limited to that which is expressly or by necessary implication permitted by that constitution, but logic would compel the conclusion that such a careful scheme of control would be undermined at the precise point at which it is most needed, namely from the point at which the nature of exercisable power is not defined at all.

The underlying question is therefore whether or not democratic government can ever claim to be free of the constraints of law as set out in a written constitution in a situation of true emergency. If not, then it is inevitably possible for a tightly-drafted constitution to give voice to all classes of crisis situation that may arise and to limit the power of the Government during such crises. If, by contrast, extra-governmental power may, in substance, always be exercised in an emergency, then it must also be the case that the courts have little, if any, power of constitutional control over the executive in that context.

In the landmark wartime ruling in *Liversidge v Anderson*,[148] the House of Lords by a majority considered that in an emergency situation the executive was outside any effective legal control. That case involved the internment (in prison) by the Home Secretary under emergency regulations of a man the Home Secretary claimed to have 'reasonable cause' to suspect of having 'hostile associations'. The majority of the House of Lords held that, as a matter of legal interpretation of the emergency regulations, the Home Secretary was permitted to exercise the emergency power of internment if he was acting in good faith. On that footing, the Home Secretary did not have to provide reasons for internment and his actions were not justiciable in the courts.

In a powerful dissenting judgment, which has largely been followed by the UK courts in more recent times, Lord Atkin considered that the question of whether there was reasonable cause for the Home Secretary's actions was an objective matter to be evaluated by the courts.

For a very long time, the exercise of royal prerogative power in the UK was also thought to be unreviewable by the courts. Since prerogative power includes a number of sweeping powers obviously capable of being assumed in an emergency (such as going to war) where there was in effect neither law governing nor parliamentary control over many potential instances of the use of emergency powers. The fact that it was in reality the Prime Minister exercising power as the delegate of the Crown (see above) is, for present purposes, neither here nor there because it is the fact that our current constitutional arrangements allow essentially dictatorial emergency power to be exercised that is the essential vice, rather than the question of who actually exercises the power.

Although the prerogative is no longer exempt from judicial control, it remains the case that only certain types of prerogative power may be the subject of judicial review in the courts. It seems safe to say that exercises of emergency

[148] *Liversidge v Anderson* [1942] AC 206.

power would not be supervised by the courts. For example, in the wake of the decision in 2003 to declare war on Iraq, challenges were mounted as to the legality of that war. None of those challenges were considered to be suitable for adjudication by the courts.

In reality, though, it may be thought that the scope of the law can be extended as far as those legitimately making the law (whether they are, in the relevant context, judges or Parliament) wish it to be extended. As can be seen from *Liversidge v Anderson* itself, the judges in that case were interpreting emergency regulations and they could as easily have interpreted the regulations so as to bring the Home Secretary within the control of the court (as Lord Atkin did) as exclude supervision by the court (as the majority did). The more recent willingness of the courts to exercise control over the use of asserted emergency power in the name of the royal prerogative provides a similar illustration that the common law control of the courts may be (and is being) extended incrementally. Even the common law doctrine of necessity, which – at least in some guises – allows for the use of extra-constitutional emergency power, subjects the exercise of such power to the control of the common law.

This Constitution takes as a premise, therefore, the potential for unlimited constitutional control over the executive, in the form of parliamentary control and/or in the form of judicial control as stipulated in the Constitution. There is no doctrinal, a priori reason for suggesting that the use of emergency powers enables governmental power to be exercised in defiance of a constitution if the constitution contains provisions that are sufficiently tightly drawn to limit its exercise.[149]

Emergency Powers in Time of War or Armed Rebellion (Arts 120–123)

The starting point is to identify the circumstances, if any, in which a constitution recognises the immunity of executive action from judicial control by virtue of its emergency nature. Article 120 is modelled on a similarly worded provision found in the Constitution of the Republic of Ireland but with significant differences. Its intention is to prevent the courts in most situations from interpreting or applying the Constitution in such a way as to invalidate laws passed during a crisis caused by war or armed rebellion. It does not include acts of terrorism since these are not considered to pose any general threat to the rule of law, even though they may constitute an 'emergency' and, hence, be subject to other provisions of this Part of the Constitution. It is perhaps for debate whether there can ever, sensibly, be a 'war against terrorism' in the sense advocated by former

[149] If the common law were to suggest otherwise, for example through the further development of the common law doctrine of necessity, then the common law itself would be susceptible to control by the provisions of the Constitution as the common law is capable of being abrogated or modified by the provisions of this Constitution.

President Bush, but, as is made clear in the interpretation provisions set out in Part 14, the expression 'in time of war' does not encompass emergency measures in response to acts of terrorism.

Draconian as Article 120 is, however, there are a number of constraints. The first is that the combined effect of this Constitution is to prevent a declaration of war without the approval of Parliament sitting as a single Assembly. The second constraint is that Article 120 is made subject to Article 119. This means that even emergency laws passed during a state of war or armed rebellion cannot interfere with the most fundamental rights, which may not be derogated from under any circumstances. This constraint has particular resonance in British society, given the concerns over torture and rendition that have emerged in recent years. The third constraint is that no emergency law – even subject to Article 120 – may derogate from certain identified provisions of the Constitution. Thus, for example, no emergency law may – however temporarily – establish a dictatorship (see the definition of the expression 'fundamental provisions of the Constitution' in Article 253 and the provisions of the Constitution there referred to which permit or authorise derogation from certain fundamental rights).

There is nonetheless an important difference between the emergency laws that may be passed if this country is at war or in a state of civil war and other emergency laws included in Article 119. Provided that an emergency law passed in time of war or armed rebellion does not interfere with non-derogable rights or other fundamental provisions of the Constitution (as defined), it may not be invalidated and no act done pursuant to such laws will be capable of being nullified by the courts (see Art 120). Nor should any constitutional provision be interpreted to have such effect. This means that an otherwise defective law passed during the extreme conditions envisaged in Article 120 will continue to have legal effect if it does not infringe particular fundamental rights or fundamental constitutional provisions. The courts have traditionally been averse to statutory provisions purporting to oust their jurisdiction. However, Article 120 is a constitutional form of ouster provision and the courts would be in defiance of the Constitution (and hence acting unlawfully) if they purported to deny its direct effect.[150]

Other Emergency Powers (Arts 119 and 122)

Laws passed in other emergency situations are treated differently. A strict constitutional regime governs the passing of such laws, with an emergency power given to the Prime Minister to pass emergency regulations in prescribed circumstances. These broadly mirror the circumstances for the making of such regulations in

[150] Importantly, however, the prerequisite for a law being passed under Art 120 is that, there is in fact, a 'time of war' or armed rebellion. It seems probable that the courts would reserve the right to inquire into whether that a state of affairs (sometimes called 'precedent fact') actually existed.

the Civil Contingencies Act 2004, which (as with this Constitution) requires Parliament to confirm them after seven days, failing which the regulations will lapse. However, those provisions of the 2004 Act that permit the monarch to make such regulations are contrary to the Constitution and are therefore invalid.

Finally, an extended emergency regime is also provided for. This allows Parliament to pass a law enabling the Prime Minister to proclaim a state of emergency and to make emergency regulations with legal effect during the period of such state of emergency.

As with emergency regulations or laws passed by Parliament, regulations made under such laws will be subject to judicial control.

The Government's Response to the Covid-19 Pandemic

Most of the powers used by the Government during the pandemic were based on two Acts. The first one was the already in force Public Health (Control of Disease) Act 1984; the second was innovative legislation, the Coronavirus Act 2020. A public inquiry into the Government's handling of the coronavirus epidemic has been set up; the inquiry Chairman is Dame Heather Hallett.[151]

It is perhaps too early to say what the inquiry process will reveal. But Lord Sumption, in a critique of the measures taken, said that of course we needed to have emergency powers but their use must be limited to the occasions when they are really necessary. Lord Sumption said that the Government ignored the fact that in their contingency plan – the Pandemic Preparedness Strategy 2011 – that there was no recommendations for a lockdown at all. Nor was a lockdown recommended in any of the other 27 states in the EU. The Government used a loophole in the Civil Contingencies Act 2004 to avoid the degree of parliamentary supervision to which that Act subjects Ministers. The other Act (the Public Health (Control of Disease Act) 1984) avoids the need for the same degree of parliamentary scrutiny and so that Act should be amended to require the same degree of parliamentary supervision as that required under the Civil Contingencies Act 2004 and 'radical measures such as lockdowns, affecting the entire population, should only be made after Ministers have considered the collateral costs, lest they prove to be catastrophic, which they have'.

EMERGENCY POWERS: KEY POINTS

- **Overview of constitutional control of emergency powers:** The term *emergency powers* is intended to refer to one of three situations: (i) acting without

[151] The fact that the appointed Chairman of the inquiry requested but was not given what she had herself asked for does not bode well for the inquiry procedure. Nor does the judicial review instigated by the Government of the time, in breach of the Chairman's request. The judicial review was dismissed on 6 July 2023.

legal authority; (ii) acting in a way contrary to rules that the Government would normally expect to obey; and (iii) taking actions that the Government would not take absent the emergency. The Constitution takes as a premise the assumption that in a tightly-drawn set of provisions there is scope for absolute control by the Constitution of all scenarios involving the use of *emergency powers*.

- **Emergency powers in time of war or armed rebellion:** The intention of Article 120 is to prevent the Courts in most situations from invalidating a law passed during a war or other forms of armed rebellion. But there are constraints: (i) war may not in general be declared by a Government without the prior approval of Parliament; (ii) nothing in Article 120 operates to allow the most fundamental rights to be infringed (such as freedom from torture); and (iii) nothing in Article 120 operates (for example) to allow a dictatorship to be formed.
- **Other emergency powers:** Laws passed in other emergency situations are treated differently. The Prime Minister is given certain powers to create emergency regulations, with Parliament exercising overall control.
- **The Government's response to the Covid-19 pandemic:** The Government used the Public Health (Control of Disease) Act 1984, which avoids the need for parliamentary scrutiny of the same kind as that required by the Civil Contingencies Act 2004. A public inquiry into the Government's handling of the pandemic is being carried out.

PART 7
POLITICAL PARTIES (ARTS 128–135)

128. Subject to this Constitution and to the law,[152] citizens have the right to form political parties and to join and to withdraw from them. However, this right may not be used to violate the fundamental liberties, the fundamental values, the democratic nature of the State or the sovereignty of the people (being the fundamental principles).[153]

129. Parties which violate the fundamental principles are unconstitutional and shall, on application duly made under this Constitution by

[152] There are, of course, a great many requirements of electoral law, including registration of political parties with the Electoral Commission and the maintaining of accounts pursuant to regulations laid down by the Commission. These detailed requirements should not, however, form part of a constitution.

[153] The term 'fundamental principles' is defined in Part 14.

the executive or by the Citizens' Council, where the Supreme Court has granted permission for the application to be made, be declared to be so by the Supreme Court. Such further relief as the Supreme Court considers within its jurisdiction to be necessary shall be granted by the Supreme Court if it makes a declaration of unconstitutionality,[154] including the banning of a political party from operating for a period not exceeding six months, such period being capable of being for further periods of six months on further application to the Supreme Court by the executive or by the Citizens' Council.

130. If the Supreme Court does not make a declaration of unconstitutionality, it must make a declaration of constitutionality[155] with such other relief acting within its jurisdiction as it considers necessary.

131. A declaration of constitutionality in respect of any political party may also be applied for in accordance with this Constitution by the Citizens' Council and must, where the Supreme Court has given permission for the application to be made, be granted by the Supreme Court with such other appropriate relief as, acting within its jurisdiction, it considers necessary if it is not, on such application, required to make a declaration of unconstitutionality by virtue of the conditions in Article 167 being satisfied and such other relief as, acting within its jurisdiction, it considers necessary.

132. Political parties and other public associations acting within the framework of this Constitution and laws shall have the right to use mass media (of whatever variety) in accordance with law.

133. No political party shall be proclaimed or affirmed as a party or ideolology of the State.

134. The State shall, subject to this Constitution, provide political parties acting within the framework of this Constitution and laws with adequate resources in a fair manner according to assets which are permitted by law in accordance with a procedure determined by law.

135. The political party which succeeds in the general election must, where following a change in Prime Minister, hold a general election within six months, unless a general election is already scheduled to occur within that six-month period.

[154] This term is defined in Part 14.
[155] This term is defined in Part 14.

POLITICAL PARTIES: OBSERVATIONS AND EXPLANATORY NOTES

Overview: Problems with the Modern Party System

Political parties are the backbone of modern politics, in that, in substance, they control the political process. This is so for two basic reasons, which are closely connected. First, the majority party is able to dominate Parliament and thereby almost invariably ensure that the laws it wishes to pass are, in fact, enacted. Second, all parties in the UK are now highly organised through the whipping system, which, amongst other things, usually guarantees that party members attend Parliament and vote according to party notice.

The reason why whipping so important is that, if it works perfectly, the majority party will always win a parliamentary vote. A carefully calibrated system of rewards and sanctions from the whips is directed towards achieving that objective. The narrower the majority, the more important effective whipping will be, since a more tightly-organised Opposition may otherwise defeat the Government and, in extreme circumstances, precipitate an election. One way in which the whipping system might be improved is avoiding whipping where there is a national crisis going beyond party politics, such as a war or other crisis.

In practice, MPs are sent a letter by the Chief Whip every week during a parliamentary session, detailing the week's debates. There appears alongside each debate a single sentence such as 'Your attendance is absolutely essential' or 'There will be a [one/two/three] line whip'. That sentence is underlined one, two or three times (hence the expression *three line whip*) depending on the importance attached by the whips to attendance and the severity of the sanction in the event of non-attendance. Sanctions are usually known in advance, sometimes negotiated in advance, and are often tailored to the individual MP, about whose life and aspirations the whips will have considerable inside information.

The party system and the way in which Parliament is organised more generally raise serious questions about the nature of representative democracy at the present time. In reality, MPs follow the party line rather than engaging with the issues, not only because of the whips but also because it is only by following the party line that they will be 'given a job'.

Because the majority party dominates Parliament there is simply no alternative career progression in Parliament. Further, if a three-line whip is defied, career demotion is inevitable, and effective expulsion from the party (by the whip being withdrawn)[156] is highly likely.

The aspiring MP, Minister or shadow Minister is therefore overwhelmingly likely to look to the party machine rather than to his or her conscience when

[156] Losing the party whip does not prevent an MP from attending Parliament. However, in practice an MP is highly unlikely to retain his or her seat if not adopted as a party candidate. The result of the whip being lost is that the MP no longer commands support of the party in Parliament and is in effect expelled from the party.

deciding how to vote. As one seasoned observer (and then serving MP) has put it with a degree of irony:

> Members of Parliament are bombarded with representations from pressure groups and others about all the issues of the day, especially in the context of legislation and votes, as though they were dispassionate and independent legislators rather than the willing slaves of the whips.[157]

These are not the only obstacles to a more effective representative democracy thrown up by the current party system in the UK. By its very nature party politics reflects a struggle for power amongst the main parties. The election manifesto of each party is not in substance an attempt by that party to represent the electorate; it is rather only a statement of which policies it intends to implement if elected. Therefore, the claim that a party is elected on the basis of the policies set out in its manifesto is, whilst true, misleading in terms of its supposed democratic credentials. The fuller truth is that a party is elected on the basis of what policies it *chooses* to include in its manifesto.

There may thus be policy areas where the major parties speak with the same voice despite the fact that the tide of public opinion is in favour of a different policy. Aspects of constitutional reform, particularly electoral reform of the FPTP system,[158] may fall into this category. Equally, parties may have different policies and voters may agree with some of the policies of one party but prefer other policies of another. How are they to vote?

Under the current system, it may be thought that political parties cannot, sensibly, lay claim to being the only legitimate vehicle for a system of representative democracy and that a better form of representative democracy would be one in which constitutional devices reduced the dominance of the parties. This is all the more so when the rapidly declining membership of our political parties is taken into account. Membership has declined across the board since the 1950s, when Labour had over a million members and the Conservatives had nearly three million. The Labour party has around 432,000 members as of December 2021 and the Conservatives around 172,000 as of September 2022. In terms of not being truly representative, declining party membership is compounded by an FPTP electoral system in which minor parties are effectively squeezed out, preventing them from having any effective representative influence in Parliament.

This suggests that whilst a dwindling number of members of one of the two major parties might be properly represented by their party, the vast majority of

[157] See Tony Wright, *British Politics: A Very Short Introduction* (Oxford, Oxford University Press, 2003).

[158] This is so despite the fact that the result of the 2011 referendum was in favour of retaining the FTPT system. As David Cameron (then Prime Minister of the UK) said: 'the AV referendum was on a system that is often less proportional than FTPT, so that the rejection of AV could not possibly be a rejection of Proportional Representation'.

the electorate are not adequately represented. For this reason there is a plausible case for open primaries to elect party candidates in which the general public, as well as party members, have a voice in choosing their MP and by which means, it might be hoped, a wider interest and engagement in the political process is engendered.[159] However, the argument for open primaries is by no means decisive and the question of whether they should be funded by the state (as opposed to the individual party choosing to do so) is probably a matter for legislation rather than constitutional provision. This Constitution therefore makes no separate provision for a system of state-funded open primaries based on the US model.

It can be seen from the above discussion that the issues regarding political parties overlap with other sections of this Constitution and are in some ways dependent for their effective resolution on being tackled as a whole. For example, a more representative electoral system engendered by PR will introduce greater pluralism into politics by reducing two-party dominance. The provisions set out in Part 5 of this Constitution, introducing changes to the relationship between Parliament and the executive, also necessarily reduce the dominance of the party in government. Paradoxically, perhaps, the weakening of parliamentary sovereignty under a written constitution of this kind will therefore strengthen rather than weaken the power of Parliament as an institution. The creation of a Citizens' Branch and Council with specific provision for referendums on important constitutional issues is another indirect way of grappling with the present constitutional imbalance caused by a party political system that has, it is strongly arguable, become far too mechanistic and serves the interests of those in power as much as it does those they are there to represent.

Part 7 of this Constitution should therefore be read in the context of more general issues raised by the need to control political parties. What it addresses are direct issues of control over the operation of the party system.

Banning Political Parties (Art 129)

It is important to emphasise that, whatever their practical deficiencies, political parties are essential to a healthy, functioning democracy. Without them, representation would simply not be possible. That is why some Constitutions state this expressly. For example, Article 8 of the Romanian Constitution provides, under the heading 'Political Parties', that 'pluralism … is a condition and safeguard of Constitutional democracy.'

[159] In *Tribune* (7 August 2009) David Miliband argued the case for open primaries. The Conservatives held an open primary in the Totnes by-election in 2009. Since then the Conservatives have held a number of by-elections and 14 primaries were held ahead of the 2015 general election. Since then, however, there was only one primary election conducted in the 2019 general election.

The overarching question is whether – given their importance – there should be direct prohibitions on the operation of political parties in a democracy, especially restrictions allowing for such parties to be banned. In principle, Article 10 of the ECHR permits the banning of political parties and there is recent precedent for the outlawing – even by some liberal democracies – of religious and radical parties considered to be undemocratic. The Spanish Law of 2002 banning Basque separatist parties is one such example.

As a general principle it is intrinsic to a liberal, and hence pluralist, society that diversity of views must be tolerated, however objectionable those views may be. Yet, there may be a danger in not restricting the scope of that principle in exceptional cases. A party that has a fundamental objection to the very existence of a democracy could, once elected, proceed to demolish those institutions it had relied upon to secure power. There is a parallel difficulty in the right of expression. The difficulty is that the benefits of permitting free expression may sometimes be outweighed by the damages that free expression causes. A similar difficulty attends the issue of emergency powers. Is the rule of law always sufficient to protect the state from destruction? Are there not at least some crisis situations in which the law itself must step back?

This Constitution starts from the premise that there are exceptional circumstances in which there should be some judicial control over the operation of political parties. Those circumstances (see Art 128) exist where a party is acting in violation certain fundamental principles as defined which materially threaten representative democracy.

However, whereas some Constitutions impose conditions on political parties, as a *sine qua non* of their continued operation, this Constitution adopts (with some modification) a device used in the German Constitution and leaves effective control with the Supreme Court provided that an application is made to it by either the executive or the Citizens' Council.

The Supreme Court may only act within its jurisdiction, but being required to declare a party to be unconstitutional if the requisite conditions are satisfied, it may decide what further relief, if any, to grant. In particular, it need not necessarily ban a party outright but may impose conditions under which that party is permitted to continue to operate. Banning orders may not be for more that six months at a time but such orders may be renewed on application to the Supreme Court. Such a power is not unheard of – the Israeli and Turkish courts have similar powers. However, given the intense political nature of the question, some may think it more desirable to give the courts a secondary rather than a primary role. A possible alternative to the proposals set out here would be for an independent commission (with no affiliation to existing parties) to be set up in order to determine the constitutionality of political parties in accordance with the 'fundamental principles', and the Supreme Court could then be given the power to judicially review the decisions of such a commission.

Whether by the method proposed in Article 129 or a suitable alternative such as that canvassed immediately above, the rival dangers of, on the one hand, the state abusing the constitutional mechanism for control of political parties and, on the other, parties flouting minimum democratic standards are sought to be reduced. A further attempt at reducing risk within the Article 129 mechanism is the above-mentioned provision (in Art 131) that enables the Citizens' Council to seek a declaration of constitutionality (as well as unconstitutionality) in respect of political parties, either of which the Supreme Court must grant if the conditions for their granting are satisfied. In this way, the Citizens' Council can act independently of the executive and seek appropriate relief from the Supreme Court.

Use of Mass Media and Party Funding (Arts 132, 134)

Of course, political parties are also subject to the general law, where applicable, and Articles 132 and 134 grant parties operating within the framework of the law the specific rights there referred to. Conformity with the law is, however, a precondition of such rights being conferred. Thus, a party such as the British National Party, which has had a controversial membership policy and which was the subject of legal action instituted by the Equality Commission alleging it to be in breach of race relations laws, would not, if that action had succeeded – however large it became – have any right to use the mass media or to receive state funding, both of which are proposed under this Constitution. The BNP has agreed to scrap its white-only policy in the light of the action commenced against it by the Equality Commission.

State funding of political parties is a somewhat controversial area. The costs of political campaigning are increasingly high and are not met by a system of state funding, although a few state grants (to opposition parties) are available and indirect costs (such as expenditure on party political broadcasts) are defrayed by the state.[160] The result of insufficient state provision (perhaps paralleled in the arena of MPs' relatively low salaries and the resultant expenses scandal) has been a lack of transparency over how parties are being financed and the true extent of loans and donations comprising important elements of funds and assets.

The law has moved quite quickly in response to increased public concern. Thus, initially, Parliament enacted the Political Parties, Elections and Referendums Act 2000, which amongst other provisions[161] required details

[160] Opposition parties receive principal state funding in the form of Short Money in the House of Commons and Cranborne Money in the House of Lords. However, there is no funding available to parties for campaign purposes.

[161] These included the establishment of an Electoral Commission to oversee the new rules. However, the Commission had no powers of prosecution under the recently passed Elections Act 2022 (see s 19(4)). Further, the Secretary of State may designate a statement which must be taken account of by the Commission when carrying out its functions (see the Elections Act 2022, s 16 amending the Political Parties, Elections and Referendums Act 2000, s 4).

of parties' income and expenditure and donations to be disclosed. However, the parties effectively circumvented these provisions by taking out *loans* (as opposed to receiving *donations*). This led to amendments being introduced to the Electoral Administration Act 2006 mandating the disclosure of loans as well as donations.[162]

A police investigation was conducted with regard to whether criminal offences might have been committed by the promising of honours in return for loans. While this investigation did not result in any prosecutions, it took place in a climate of hostile public opinion reminiscent of the expenses furore that later occurred in the early summer of 2009.

It against this unsatisfactory historical background that the need for state funding of parties is being advocated. There are advantages and disadvantages. The advantages lie in the fact that, as noted above, political parties are an essential parts of the democratic process. Absence of state funding carries with it risks such as business interests exerting control over party policy and a loss of public confidence in the honours system, which is particularly susceptible to abuse in this context. The main disadvantages of state funding are (in the present financial climate) the increased burden on public spending and, perhaps, concerns over whether it is appropriate to force the taxpayer to support a party financially when he does not support that party.

In this Constitution there is a proposal for state funding of political parties. The requirement, however, is couched in the most general terms. A number of studies investigating possible funding mechanisms have been undertaken. For example, the review[163] conducted by Sir Hayden Phillips, which was published in 2007, recommended that donations should be capped at £50,000, that there should be increased state funding as the present situation was unsatisfactory, that there should be greater regulation and transparency with stricter control of donations and loans from third parties, and that there should be a reduction in allowable expenditure on general elections.

However, taking this by way of example, Sir Hayden Phillips' proposals have not resulted in consensus. This is unsurprising. Whilst capping donations seems sensible in principle, and would eliminate scandals such as the Ecclestone affair,[164] there is asymmetry between the parties, which makes the practical detail of party funding – even if accepted in principle – significant. To take one example, Labour derives around 30 per cent of its income from trade union donations and, though there may be ways of structuring a cap on the political

[162] Donations in excess of £7,500 to national parties must be disclosed, as must be donations of £1,500 or more to local associations.

[163] There have been other attempts at a review. Examples include the 2008 Ministry of Justice Report and the Committee of Justice Report of 2011.

[164] This involved a £1 million donation to the Labour Party by Bernie Ecclestone, which was made just before the announcement that Formula One (Ecclestone's company) would be exempt from the ban on smoking in sport.

levy paid by individual members,[165] a simple £50,000 cap on union donations as a class would not seem to be equitable. The size of any cap is also controversial. Some, such as James Purnell the former Labour MP, argue that it should be in the hundreds of pounds in order to encourage small donors, in the spirit of those who swept Barack Obama to power in the 2008 US presidential election. Others argue that this is simply unrealistic and too uncertain to produce an adequate level of funding.

Matters of detail such as these, although extremely important, do not obviously raise issues of constitutional principle. This is why Article 134 leaves the details to be worked out in legislation.

The Prime Minister (Art 135)

The one detail which requires a general election, within a relatively short period (six months is the period suggested by the Constitution), is where there is a change of Prime Minister. Although the general public votes for a party rather than a Prime Minister, the person who is Prime Minister exercises the most draconian powers and it is hardly right that the choice of premiership should lie with either the party or a small circle of supporters (Art 135).[166]

Tim Bale, Professor of Politics at Queen Mary University of London, points to what he calls the 'presidentialisation' of the UK's parliamentary system as one of the reasons that Prime Ministerial terms are not lasting as long. 'There is far more focus from voters and politicians on party leaders and rather less on the party as a whole – that means that the leader is often held personally responsible for anything that goes wrong', he says.

POLITICAL PARTIES: KEY POINTS

- **Problems with the modern party system:** Political parties are the backbone of modern politics. This is so for two closely connected reasons: (i) the majority party almost invariably passes the laws it wishes to enact; (ii) the whipping system – this usually guarantees that MPs will turn up and vote as the party machine dictates because if whipping is taken away party membership is effectively removed. Whipping is one of the things that in a system of representative democracy ought not to exist. But the truth is that there is a logic to it which is that the entire system would need a profound change. Political parties in their modern form would cease to exist.

[165] As suggested by a former MP of the Labour Party: see James Purnell, 'It's All about the Money', *The Guardian*, 29 May 2009.

[166] Especially when there have been six Prime Ministers in the last eight years.

- **Banning political parties:** The question is, given their importance, whether there should be prohibitions on political parties. There is some scope for limited prohibitions by the highest court (the Supreme Court) and the Constitution starts from the premise that there should be quite exceptional circumstances in which a temporary prohibition (6 months renewable) may be imposed (see Arts 129–130). The Citizens' Council may (see Art 129) seek a declaration of constitutionality.
- **Use of mass media and party funding:** Articles 132 and 134 grant political parties operating within the legal framework the specific rights there referred to (state funding and media coverage). State funding of political parties is a highly controversial area; the arguments are discussed in the Notes. The state has moved quite quickly to allay some public concerns in this area. The passing of the Political Parties, Elections and Referendums Act 2000 was part of the process of requiring political parties to disclose of details income, expenditure and donations. The question of whether the state should actually fund political parties remains unresolved. This Constitution proposes that it should.
- **The Prime Minister:** A change of Prime Minister without a general election has happened several times recently (including three in one year, in 2022). It is highly unsatisfactory that a new Prime Minister should be chosen by a small clique. This Constitution proposes that where a new Prime Minister is appointed, a general election should be called within six months (unless a general election is scheduled to be called anyway) (see Art 135).

PART 8
THE JUDICIARY (ARTS 136–173)

Judicial Power

136. The structure, powers and functions of the courts and judges of the United Kingdom at all levels shall be as prescribed by this Constitution or contained in laws compatible with this Constitution.[167]

137. Subject to this Constitution, judges shall hold their office during good behaviour for such period as shall be laid down by law, except that the maximum age, if any, at which the law may stipulate compulsory

[167] Some Constitutions contain specific provisions as to the structure of the judiciary. Such detailed provisions are not considered appropriate for a written constitution (and in any event, the structures differ as between the different nations of the UK). As can be seen, the general intention is not to disturb the overall judicial structure but to leave that to be addressed in legislation if necessary.

retirement for any judge shall not be lower than 65 years of age. Judges shall be paid a salary and pension to be determined by law for their service.

138. Subject to this Constitution, the appointment and removal from office of judges shall be governed by law.

139. In the exercise of its jurisdiction, the judiciary is independent of the legislative and executive branches of government and is also independent of the Citizens' Branch.

140. Judges must, within their jurisdiction, interpret and apply the provisions of this Constitution and law compatibly with this Constitution.

141. The judiciary shall, as prescribed by law, be accountable both in terms of the individual judges and as an institution for the undertaking of functions under the Constitution and the law.

142. As an institution, the judiciary derives its constitutional status from this Constitution and from such laws as may be, and are, made that are compatible with this Constitution.

143. The rights and obligations of the United Kingdom under international treaties that have been ratified by the United Kingdom shall form part of this Constitution to the extent that such rights and obligations shall inform the judicial interpretation of the provisions of this Constitution and of the law. However, rights and obligations under international treaties shall not, save as otherwise provided for by this Constitution, be enforceable at the suit of parties in the courts.

144. In the case of the European Convention on Human Rights, the rights and obligations therein contained shall, subject to this Constitution, be directly enforceable in the courts against public authorities within the meaning of the Human Rights Act 1998, and laws that violate the European Convention on Human Rights shall also violate this Constitution.

145. The highest judicial power and jurisdiction shall vest in the Supreme Court established by this Constitution. The composition, constitutional power and jurisdiction of the Supreme Court are derived solely from this Constitution and must be exercised subject to this Constitution. However, nothing affects the distinctions between separate legal systems of the parts of the United Kingdom.

146. Judicial power shall otherwise vest as prescribed by this Constitution and by law provided that such laws are compatible with this Constitution.

147. Laws shall make provision, or continue to make provision, for both superior courts of record and inferior courts and tribunals in the United Kingdom and for a comprehensive system of appeals. No court or tribunal below the level of the Supreme Court shall have greater power than the Supreme Court in the application of the law to the proceedings before it. No court or tribunal below the level of the Supreme Court shall have the constitutional powers conferred on the Supreme Court in this Constitution, or, in particular, the power to declare primary legislation to be unconstitutional.

The Supreme Court

148. The permanent judges of the Supreme Court comprise the President and eleven Justices. The President is elected by majority vote of the other judges. One of the permanent judges who is not the President shall be appointed Deputy President by majority vote of the other permanent judges.

149. The Court is to be taken to be duly constituted despite any vacancy among the judges of the Court or in the office of President. However, in order to be duly constituted the Court must consist of at least five judges.[168]

150. Each permanent judge must as a condition of exercising office, take an oath of allegiance to this Constitution as set out in Schedule [...] and in the manner there prescribed.

151. Additional members of the Supreme Court may at the request of the President or, if the President is not available, the Deputy President, and provided that the Court is duly constituted sit on the Supreme Court as non-permanent judges if they fulfil the qualifications specified by law and may sit on the Supreme Court for such periods as may be specified by law.

152. The Supreme Court shall, subject to this Constitution, have final responsibility for interpreting this Constitution and shall accept references

[168] There is a strong case for a greater number of Supreme Court judges hearing the most important cases, which by definition come to the Supreme Court. The Supreme Court has published on its website the criteria for considering whether a case is of sufficient importance to justify increasing the panel. They include: (i) if the court is being asked to defect or may decide to depart from a previous ruling; (ii) cases of great constitutional importance; (iii) cases of great public importance; (iv) cases where a conflict between decisions of the House of Lords, the Judicial Committee of the Privy Council and/or the Supreme Court have to be reconciled; (v) cases raising an important point in relation to the European Convention on Human Rights.

on questions of constitutional interpretation that are made to it in accordance with this Constitution by other courts or tribunals. Where such a question is raised before any such court or tribunal, that court or tribunal may, if it considers that a decision on the question is necessary to enable it to give judgment, request the Supreme Court to give a ruling thereon provided that it considers that the conditions for exercise of the jurisdiction of the Supreme Court are satisfied.

153. Where any such question is raised in a case pending before a court or tribunal against whose decisions there is no judicial remedy, that court or tribunal shall bring the matter by way of request for a preliminary ruling before the Supreme Court provided that it considers that the conditions for exercise of the jurisdiction of the Supreme Court are satisfied. There shall be a right to seek permission to appeal to the Supreme Court from a court or tribunal required to seek a preliminary ruling by any party whose application for a referral to the Supreme Court has been refused and who contends that such referral ought to have been made.

154. If the Supreme Court needs to interpret the provisions of this Constitution concerning affairs which are the express responsibility of the Prime Minister or executive, the Supreme Court shall, before making any final judgment, ruling or opinion which is not appealable, seek an interpretation of the relevant provisions from the Cabinet. The Supreme Court shall take such interpretation into account when giving its judgment, ruling or opinion.

155. Where a reference is made to the Supreme Court by another court or tribunal in accordance with this Constitution or on appeal by a party entitled to seek permission to appeal, the Supreme Court shall, if it grants permission for the making of such reference, give a preliminary ruling on the questions referred to it.

156. The Prime Minister may in the public interest and on the advice of the Cabinet refer to the Supreme Court for its opinion on any question as to the effect of a provision of this Constitution that has arisen or appears likely to arise, and the Supreme Court must, if the application is properly brought and it has given permission for the reference to be made, state its opinion on the question.

157. The Citizens' Council may in the public interest and subject to this Constitution refer to the Supreme Court for its opinion any question as to the effect of a provision of this Constitution that has arisen or that appears likely to arise, and the Supreme Court must, if the application is brought in accordance with this Constitution and it has given permission for the reference to be made, state its opinion on the question.

158. Bills proposed to be enacted by Parliament must, if the Attorney-General advises that a question arises as to the compatibility of the Bill with this Constitution, be referred by the Prime Minister to the Supreme Court for a declaration that such Bill would, if enacted, be compatible with this Constitution. If, on such reference made in accordance with this Constitution, the Supreme Court considers, having given permission for the reference to be made, that such Bill would, if enacted, not be compatible with this Constitution it must make a declaration to that effect.[169]

159. The Supreme Court shall have jurisdiction to hear appeals from other courts and tribunals according to law. In any case where the Supreme Court is entitled by law to refuse permission for the making of an appeal and does refuse permission it shall state its reasons for refusing permission to appeal. In any case where the Supreme Court is entitled by law to refuse permission for the making of an appeal and does refuse permission it shall state its reasons for refusing permission to appeal.

160. Nothing in the content or legal effect of the jurisdiction of the Supreme Court under the Constitutional Reform Act 2005 in relation to devolution matters as defined in the Constitutional Reform Act 2005 shall be affected by this Constitution save insofar as it is amended by law. However, exercise of the jurisdiction of the Supreme Court in respect of devolution matters must otherwise conform to this Constitution and be consistent and compatible with the powers granted by this Constitution.

161. The Supreme Court shall have power to determine any question necessary to be determined for the purpose of doing justice in proceedings before it.

162. Apart from its jurisdiction conferred by this Constitution, including the power to grant preliminary rulings on questions of law referred to it by other courts or tribunals, declarations of constitutionality and declarations of unconstitutionality under specific provisions of this Constitution, and to give advisory opinions, the Supreme Court shall have power to grant any relief in proceedings before it which the Supreme Court as defined in the Constitutional Reform Act 2005 could have granted, or would have been required to grant, immediately before the coming into force of this Constitution.

163. In any case before it the Supreme Court must grant a declaration of unconstitutionality in respect of legislation, including primary legislation, and any other act or omission which it finds to be in breach of this Constitution.

[169] The Supreme Court here grants a declaration of *incompatibility* rather than a declaration of *unconstitutionality* as the Bill, not having received assent, is not yet law.

Constitutional Applications and References to the Supreme Court

164. No application or reference permitted to be made direct to the Supreme Court as provided for in this Constitution may be entertained by the Supreme Court unless the Supreme Court has granted permission for the making of the application or reference.

165. The Supreme Court may refuse permission for the making of any such application or reference made to it but must give its reasons for declining to entertain such application or reference. However, permission for the making of any such application or reference may only be refused in accordance with this Constitution.

166. The Supreme Court must refuse permission for the making of such application or reference unless the conditions for the exercise of its jurisdiction are satisfied.

167. The conditions for the exercise of the Supreme Court's jurisdiction are that the application or reference in question involves a question of interpretation of this Constitution, or the validity under this Constitution of acts or omissions which give rise to constitutional obligations or rights.[170] The Supreme Court may refuse to allow such application or reference to be made unless it considers that the application or reference raises issues of constitutional importance or that it is in the public interest that the application or reference in question should be determined.

Appointment and Removal of Judges, Administrative Provisions

168. Provision shall be made in law for the appointment of judges of courts and tribunals at all levels by an independent Judicial Appointments Commission. The composition and manner of selection of the members of the Commission shall be determined by law but it must be independent of the legislative, executive and judicial branches of government.

169. The procedure for making judicial appointments by the Commission shall be specified in law but must be independent of the legislative,

[170] Some jurisdictions (eg the US) have adopted the doctrine of constitutional avoidance, which provides that the court should avoid interpreting statutes etc in a way that would raise constitutional questions. The motivation is to avoid making issues constitutional issues if they can be dealt with in some other way. Consideration should perhaps be given to entrenching such a doctrine in the Constitution as a canon of interpretation in order to avoid unnecessary disputes under provisions such as these.

executive and judicial branches of government. In making decisions on judicial appointments the Commission must follow a fair and transparent process and shall make the final decision as to which judges are to be appointed. The Commission shall select only the best candidates in terms of merit by reference to selection criteria which must give priority to independence of mind, high intellect, excellent judgement and integrity, and also taking into account any other general obligations under this Constitution. However, no candidate may be considered who fails to fulfil the qualifications prescribed by law in terms of legal experience.

170. Subject to this Constitution, judges shall not be dismissed, or retired before the age prescribed by law, nor shall they be deprived in real terms of the whole or part of their salaries, allowances or other rights relating to their status.

171. Exceptions may be indicated in law relating to those convicted of an offence requiring automatic dismissal from the profession, those who are established as unable to perform their duties on account of ill-health, and those determined to be unfit to continue in judicial office.

172. The manner by which judges may, subject to this Constitution, be removed from office shall be specified by law except that judges of the Supreme Court or of any Superior Court of Record may only be removed by the Head of State on an address[171] by both Houses of the Parliament.

173. Administrative arrangements for courts, tribunals and judges, including the payment of judicial salaries and pensions, and all other matters relating to those courts, tribunals and judges which are not otherwise regulated by this Constitution, shall be governed by law.

THE JUDICIARY: OBSERVATIONS AND EXPLANATORY NOTES

Overview: Constitutional Role of Judges

Some constitutional tensions arise when considering what the constitutional position of judges should be in society.[172] Judges are not legislators. This is a necessary consequence of the doctrine of separation of powers. Nonetheless, the

[171] An 'address' in the sense here means a statement or opinion of both of the Houses of Parliament that is sent to the monarch.

[172] For an analysis of the various factors involved see House of Lords Select Committee on the Constitution, *Judicial Appointments: Report* (March 2012).

judiciary is an important branch of government because it interprets and applies the laws that the legislature enacts.

The first tension is that between *making* law and *deciding* law. The reality is that in interpreting and applying laws, judges are being forced into something of a political role. It is hard to deny that one of the consequences of the introduction of recent legislation, including devolution statutes and the Human Rights Act 1998, is that a measure of political power has passed from Parliament and the executive to the judiciary.

Though classed as legal rulings, many of the judgments made in court are now capable of overturning parliamentary legislation or executive acts. In recent years there have been challenges in court to highly politically controversial government decisions such as the legality of the Iraq War, the validity of the Parliament Act and the internment without trial of foreign terrorist suspects.

It is the constitutional tussle between the executive on the one hand and Parliament on the other, mediated by the court, which has given rise to the most concern. The two *Miller* cases, for example, both of which resulted in heavy Government defeats, are illustrations of the fact that the judiciary now exercises real political power.

In *Miller (1)*[173] the majority in the United Kingdom Supreme Court held that the European Communities Act 1972 operated as a partial transfer of lawmaking powers from Parliament to the EU but that at the same time Parliament remained sovereign during this country's membership of the EU because during that period Parliament had the capacity to expressly repeal EU law. Further, the United Kingdom Supreme Court was of the view that a change affecting the 1972 Act was of such fundamental constitutional importance that it could not be introduced using the prerogative power but would require primary legislation enacted by Parliament. This was because (see para 61) '… it is unrealistic to deny that, as long as that Act remains in force, the EU Treaties, EU legislation, and the interpretations placed on these instruments by the Court of Justice are direct sources of UK law.' So the majority of the United Kingdom Supreme Court was perfectly happy to declare that an order, supposedly emanating from the prerogative, was invalidly made.

In *Miller (2)*[174] the United Kingdom Supreme Court understood that the advice given to the Crown was inherently political in nature but it held that the lawful limits of that power was a legal matter that the Court was required to establish (see para 52):

> … the standard which determines the limits of the power, marking the boundary between the prerogative power on the one hand, and the operation of the constitutional principles of the sovereignty of Parliament and responsible government on the other hand …

[173] *R (on the application of Miller) v the Secretary of State for Exiting the European Union* [2019] UKSC 5.

[174] *R (on the application of Miller) v the Prime Minister* [2019] UKSC 41.

After having analysed justiciability, the Supreme Court went on to assess whether the advice given to the Queen had been lawful. The Court stated (see para 50)

> … a decision to prorogue Parliament … will be unlawful if the prorogation has the effect of frustrating or preventing, without reasonable justification, the ability of Parliament to carry out its constitutional functions as a legislature and as a body responsible for the supervision of the executive …

On the facts, the Court held that the advice given was unlawful. It quashed the order in council approving the prorogation and declared the advice to have been unlawful.

As a result, the Conservative party, which was furious at the result of *Miller (1)* and *Miller (2)* launched an inquiry headed by Lord Faulks:

> on how well or effectively judicial review balances the legitimate interest in citizens being able to challenge the lawfulness of executive action with the role of the executive in carrying on the business of government, both locally and centrally.

But in the end the review undertaken[175] produced the conclusion that 'the Panel consider that the independence of our judiciary and the high reputation in which it is held internationally should cause the government to think and hard before seeking to curtail its powers'.

The truth is that law is not abstract entity with an identity always easily separable from that of political and executive decision-making. In substance, when judges decide that legislation is contrary to law, one constitutional body (the judiciary) is usually making a value judgement as to the appropriateness of a set of rules decided on by another constitutional body (the executive), because we have an over-strong executive only formally legislated for by a third constitutional body (the legislature – Parliament).

Judges are empowered to make such value judgements because the language of the law is, in such a context, largely open-ended. Interferences with many fundamental rights, for example, are unlawful under the ECHR if they are not *necessary in a democratic society.* Yet whether a measure is or is not necessary in a democratic society is not a hard-edged question of law. It represents a subjective decision with implicit policy content.

Responses to these tensions are not always logical. It is sometimes suggested that there is a conflict between unelected judges and an elected Parliament which is contrary to democracy. Yet, as has been seen, the process by which laws come to be made is largely executive-driven, with an essentially complaisant Parliament. Judges, it may be argued, provide an essential check on an over-mighty executive which is not otherwise effected in an organic fused-powers constitution of the kind we currently have in the UK (*Miller (1)* and *Miller (2)* were both instances of the judiciary standing up for Parliament). Nonetheless, even if this is true – and whatever the imperfections of our present electoral system – it leaves a

[175] The Report was published in March 2021.

wholly unelected body potentially capable of interfering with the decisions of an elected body on a basis that is arguably too imprecise and too uncertain.

A series of body-blows to the principle of parliamentary sovereignty, even in terms of constitutional theory, can now be seen to have been delivered by various events over the past 50 years or so. Accession to the EU and the enactment of the European Communities Act 1972[176] were the first of these events. The clear result of the incorporation of EU law into national law was that – because of the well-established EU principle of EU law supremacy over national law – parliamentary legislation could not be applied if was found by the domestic court to breach EU law. Although efforts have been made to explain why this is not an abandonment of sovereignty,[177] the reality was that EU law prevailed over laws enacted by Parliament, during membership, whenever there was a conflict.

Another development that has made it difficult to rely on parliamentary sovereignty as an explanation for what judges actually do is the expansion of judicial review to encompass control by the judiciary over bodies which have not been created by Parliament at all. This development was introduced in 1987 by the Court of Appeal's ruling in the *Datafin* case,[178] in which a non-statutory body (the Panel on Takeovers and Mergers) was held to be amenable to judicial review. The difficulty, as many commentators noted at the time, was that this otherwise welcome judicial activism had no obvious constitutional source of authority and certainly could not be explained by invoking parliamentary sovereignty.

A more recent body-blow to the supposed axiom of sovereignty came, perhaps ironically, from the constitutional reforms introduced by the Blair Government from 1997, and especially from the enactment of the HRA 1998. Taking that Act as the best example, ingenious attempts were made in its drafting to preserve parliamentary sovereignty by not allowing the courts to strike down legislation in the manner of the US Supreme Court. Instead, the courts could only grant a declaration of incompatibility between laws found to offend against human rights and the requirements of the ECHR.

However, nearly all declarations of incompatibility made by the courts have either been complied with or are intended to be complied with but with the defective Act being permitted to stand.[179] They could, it may be thought, hardly not be. It would be impossible, politically, for a Government to defy such a declaration. In this context it may therefore be seen that whilst parliamentary

[176] Now repealed by the European Union (Withdrawal) Act 2018.

[177] See eg Lord Bridge in *R v Secretary of State for Transport, ex p Factortame Ltd* [1990] 2 AC 8,5 who suggested that the exercise of sovereignty lay precisely in the fact Parliament chose when passing the 1972 Act to permit EU law to have supremacy over parliamentary law. A more recent example is *Miller (1)*, where the majority held that during the period of EU membership Parliament retained the capacity to repeal EU law.

[178] *R v Panel on Takeovers and Mergers plc, ex p Datafin* [1987] QB 815.

[179] The very few exceptions to this are immaterial for the purpose of the point being made here.

sovereignty survives with its analytic integrity intact, we are left with more words than substance.

The absence of an adequate explanation in constitutional terms for what judges are doing is easily solved by a written constitution. This is because in a written constitution the source of authority for what each of the different branches of government may do is the constitution itself. The more difficult question is what to include in such a constitution, since the tension between unelected judges and elected politicians remains, has the potential for friction, and needs to be carefully addressed.

It should first be noted that the very fact of a written constitution should eliminate the prospect (whether heretical or not) of continued judicial assertion of some undefined common law control over Parliament. In recent years some senior judges have made statements to the effect that parliamentary sovereignty may itself be a construct of the common law rather than a separate constitutional doctrine.[180] The result, if this were correct, would be that the judges would enjoy uncontrolled power despite being wholly unelected. This is, on any view, antithetical to the idea of a representative democracy. With a written Constitution this could not happen because common law (which provides the only basis for such assertion of power) is, necessarily, subordinate to the terms of the constitution.

What a written constitution must do is to grapple with the fact that judges are not elected. There are different means of addressing this. One possibility is to provide for the election of judges, as in the US system below the federal Supreme Court. The advantage of an elected judiciary is that it would be less likely to lose touch with the people. Moreover, it would, on one view, lend legitimacy to judicial rulings precisely because they would be the rulings of an elected body.

But the disadvantages of allowing judges to be elected are, it is suggested, fundamental. The essential requirement of a judiciary, at all levels, is that it is both independent and impartial (as well as being perceived to be so). It is often believed that judicial independence requires only a guarantee of independence from the executive and impartiality in the individual case.

However, independence from the people is equally important. The systemic dangers of judges having to campaign for election or re-election whilst sitting on a controversial cases are graphically illustrated by the observation of a former California Supreme Justice who described it as 'like finding a crocodile in your bathtub when you go in to shave in the morning. You try not to think about it, but it's hard to think about much else while you're shaving'.[181]

It is important, therefore, to view the non-electability of judges as a component of judicial independence rather than as evidencing a democratic deficit.

[180] See Chapter 1 'Setting the Scene' above.

[181] Cited in John D Fabian, 'Paradox of Elected Judges – Tension in the American Judicial System' (2001) 15 *Georgetown Journal of Legal Ethics* 155.

Representative democracy is served better by an integrated system, endorsed by the people and reflected in a constitution in which the different branches of government and civic activity can readily be justified and harmonise with each other.

In order to achieve these objectives, the starting point is an independent judiciary constitutionally entrenched by constitutional guarantees of full independence from all other branches of a constitution. Then, the greatest care needs to be taken in appointing judges. Those who are selected must be independent-minded, must be of the highest intellectual calibre, must possess excellent judgement and common sense, and must be in touch with contemporary ideas and values. It is important, too, that judges are – to a material extent – representative of the society in which we live.

Providing the necessary constitutional guarantees of independence once judges have been appointed to office is relatively easy and is a feature of most written Constitutions. However, such guarantees are empty words unless an objectively independent and transparent appointments system is established in which selection criteria are fairly and consistently applied.

The key issue here is the extent, if any, to which judges, executive Government and Parliament should be able to participate in a judicial appointments process. In the US Supreme Court justices are appointed by the President but have to undergo extensive and potentially gruelling confirmation hearings by the Senate before the appointment is confirmed.

During these confirmation sessions the personal life and judicial record of the potential candidate is exposed to exhaustive public scrutiny. The problem is that the dynamics of such a process can lead to (and have been argued to have led to) not much more than an extension of the legislative work of the Senate as well as being 'an arena for competition among warring factions of interest groups and senators'.[182] In other words, the appointments process itself is vitiated by a breach of the separation of powers principle.

There is arguably no principled basis for permitting any of the other constitutional branches of government (including the judiciary itself) to intrude into the process of selecting judges. It is sometimes contended that an appointments commission will produce bland appointments, but there is no reason of principle why this should be so, especially if the selection criteria are sufficiently tightly drawn.

Finally, the logical consequence of having a written constitution is that provisions need to be made for its interpretation and application. Such provisions are likely to require the creation of, effectively, a Constitutional Court with special principles relating to its composition and jurisdiction.

[182] LC Bell, *Warring Factions: Interest Groups, Money and the New Politics of Senate Confirmation* (Columbus OH, Ohio State University Press, 2002).

Judicial Independence (Art 139)

Against the background of these considerations (few of which are confronted in the Constitutional Reform Act 2005 which, nonetheless, made some extremely important changes to the running of the judicial system, including the creation of a Supreme Court and a new judicial appointments system), the section of this Constitution dealing with the judiciary (Part 8) begins by laying down certain general principles relating to the holding of judicial power in the UK.

Article 139 is directly concerned with judicial independence. For the reasons set out earlier, Article 139 states in terms that the judiciary is independent not merely of the executive and legislative branches of the Constitution but also of the Citizens' Branch.

Judicial independence is thus an express guarantee of this Constitution (as it is of most Constitutions and, indeed, as it is currently enshrined in statute: see s 3 of the Constitutional Reform Act 2005). It is indirectly backed up by a number of other provisions. Articles 141 and 142, for example, prevent all restrictions on judges that are not grounded in law. The constitutional crisis engendered by the false convictions of several hundred managers of post offices is not grounded in law by legislation to remove the convictions because the law is contrary to the constitutional guarantee of independence because independence is not guaranteed by intervention from government.

Accountability of Judges (Art 141)

The Constitutional Reform Act 2005 introduced other constitutional reforms besides the creation of a Judicial Appointments Commission. As well as creating a Supreme Court (discussed below), it displaced the Lord Chancellor as head of the judiciary. In doing so, it altered the traditional mechanism by which the judiciary were accountable as an institution. As a Government Minister, the Lord Chancellor was formerly accountable to Parliament in the normal way for the acts and omissions of the judiciary.

Article 141 deals, therefore, with the related, but often neglected, topic of judicial accountability by requiring laws to ensure the accountability of individual judges and of the judiciary as institution. Accountability should be distinguished from the separate laws governing the effective running of the court system and deployment of resources, which are currently regulated by law and continue to be so regulated under the Constitution.

The accountability of *individual* judges causes few constitutional problems. Apart from the appeal system, whereby higher courts oversee how specific cases have been handled, there is a Judicial Investigations Office, which is part of the Ministry of Justice and addresses complaints about the conduct of individual judges.

However, the judiciary as an *institution* causes more problems. If it is accepted as a principle that, to ensure the rule of law, there must be an independent and unelected judiciary capable, at the at the highest level, of wielding considerable political power, it ought to follow logically that there should be a substantial degree of judicial accountability in terms of the performance of the judiciary as a whole. However, this is not universally accepted. For example, the late Lord Cooke of Thorndon argued that external accountability and judicial independence were contradictions in terms and that accountability could only properly take the form of self-policing.

It may depend on what one means by *accountability*. This is sometimes thought in terms of what Professor Vernon Bogdanor calls *sacrificial* accountability,[183] which is the political doctrine by which Ministers are accountable to Parliament for the mistakes of their department. Any such doctrine applied by analogy to the judiciary would compromise its independence.

In a different application of accountability, though, Professor Bodgdanor suggests that judges may be accountable in an *explanatory* sense. What this means is that the judiciary ought, as a matter of principle, to enter into a dialogue with other branches of government. By this means its distinct role in the Constitution will be better understood. Added to this, however, it is suggested that the judiciary needs to be accountable in being *required* to explain to the other branches of government (which are electorally accountable) how it has exercised its functions; otherwise, the judiciary is accountable only to itself.

The ways in which accountability in this sense is guaranteed will (as Art 142 recognises) require special legislation. Central to that legislation will be a need to ensure that the mechanisms of accountability do not in any way impinge on judicial independence and that the judiciary is made accountable only for those matters for which it – and not another entity (such as the Lord Chancellor) – has been made responsible. Legislation that fails to make these distinctions will, to that extent, be invalid under the Constitution.

Hierarchy of Judicial Control (Arts 136, 142, 145 and 147)

These provisions address the structure of the legal regimes that affect judicial decision-making in the UK. Article 136 preserves the structure of the courts' decision-making process. Article 142 makes it clear that the judges in the UK derive their constitutional status from the Constitution. Any laws made under Articles 145 and 147 provide that the Supreme Court retains all ultimate power and that the future is conditioned by laws always provided that they are compatible with the Constitution.

[183] See Vernon Bogdanor, 'Accountability and the Media: "Parliament and the Judiciary: The Problem of Accountability"', 2006 Sunningdale Lecture (9 February 2006), https://ukpac.wordpress.com/bogdanor-speech/.

The Supreme Court (Arts 148–163)

A Supreme Court has only relatively recently (as from October 2009) been established, under the Constitutional Reform Act 2005. However, the reason for creating it was to avoid the continuation of a breach of the separation of powers principle (see above), not to invest it with new powers. In the absence of a written constitution, this would have required primary legislation. The Supreme Court that we currently have is simply a merger of the two committees that the 12 former Law Lords used to sit in the House of Lords, which were the Appellate Committee of the House of Lords (which dealt with final appeals in domestic civil and criminal cases) and the Judicial Committee of the Privy Council (which dealt mainly with overseas appeals and devolution questions). There are a number of modern features, such as updates on hearings via the internet and televised proceedings, but there is no essential difference between the Supreme Court sitting in the newly renovated Middlesex Guildhall and the former judicial committee of the House of Lords that sat in Westminster.

However, as noted above, the logic behind a written constitution is that a real Constitutional Court should be established. This is because, amongst other things, the Constitution takes primacy and all branches of government are therefore subject to it. The consequence of this is that enforcement powers must be vested in such a court to decide, where necessary, that laws passed by the Government are invalid and to make such orders as may be necessary to secure enforcement of the Constitution against even the Government itself.

This creates an entirely new jurisdiction and one that is logically inconsistent with the notion of parliamentary sovereignty, which underpins our present constitutional settlement. The strong new powers that are required should, it may be thought, be vested at the highest level in a new Supreme Court with a special constitutional jurisdiction. That is the aim of the specific provisions in this Constitution that confer discrete powers of a constitutional nature on the Supreme Court. None of these special powers is to be exercisable by any other court and no court or tribunal below the level of the Supreme Court may declare primary legislation to be unconstitutional.

The main features of the proposed changes insofar they affect the powers of the Supreme Court (subject to the detail of specific laws passed separately) are essentially as follows:[184]

- The Supreme Court retains its current appellate jurisdiction. This includes its existing jurisdiction over devolution issues, which was transferred to it under s 40 of the Constitutional Reform Act 2005 and is expressly preserved.

[184] Different powers from those proposed in this Constitution may also be envisaged. For example, a Supreme Court might be given a power (consistent with the Canadian approach) to declare a measure to be incompatible with the Constitution but with the legislature being able to override such declaration for a limited period.

The principles governing composition are very similar to those contained in the Constitutional Reform Act 2005.

- The present jurisdiction to grant declarations of incompatibility under the HRA 1998 remains, but where such a human rights case reaches the Supreme Court that Court is under a duty to make a declaration of unconstitutionality – as opposed to a declaration of incompatibility – if primary legislation, by breaching a fundamental right, contravenes the Constitution.
- The Supreme Court is invested with a duty to make a declaration of unconstitutionality if it considers that an existing legislative provision, act or omission is unconstitutional; sometimes, alternatively, it is required to make a declaration of constitutionality.
- There is a much softer version of a provision contained in the Hong Kong Basic Law which requires the Supreme Court to refer the interpretation of certain sensitive legislation to a central Government committee which provides an 'authoritative' interpretation that the courts must take into account. Such a provision would not be acceptable in most democracies underpinned by the rule of law where questions of law are treated as matters solely for the judiciary. However, what this Constitution does is to mandate the referral by the Supreme Court of a proposed judicial interpretation of a constitutional provision which impinges on expressly defined executive functions in order to the obtain the executive's view of the matter which the Court must take into account before deciding the matter. This provision is designed to strengthen the links between the Supreme Court and the executive rather than (as in the Hong Kong model) to tie the court's hands, and is considered to be useful in that it affords the Supreme Court a somewhat better insight into the thought processes of executive government in sensitive areas.
- New regimes, not wholly dissimilar to those adopted in the German Constitution, are created for the Supreme Court to determine the constitutionality or otherwise of political parties. There is also a power granted to the Supreme Court to give preliminary rulings and opinions. The preliminary ruling procedure has obvious and intended affinities with the reference procedure to the European Court of Justice by national courts and tribunals, although references on constitutional questions will effectively be compulsory where the lower court or tribunal (even if not a court or tribunal 'of last resort') needs a ruling on whether a legislative provision or other act or omission is unconstitutional, since only the Supreme Court may make a declaration of unconstitutionality.
- The power to review the constitutionality of Bills is a significant enhancement of the Supreme Court's powers and needs to be carefully considered in terms of its potential implications for representative democracy. The argument against conferment of such power is that the will of the elected Parliament ought not to be capable of being stifled by an unelected court. However, if proposed legislation is indeed unconstitutional, a power to declare it

as such before it is enacted may be thought to be valuable. Both the Irish Supreme Court and the French Conseil Constitutionnel have such a power.

- However, the proposed scope for further constitutional references and applications to the Supreme Court under the Constitution is much wider than permitting/requiring lower courts to make references. It enables (and sometimes requires) references and applications to be made direct to the Court not only by courts and tribunals but also by the executive and by the Citizens' Council on questions of constitutional importance.
- Nonetheless, in all constitutional cases coming directly before the Supreme Court, it must give permission for the application or reference to be heard before it may be entertained on a full hearing. These provisions are designed to prevent abuse by the bringing of wholly unmeritorious applications. However, the Supreme Court must give permission on matters relating to its appellate jurisdiction; it must also give its reasons for declining to grant permission for the making of a constitutional application or reference.

Overall, the new Supreme Court created by this Constitution has the widest constitutional powers – both in relation to proposed legislation and to existing measures including administrative acts and omissions – to ensure that the Constitution is being interpreted and implemented lawfully. It has the widest power to entertain applications from the executive, and from the Citizens' Council. There is much scope for debate as to the exact nature of the constitutional jurisdiction that could or should be conferred on the Court, but it is suggested that it is intrinsic to the nature of a constitution embodying the values of a representative democracy that some form of constitutional jurisdiction of this kind is both necessary and desirable.

Appointment and Removal of Judges and Administrative Provisions (Arts 168–173)

Articles 168–173 address the question of the appointment and removal of judges as well as salary and other financial benefits.

The process of appointing judges also raises important issues as to judicial independence. Here, the requisite considerations include not merely the provision of objective protections but must also include devising mechanisms for ensuring that persons of independent mind are selected and that pressure is not brought to bear in the selection process from other branches of the Constitution.

Articles 168–173 are designed to give effect to these considerations. The Constitution entrusts the appointment of judges to an independent Judicial Appointments Commission, which must make its decisions in such a way as to be independent of the legislative, executive and judicial branches of government.

The composition of the current Judicial Appointments Commission (JAC) set up under the Constitutional Reform Act 2005 is, it is suggested, entirely independent. Neither the executive nor Members of Parliament take part in the selection process. There is a requirement that the JAC include five judicial members. But since the number of Commissioners is 15 there is no issue of composition relating to its independence from the judiciary. This is all the more so given the current statutory requirement that the Chairman must be a lay person.

There are, however, issues relating to the nature and 'reach' of the current decision-making process of the JAC contained in the 2005 Act that are arguably relevant to judicial independence.

First, under the Constitutional Reform Act 2005 the JAC's decisions may be rejected by the Lord Chancellor. Although, following such rejection, the Lord Chancellor cannot make the appointment himself but must remit the decision to the JAC, the reality that executive influence is built into the statutory framework.

Second, judicial influence is also present. Even at the level of the High Court, senior members of the judiciary must, under the 2005 Act, be consulted, and their views will sometimes determine whether an appointment is made.[185] At higher levels, senior members of the judiciary are required by the same Act to be on the selection panel and have a potentially decisive influence on the appointment that is made. Whilst it is arguable that judges ought to have an influence on who is appointed, the perception that an elitist 'club' will select by a tap on the shoulder those conforming to a middle-aged, Oxbridge stereotype with out-of-touch-values continues to prevail, especially at the Supreme Court level.

Third, the JAC has no direct remit in the selection of justices of the Supreme Court. At first sight, this is a surprising omission. Instead of involving the JAC directly, the Constitutional Reform Act 2005 establishes a *selection commission* which consists of the President of the Supreme Court and a senior UK judge who is not a UKSC justice, as well as individual members of the respective JACs for the UK. The appointments process requires recommendations to be made to the Prime Minister, who must choose one of the names notified. That means that in practice there is heavy judicial input in the selection process from the very body into which the new appointment is to be made. Given the small size of the Supreme Court, it may be difficult, in practice, to avoid giving the impression that new appointments are decided from the 'inside', especially as Supreme Court justices may now be appointed from outside the serving judiciary altogether.

[185] There is, for example, strong anecdotal evidence of instances (a specific incident occurring most recently in the 2008 appointment process for High Court judges) where the JAC has, following interview, assessed a candidate as fully meeting the requirements for appointment to the High Court and prepared a report 'recommending' such candidate, but following 'consultation' the judges statutorily to be consulted have in practice had an effective veto over the appointment. The process operates unfairly in that the rejected candidate has no opportunity to learn the reasons for the veto or to know the case against him or her. As importantly, the senior judges with the 'veto' do not hear the tape of the interview with the rejected candidate.

Amongst other things, this Constitution does away with the currently heavy behind-the-scenes judicial influence in the decision-making process leading to the selection of judges at all levels. It also requires decisions to be made by the JAC.

The general criteria by which judges are to be selected is also specified. These are necessarily general, and because they cannot be precisely quantified in isolation let alone in relation to each other they are not expressed to be determinative. The JAC must 'give priority to' independence of mind, high intellect and excellent judgement, and must take into account any other requirement of the Constitution. Most notable of these will be the requirement to appoint more women to these positions provided that doing so is consistent with the specific selection criteria. However, the central requirement for selection is the 'best' candidate 'in terms of merit' is selected. This is effectively the present position under the Constitutional Reform Act 2005, which requires candidates to be selected on 'merit'.

Judicial selection has been the subject of much recent academic work, particularly the question whether appointment on merit needs to be rethought having regard to the requirements of diversity in a modern and pluralistic society.[186] However, the approach adopted in this Constitution is to emphasise that merit in terms of individual excellence (irrespective of gender and race) is the overriding criterion. There will be those who disagree with this approach,[187] but the danger is that an appointments system based on diversity (including gender)[188] rather than merit would be more likely to reduce the high regard in which the judiciary must be held if the rule of law is to be preserved.

As to removal of judges, the present position is essentially preserved but with more uniformity across all levels of the judiciary in terms of the criteria for removal. The current position is that judges of the Supreme Court, the Court of Appeal and the High Court may only be removed if they misbehave, and only then by the Crown on an address by both Houses of Parliament. However, this little-used procedure has not been invoked since 1830 (when it was used to remove an Irish judge found to have misappropriated funds). Below that level, the Lord Chief Justice may remove circuit judges on grounds of misbehaviour

[186] Most notable perhaps in this area is the work of Professor Kate Malleson at Queen Mary University of London. She has written numerous works on this including 'Rethinking the Merit Principle in Judicial Selection' (2006) 33 *Journal of Law and Society* 126. She is co-director of the Centre for Research of Law, Equality and Diversity which was established at Queen Mary in 2015, and co-founded the Equal Justices Initiative to monitor developments in judicial appointments and to promote the appointment of equal numbers of women and men to the bench in the UK.

[187] Baroness Hale in particular has argued that without a more diverse judiciary, judicial decisions will, amongst, other things, lack democratic legitimacy and will not command public confidence: Brenda Hale, 'Equality and the Judiciary: Why Should We Want More Women Judges?' [2001] *Public Law* 495. See also Brenda Hale, 'Lady Hale: at least half of UK judiciary should be female', *The Guardian*, 24 March 2019.

[188] The South African Constitution contains an express requirement that the judiciary should reflect the racial and gender composition of the nation.

or incapacity. Other similar but less stringent provisions apply to the removal of stipendiary and lay magistrates.

The US Constitution expressly prohibits reduction of salary whilst in office and a similar provision is contained in this Constitution. This provision, once perhaps uncontroversial, may be more contentious in times of economic recession, and there have recently been calls for pay and pension cuts in the public sector and even in government.

Nonetheless, the purpose of maintaining the level of judicial salary in real terms is to ensure that judges remain in office and are not deterred from seeking office, and also to avoid judicial corruption in the form of bribes and other inducements where salaries are very low. This danger, happily rare at present in the UK, is a real and current problem, especially in some African countries.

THE JUDICIARY: KEY POINTS

- **The constitutional role of judges:** Judges are not legislators. Behind this apparently uncontroversial statement lie some inconvenient truths. Judges do interpret laws and, because opinions differ, it is possible that a judicial interpretation will be different to that of some politicians. Judges have been given a raft of political powers and not only in human rights cases. There has recently been a spate of cases involving constitutional issues. The two *Miller* cases, for example, resulted in heavy defeats for the Government. The truth is that law is not an abstract entity with an identity necessarily easily separable from political and executive decision-making. In substance, what the judiciary is doing is passing a value judgement on a set of issues decided upon by the Cabinet (or, indeed, Prime Minister). A written constitution with a place for an independent judiciary, some inbuilt restrictions on what the Government can and cannot do and above all public participation in the whole process is what is necessary.
- **Judicial independence:** Article 139 is directly concerned with judicial independence. It states in terms that the judiciary is independent not only of the executive and legislative branches but also of the Citizens' Branch.
- **Accountability of judges:** The accountability of judges was often, in the past, a neglected field of activity. Laws to ensure the individual accountability of judges are guaranteed by the Judicial Conduct Investigations Office, which addresses complaints about the behaviour of individual judges. More difficult is the behaviour of the judiciary as an institution. A useful distinction is made by Professor Vernon Bogdanor who suggests there is a difference between *sacrificial* accountability and *explanatory* accountability. *Sacrificial* accountability means giving up independence. But *explanatory* accountability means that the judiciary is required to bring the operation of the judiciary as an institution to the attention of other branches of the constitution (Art 141).

- **Hierarchy of judicial control:** There is a hierarchy of judicial control, addressed by Articles 136–147. Article 142 clarifies that judges derive their status from the Constitution and any laws made under it.
- **The Supreme Court:** The Supreme Court is a constitutional court. This is because the Constitution takes primacy and all players under it derive their legal status and powers from it. The legal status of the Supreme Court is, thus, inconsistent with the idea behind the sovereignty of Parliament. The powers and legal status of the Supreme Court are addressed in Articles 148–167 and a summary is included in the explanatory Notes.
- **Appointment and removal of judges and administrative provisions:** Articles 168–173 address the question of the appointment and removal of judges as well as salary and other benefits. The appointment of judges raises important issues relating to independence. The Constitution opts for a system as close to the present system as possible but with a few qualifications: (i) currently, decisions of the Judicial Appointments Commission may be rejected by the Lord Chancellor – this power is removed; (ii) currently senior members of the judiciary must be consulted and even have a voice, in the selection process of judges – this also is not part of the Constitution; (iii) the Judicial Appointments Commission has no effective say in appointments to the Supreme Court – again, this is remedied in the draft Constitution. The process of removal from the Bench would be specified by law except the Supreme Court, where removal by an address of both Houses of Parliament would be required.

PART 9

FUNDAMENTAL RIGHTS, FREEDOMS AND RESPONSIBILITIES (ARTS 174–224)

Constitutional Effect of Rights, Freedoms and Responsibilities

174. This part of the Constitution is subject to the provisions of Part 6.

175. Subject to the terms of this Constitution, the provisions of the European Convention on Human Rights and the European Charter of Fundamental Rights and the rights contained in them are guaranteed by this Constitution in their entirety whatever their status as international obligations imposed on the United Kingdom and, in the case of the European Charter of Fundamental Rights, subject to no international obligations at all.[189]

[189] The 'rights' granted by EU law up to the exit of the UK from the EU and beyond are quite complicated.

176. In particular, the fundamental rights and freedoms contained in this Constitution which correspond with rights guaranteed by the European Convention on Human Rights and the European Charter of Fundamental Rights shall be interpreted as having at least the same scope as those Convention and Charter rights. However, nothing in this Constitution shall prevent the fundamental rights and freedoms contained in this Constitution from being interpreted as providing more extensive protection than the corresponding Convention and Charter rights.

177. Nothing in the provisions of this Part of the Constitution shall prevent the rights and responsibilities recognised by this Constitution from being developed further by law or so as to provide additional rights and responsibilities through the devolved government institutions of the United Kingdom enacting legislation within the limits of their jurisdiction, provided that nothing in the recognition of any additional responsibilities shall affect either the existence or the availability of the fundamental rights and freedoms under this Constitution.

178. Nothing in the provisions of this Part of the Constitution shall affect the rights, remedies and obligations contained in the Human Rights Act 1998 which shall form part of this Constitution. However, any limitation of rights and remedies contained in that Act that are incompatible with the provisions of this Constitution shall no longer apply.

179. Nothing in this Constitution denies the existence, or restricts the scope, of any other rights or freedoms recognised or conferred by common law, statute, or customary international law, to the extent that they are consistent with the rights and freedoms contained in this Constitution.

180. Any person or body who has a sufficient interest in a matter may bring legal proceedings in the appropriate court or tribunal concerning the alleged breach of any provision of this Constitution.

181. No derogation from any of the rights and freedoms in this Constitution shall be lawful unless emergency powers are lawfully exercised under Part 6 of this Constitution. Any legislation enacted in consequence of the exercise of emergency powers may derogate from any right or freedom in this Constitution only as permitted under this Constitution and only then to the extent that the derogation is strictly required by the emergency and is consistent with the UK's other international obligations.

182. Subject to this Constitution the rights and freedoms contained in this Constitution may, where capable of being restricted, be subject only to

such reasonable limits,[190] provided for by law, as can be demonstrably justified in a society based on the values of liberty, democracy, fairness, civic duty and the rule of law, and to the extent compatible with international human rights treaties to which the UK is a party, taking into account all relevant factors, including –

(i) the nature of the right;
(ii) the importance and legitimacy of the purpose of the limitation;
(iii) the nature and extent of the limitation;
(iv) the relation between the limitation and its purpose; and
(v) the availability of less restrictive means to achieve the purpose.

183. Any person or body who has a sufficient interest in a matter may bring legal proceedings in the appropriate court or tribunal challenging, to the extent permitted by Part 6 of this Constitution, the validity under this Part of the Constitution of –

(i) the exercise of emergency powers under Part 6 of this Constitution; or
(ii) any legislation enacted, or other action taken, in consequence of the exercise of such emergency powers.

184. No legislation enacted in consequence of emergency powers under Part 6 of this Constitution may permit or authorise any derogation from the rights and freedoms contained in the fundamental provisions of the Constitution.

Civil and Political Rights and Freedoms

185. All persons shall be equal before the law. Everyone is equal before the law and has the right to equal protection and benefit of the law. Equality includes the full and equal enjoyment of all rights and freedoms under this Constitution. To promote the achievement of equality, legislative and other measures designed to protect or advance persons, or categories

[190] This is one of various provisions in the draft Constitution that are likely to be the focus of extensive discussion as to how they should be interpreted (eg phrases such as 'sufficient interest' when interpreting standing to commence proceedings under the Constitution and 'consistently with the needs of a representative democracy in a modern and developing society' (Art 6(i)) as well as the general limitations clause for rights in Article 182. For such provisions it will be important to balance the need for flexibility (and therefore leave the phrases open-textured) and the need for prescription to assist the courts in their adjudication of constitutional questions. For reasons of flexibility it may not be desirable to include too many definitions for such terms (indeed, it is not possible).

of persons, disadvantaged by unfair discrimination may be taken.[191] The state may not unfairly discriminate directly or indirectly against anyone on one or more grounds, including race, gender, sex, pregnancy, marital status, ethnic or social origin, colour, sexual orientation, age, disability, religion, conscience, belief, culture, language and birth. National legislation must be enacted to prevent or prohibit unfair discrimination. Discrimination on one or more of the grounds listed in this article is unfair unless it is established that the discrimination is fair.

186. Human dignity is inviolable.[192] It must be respected and protected.

187. Everyone's right to life shall be protected by law. No one shall be deprived of life intentionally. No one shall be condemned to death or executed. Deprivation of life shall not be regarded as inflicted in contravention of this Constitution when it results from a use of force which is no more than absolutely necessary in defence of any person from unlawful violence or lawful violence in terms of war, in order to effect a lawful arrest or to prevent the arrest of a person lawfully detained or in action lawfully taken for the purpose of quelling a riot or insurrection.

188. Everyone has the right to respect for his or her physical and mental integrity. In the fields of medicine and biology, the following must be respected in particular –

(i) the free and informed consent of the person concerned, according to the procedures laid down by law;
(ii) the prohibition of eugenic practices;
(iii) the prohibition of making the human body a source of financial gain; and
(iv) the prohibition of reproductive cloning of human beings.

189. No one shall be subjected to torture or to inhuman or degrading treatment or punishment.

190. No one shall be held in slavery and servitude or required to perform forced or compulsory labour. Trafficking in human beings is prohibited.

[191] Some instruments (such as the UN's Convention on the Elimination of All Forms of Racial Discrimination) include a time limit for affirmative action policies, such as 'for so long as necessary to achieve objectives'. This is a useful limit as it provides a balance between the interests of the various affected parties.

[192] 'Dignity' is an interesting contemporary inclusion in modern Constitutions. Such guarantees are a difficult basis for adjudicating claims (see C McCrudden, 'Human Dignity and Judicial Interpretation of Human Rights' (2008) 19(4) *European Journal of International Law* 655). As a result of these difficulties, some have suggested that guarantees of dignity may be better placed in a preamble rather than as a norm within the operative provisions of a constitution.

However, the term 'forced or compulsory labour' shall not include any work required to be done in the ordinary course of lawful detention, or during conditional release from any such detention, or as part of legitimate punishment imposed by a court or tribunal according to law, or as part of any service of a military character or, in case of conscientious objectors in countries where they are recognised, service exacted instead of compulsory military service, or any work or service which forms part of normal civic obligations including as part of the responsibilities under this Constitution.

191. Everyone has the right to liberty and security of person. No one shall be deprived of his or her liberty save in the following cases and in accordance with a procedure prescribed by law –

(i) the lawful detention of a person after conviction by a competent court;
(ii) the lawful arrest or detention of a person for non-compliance with the lawful order of a court or in order to secure the fulfilment of any obligation prescribed by law;
(iii) the lawful arrest or detention of a person effected for the purpose of bringing him or her before the competent legal authority on reasonable suspicion of having committed an offence or when it is reasonably considered necessary to prevent his or her committing an offence or fleeing after having done so;
(iv) the detention of a minor by lawful order for the purpose of educational supervision or his or her lawful detention for the purpose of bringing him or her before the competent legal authority;
(v) the lawful detention of persons for the prevention of the spreading of infectious diseases, or of persons of unsound mind, alcoholics or drug addicts or vagrants;
(vi) the lawful arrest or detention of a person to prevent his or her effecting an unauthorised entry into the country or of a person against whom action is being taken with a view to deportation or extradition.

192. All persons who are arrested shall be informed promptly, in a language they understand, of the reasons for their arrest and of any charge against them. All persons arrested or detained in accordance with the provisions shall be brought promptly before a judge or other officer authorised by law to exercise judicial power and shall be entitled to a trial within a reasonable time or to release pending trial. Release may be subject to a requirement of guarantees from third parties that an accused person will appear for trial. All persons who are deprived of their liberty by arrest or detention shall be entitled to take proceedings by which the lawfulness of their detention shall be decided speedily by a court and their release

ordered if the detention is not lawful. All persons who have, since the coming into force of this Constitution, been the victim of arrest or detention which is judged to be unlawful shall have a right to compensation.

193. Everyone has the right to respect for his or her private and family life, his or her home and his or her communications. There shall be no interference by a public authority with the exercise of this right except such as is in accordance with the law and is necessary in a democratic society in the interests of national security, public safety or the economic well-being of the country, for the prevention of disorder or crime, for the protection of health or morals, or for the protection of the rights and freedoms of others.

194. Everyone has the right to freedom of thought, conscience and religion. This right includes a person's freedom to change his or her religion or beliefs, and freedom, either alone or in community with others and in public or private, to manifest his or her religion or beliefs, in worship, teaching, practice and observance. Freedom to manifest one's religion or beliefs shall be subject only to such limitations as are prescribed by law and are necessary in a democratic society in the interests of public safety, for the protection of public order, health or morals, or for the protection of the rights and freedoms of others. The right to conscientious objection is recognised, in accordance with the national laws governing the exercise of this right.

195. Everyone has the right to freedom of expression. This right shall include freedom to hold opinions and to receive and impart information and ideas without interference by public authority and regardless of frontiers. This article shall not prevent States from requiring the licensing of broadcasting, television or cinema enterprises. The exercise of these freedoms, since it carries with it duties and responsibilities, may be subject to such formalities, conditions, restrictions and penalties as are prescribed by law and are necessary in a democratic society, in the interests of national security, territorial integrity or public safety, for the prevention of disorder or crime, for the protection of health or morals, for the protection of the reputation or the rights of others, for preventing the disclosure of information received in confidence, or for maintaining the authority and impartiality of the judiciary. The freedom and pluralism of the media shall be respected.

196. Everyone has the right to hold unarmed and peaceful demonstration marches, the right of freedom of peaceful assembly and of freedom of association with others, including the right to form and to join trade unions for the protection of his or her interests. No restrictions shall be placed on the exercise of these rights other than such as are prescribed by

law and are necessary in a democratic society in the interests of national security or public safety, for the prevention of disorder or crime, for the protection of health or morals, or for the protection of the rights and freedoms of others. However, this article shall not prevent the imposition of lawful restrictions on the exercise of these rights by members of the armed forces, of the police or of the administration of the State.

197. Men and women of marriageable age have the right to marry and to found a family, according to the national laws governing the exercise of this right. The right to marry shall not be restricted to marriage between members of the opposite sex.

198. Every natural or legal person is entitled to the peaceful enjoyment of his or her possessions. No one shall be deprived of his or her possessions except in the public interest and subject to the conditions provided for by law and by the general principles of international law. These provisions shall not, however, in any way impair the right of a State to enforce such laws as it deems necessary to control the use of property in accordance with the general interest or to secure the payment of taxes or other contributions or penalties. Intellectual property shall be protected under the same terms.

199. Everyone lawfully within the territory of the United Kingdom shall, within that territory, have the right to liberty of movement and freedom to choose his or her residence. Everyone shall be free to leave the United Kingdom. No restrictions shall be placed on the exercise of these rights other than such as are in accordance with law and are necessary in a democratic society in the interests of national security or public safety, for the maintenance of public order, for the prevention of crime, or for the protection of the rights and freedoms of others. These rights may also be subject, in particular areas, to restrictions imposed in accordance with law and justified by the public interest in a democratic society.

200. The right to asylum shall be guaranteed with due respect for the rules of the Geneva Convention of 28 July 1951 and the Protocol of 31 January 1967 relating to the status of refugees.

Fair Process Rights

201. Everyone who is arrested for allegedly committing an offence has the right –

(i) to remain silent;

(ii) to be informed promptly –
   (a) of their right to remain silent, and
   (b) of the consequences of not remaining silent;

(iii) not to be compelled to make any confession or admission that could be used in evidence against that person;

(iv) at the first court appearance after being arrested, to be charged or to be informed of the reason for the continuation of the detention, or to be released; and

(v) to be released from detention if the interests of justice permit, subject to reasonable conditions.

202. Everyone who is detained, including every sentenced prisoner, has the right –

(i) to be informed promptly of the reason for the continuation of the detention;

(ii) to choose, and to consult with, a legal practitioner, and to be informed of this right promptly;

(iii) to have a legal practitioner assigned by the state and at state expense, if substantial injustice would otherwise result, and to be informed of this right promptly;

(iv) to challenge the lawfulness of the detention in person before a court and, if the detention is judged to be unlawful, to be released;

(v) to conditions of detention that are consistent with human dignity, including at least reasonable exercise and the provision, at state expense, of adequate accommodation, nutrition, reading material and medical treatment; and

(vi) to communicate with, and be visited by, that person's –
   (a) spouse or partner,
   (b) next of kin,
   (c) chosen religious counsellor, and
   (d) chosen medical practitioner.

203. In the determination of civil rights and obligations or of any criminal charge, everyone is entitled to a fair and public hearing within a reasonable time by an independent and impartial tribunal established by law. Judgment shall be pronounced publicly. The press and public may be excluded from all or part of the trial or hearing in the interest of morals, public order or national security in a democratic society, where the interests of juveniles or the protection of the private life of the parties so requires, or to the extent strictly necessary in the opinion of the court in special circumstances where publicity would prejudice the interests of justice.

204. Everyone charged with a criminal offence shall be presumed innocent until proved guilty according to law. Everyone charged with a criminal offence has the following minimum rights –

(i) to be informed promptly, in a language he or she understands and in detail, of the nature and cause of the accusation against him or her;
(ii) to have adequate time and facilities to prepare his or her defence;
(iii) to defend himself or herself in person or through a legal representative of his or her own choosing or, if he or she has not sufficient means to pay for legal assistance, to be given legal assistance without charge when the interests of justice so require;
(iv) to examine or have examined witnesses against him or her and to obtain the attendance and examination of witnesses on his or her behalf under the same conditions as witnesses against him or her;
(v) to have the free assistance of an interpreter if he or she cannot understand or speak the language used in court.

205. No one shall be held guilty of any criminal offence on account of any act or omission which did not constitute a criminal offence under national or international law at the time when it was committed. Nor shall a heavier penalty be imposed than the one that was applicable at the time the criminal offence was committed. If, subsequent to the commission of a criminal offence, the law provides for a lighter penalty, that penalty shall be applicable. This article shall not prejudice the trial and punishment of any person for any act or omission which, at the time it was committed, was criminal according the general principles of law recognised by civilised nations. The severity of penalties must not be disproportionate to the criminal offence.

206. Everyone whose rights and freedoms as set forth in this Part of the Constitution are violated shall have an effective remedy before a national authority notwithstanding that the violation has been committed by persons acting in an official capacity.

207. Everyone has a right of access to any information held by the State, and any information that is held by another person, that is required for the exercise or protection of any of their rights protected by this Constitution. Laws must be enacted to give effect to this right, and may provide for reasonable measures to alleviate the administrative and financial burden on the State.

208. Everyone has the right to receive administrative treatment that is lawful, reasonable and procedurally fair. Everyone whose rights have

been adversely affected by administrative action has the right to be given written reasons. Laws must be enacted to give effect to these rights, and must –

(i) provide for the review of administrative action by a court or, where appropriate, an independent and impartial tribunal; and
(ii) impose a duty on the state to give effect to these rights and promote an efficient administration.

Democratic Rights

209. There shall, subject to this Constitution, be provision by law for the acquisition and termination of citizenship and all other matters relating to citizenship.

210. Every citizen shall have the right and the opportunity –

(i) to take part in the conduct of public affairs, directly or through freely chosen representatives;
(ii) to vote and to be elected at genuine periodic elections which shall be by universal and equal suffrage and shall be held by secret ballot, guaranteeing the free expression of the will of the electors; and
(iii) to have access, on general terms of equality, to public service in his or her country.

Rights of Special Groups

211. A child's[193] best interests are of paramount importance in every matter concerning the child and must be identified and protected with the minimum of delay. Every child has the right –

(i) to a name and a nationality from birth;
(ii) to parental care, or to appropriate alternative care when removed from the family environment;
(iii) to basic nutrition, shelter, basic health care services and social services;
(iv) to be protected from maltreatment, neglect, abuse and degradation;
(v) to be protected from exploitative labour practices;

[193] The word 'child' is defined in Article 241 as including everyone under the age of 18.

(vi) not to be required or permitted to perform work or provide services that –

(a) are inappropriate for a person of that child's age, or

(b) place at risk their well-being, education, physical or mental health or spiritual, moral or social development;

(vii) not to be detained except as a measure of last resort, in which case, in addition to the rights a child enjoys as a detained person under this Constitution, the child may be detained only for the shortest appropriate period of time, and has the right to be –

(a) detained separately from persons over the age of 18 years, and

(b) treated in a manner, and kept in conditions, that take account of the child's age;

(viii) to have a legal practitioner assigned by the state, and at state expense, in civil proceedings affecting the child, if substantial injustice would otherwise result; and

(ix) to be protected in times of armed conflict.

212. This Constitution recognises and guarantees, subject to its other provisions, the right of persons belonging to national minorities to the preservation, development and expression of their ethnic, cultural, linguistic and religious identity and to the right of such persons to be treated in conformity with the principles of equality and non-discrimination in relation to other citizens of the United Kingdom.

213. This Constitution recognises the equal right of all persons with disabilities to live in the community, with choices equal to others, and laws shall facilitate full enjoyment by persons with disabilities of this right and their full inclusion and participation in the community, including by ensuring that –

(i) persons with disabilities have the opportunity to choose their place of residence and where and with whom they live on an equal basis with others and are not obliged to live in a prescribed arrangement;

(ii) persons with disabilities have access to a range of in-home, residential and other community support services, including personal assistance necessary to support living and inclusion in the community, and to prevent isolation or segregation from the community;

(iii) community services and facilities for the general population are available on an equal basis to persons with disabilities and are responsive to their needs. Laws shall also ensure personal mobility with the greatest possible independence for persons with disabilities, including by –

(a) facilitating the personal mobility of persons with disabilities in the manner and at the time of their choice, and at affordable cost,
(b) facilitating access by persons with disabilities to quality mobility aids, devices, assistive technologies and forms of live assistance and intermediaries, including by making them available at affordable cost,
(c) providing training in mobility skills to persons with disabilities and to specialist staff working with persons with disabilities, and
(d) encouraging entities that produce mobility aids, devices and assistive technologies to take into account all aspects of mobility for persons with disabilities.

214. The rights of persons who have sustained harm as a result of crimes shall be protected by law. In particular, the rights of such persons to access to justice and to compensation for damage are guaranteed by this Constitution.

Economic and Social Rights

215. Subject to this Constitution, all persons are entitled to an adequate standard of living sufficient for themselves and for their dependants. Everyone has the right to have access to –

(i) sufficient food, water, clothing and housing; and
(ii) social security, including, if they are unable to support themselves and their dependants, appropriate social assistance.

Reasonable legislative and other measures, within the available resources of the State, must be taken to achieve the progressive realisation of each of these rights.

216. Subject to this Constitution, everyone has the right to have access to appropriate health and social care services free at the point of delivery and within a reasonable time. No one may be refused emergency health treatment or emergency social care services. Reasonable legislative and other measures within the available resources of the State must be taken to achieve the progressive realisation of these rights.

217. This Constitution recognises the right of everyone to education. It recognises that education shall be directed to the full development of the human personality, the sense of its dignity, and the respect for human rights and fundamental freedoms. It also recognises that education shall be designed to enable all persons to participate effectively in a free society, promote understanding, tolerance and friendship among all nations and all racial, ethnic or religious groups, and further the maintenance of peace.

218. Subject to this Constitution, everyone of compulsory school age has the right to receive free, full-time education suitable to their needs and the right to have access to further education and to vocational and continued training.

219. Subject to this Constitution, everyone has the right to live in an environment that is not harmful to their health. Everyone has the right to access information that enables them to assess risks to their health from their environment. Everyone has the right to a high level of environmental protection, for the benefit of present and future generations, through reasonable legislative and other measures that –

(i) prevent pollution and ecological degradation;
(ii) promote conservation; and
(iii) ensure that economic development and use of natural resources are sustainable.

Responsibilities

220. Every person has both individual and civic duties towards his or her family and society, the State and other legally recognised communities as well as the international community. The rights and freedoms of each individual protected by this Constitution shall be exercised with due regard to the rights of others, collective security, morality and the just demands of general welfare in a democratic society.

221. Every individual shall have the duty to respect and consider his or her fellow beings without discrimination, and to maintain relations aimed at promoting, safeguarding and reinforcing mutual respect and tolerance.

222. Nothing in the provisions of this Part of the Constitution shall permit or be interpreted or applied as permitting or having the effect of permitting any person, group or body to engage in any activity or perform any

act aimed at the destruction of any of the rights and freedoms contained in, or guaranteed by, this Constitution or at their limitation to a greater extent than is provided for in this Constitution.

223. The responsibilities recognised by this Constitution shall not affect the existence and availability of the fundamental rights and freedoms under this Constitution.[194]

224. No responsibility recognised by this Constitution shall be legally enforceable against individuals or create legal responsibilities of any kind.

FUNDAMENTAL RIGHTS, FREEDOMS AND RESPONSIBILITIES: OBSERVATIONS AND EXPLANATORY NOTES

Overview: The Case for a Domestic Bill of Rights

Part 9 represents what is sometimes referred to as a domestic Bill of Rights.

Of itself, the need for a domestic Bill of Rights is by no means self-evident. Underlying the enactment of the HRA 1998, which came into force on 2 October 2000, was the desire to 'bring rights home'. In essence, the rights in question were those to which the UK had subscribed by ratifying the ECHR. It could be said, therefore, that – at least by that stage – there was already a Bill of Rights and that to overlay it with further human rights provisions was both unnecessary and confusing.

This was the general view expressed by several witnesses who gave evidence to the Joint Committee on Human Rights in the course of its extensive inquiry during its 2007/2008 session into whether there was a good case for a domestic Bill of Rights.[195]

Explicit in many of the concerns expressed to the Committee was a suspicion that the real motive of the main political parties in espousing the need for a domestic Bill of Rights – possibly engendered by media highlighting of cases where it was suggested that rights protection was being given priority over public safety – was the wish to dilute existing fundamental rights protections in the HRA 1998. The Tory party, in particular, appeared keen on the idea of a Bill

[194] The inclusion of responsibilities on the part of citizens is not without its difficulties. They have been incorporated in benign ways in some Constitutions, but there are also some more damaging inclusions (eg the Chinese Constitution, where it is argued that the emphasis is on responsibilities versus rights). There is a case to be made for emphasising more strongly than in the current version – perhaps in the form of a presumptive interpretation principle – that it is *not* a question of responsibilities versus rights.

[195] The Committee's Report *A Bill of Rights for the United Kingdom* was published on 21 July 2008.

to minimise the protection afforded by the ECHR and only the resignation of Dominic Raab for bullying seems to have been responsible for the jettisoning of the Bill of Rights Bill on 27 June 2023; the Bill had gathered much opposition.[196] The blog 'Public Law for Everyone'[197] (by Professor Mark Elliot of Cambridge University) has an excellent section on the now-withdrawn Bill, to show the potential difficulties raised by the Bill of Rights Bill.

Whatever may have been the trigger for the initial political articulations of the desirability of a UK Bill of Rights, there is now consensus in the Labour government that supports the HRA and that the UK's position as a party to the ECHR will be unaffected.[198]

There are in fact many arguments which support the idea that a domestic Bill of Rights should contain rights additional to those enshrined in the ECHR. Perhaps the most important consideration is that the ECHR was adopted as long ago as 1950 and arguably needs modernising and broadening to achieve maximal human rights protection.

The primary purpose of the ECHR, following the Holocaust, was to cement a *moral* foundation for protecting individuals against the tyranny of the state. Indeed, a general Enlightenment morality designed to protect individuals from state interference may be thought to have characterised earlier rights-driven landmarks of our constitutional history such as Magna Carta and the 1689 English Bill of Rights.

In more recent times a combination of higher living standards (at least in western liberal democracies) and the development of political and philosophical thought has led to a broader way of looking at human rights protection which encompasses, amongst other things, economic and social rights (which are not mentioned in the ECHR) often requiring state intervention that enable individuals to lead more fulfilling lives. Thinkers such as Isaiah Berlin, albeit drawing on Kantian political theory, have demonstrated that there is a significant distinction between *negative* liberty (the absence of constraint) and *positive* liberty (the potential to exercise personal autonomy).[199] International treaties – such as the International Covenant on Economic, Social and Cultural Rights – have increasingly focused on the protection of such economic and social rights.

It may be thought that the rationale for developing a Bill of Rights becomes more difficult to refute once the argument for a written constitution is accepted.

[196] The Tory party was also responsible for the Rwandan policy (some asylum seekers would be sent to Rwanda to have their applications dealt with and processed there) which Sir Keir Starmer promised to repeal. The Court of Appeal by a majority held that the policy was unlawful and the Supreme Court has also held that the Rwandan policy is unlawful.

[197] 'The UK's (New) Bill of Rights', *Public Law for Everyone*, 22 June 2022.

[198] The new Labour Government supports the HRA 1998. What a future Tory Government might do is unfortunately not known.

[199] Isaiah Berlin, 'Two Concepts of Liberty' in Isaiah Berlin, *Four Essays on Liberty* (Oxford, Oxford University Press, 1969). Even earlier, in his 'four freedoms' speech in 1941, President Roosevelt had emphasised the importance of freedom from want and freedom from fear, each of which could be viewed as giving rise to rights of an economic and social nature.

This is because, whatever view one takes of the current strength of fundamental rights protection under the HRA 1998, that Act is a statute and may be amended or repealed so as to weaken rather than strengthen rights protection. By contrast, in a written constitution the desired level of rights protection is constitutionally entrenched because the Bill of Rights forms part of the Constitution. A Bill of Rights has the additional advantage that the drafting of such a Bill affords an opportunity to codify wider principles of administrative law such as a right to good administration as well as strengthening rights protection more generally.

It is interesting to note that many of the other arguments in favour of a domestic Bill of Rights, as expressed to the Joint Committee on Human Rights, are also arguments in favour of a written constitution. Thus, witnesses to the Committee variously thought that amongst other things a Bill of Rights would provide 'human rights with superiority over all ordinary law', 'constitutional stability' and 'a unifying force in a diverse society', and that it would 'reinvigorate our democracy' and 'ingrain fundamental principles that otherwise might remain implied or implicit'.[200]

This Constitution therefore proceeds on the basis that a constitutionally entrenched statement of fundamental rights is a considerable improvement on the present position. But a number of issues require consideration before such an entrenched rights model can be developed.

Constitutional Mechanisms for a Domestic Bill of Rights (Arts 174–184)

As explained above, it appears to be accepted by the Labour Government that any new formulation of fundamental rights should not detrimentally affect the UK's adherence to the ECHR. It follows from this that neither the content nor the scope of the rights contained in this Constitution can be allowed to limit in any way the scope of the rights set out in the ECHR.

This is achieved by Articles 175–180, which in effect incorporate the ECHR into the Constitution (including, significantly, rights not ratified by the UK such as freedom of movement). Since there are many rights in the Constitution that are largely updates of ECHR rights or that contain only slightly modified wording of ECHR provisions it is necessary to include a provision that enables constitutional rights that overlap with the ECHR to be interpreted as conferring at least as much protection as the ECHR version, and Article 176 (modelled on a similarly worded provision in the Joint Committee's outline of a Bill of Rights) makes it clear that the courts may interpret the constitutional provision in question as conferring *greater* protection than that conferred by the ECHR. It is questionable whether this result could have been achieved under HRA 1998 principles of interpretation, since the interpretative obligation on the courts

[200] See Joint Committee on Human Rights, Twenty Ninth Report, Session 2007–08, para 35.

under section 3 of the HRA 1998 is to interpret a statute so far as possible to be compatible with the ECHR.

Importantly, the ECHR is given domestic effect in the UK courts through the HRA 1998. There is thus a significant question as to whether (and if so how) the Act – as opposed to the ECHR – will be affected by a written constitution (or, in fact, a domestic Bill of Rights). It is one thing to accept that the UK's international obligations under the ECHR will not be affected by new domestic legal provisions; it is quite another to make the same concession in respect of rights protection mechanisms in the HRA 1998. It would, however, be a pyrrhic victory if the individual litigant were to have a brand new statement of rights which could not, in practice, be enforced save through petitioning the European Court of Human Rights in Strasbourg (a process that usually takes several years) because the HRA 1998 had been amended or repealed so as to weaken or even remove effective judicial domestic human rights protection.

However, in certain respects, the HRA 1998 is less than adequate. The Constitution is designed to strengthen rather than weaken existing judicial protection of fundamental rights. As already seen in the section on Judges, this Constitution proposes a radical new role for the new Supreme Court in terms of being empowered to strike down statutes. This is not possible under the HRA 1998, which permits only (at the level of the High Court or higher) the granting of declarations of incompatibility in respect of primary legislation that breaches the Convention rights.

For that reason, some limited changes to the HRA 1998 would be needed to give effect to the expanded constitutional powers of the Supreme Court. However, it is proposed that the other HRA 1998 mechanisms for protecting fundamental rights are left unchanged. Rather than repealing or amending the HRA 1998, Article 178 adopts the simple expedient of leaving it in full force save and insofar as any statutory limitations set out in that Act are incompatible with the Constitution, in which case the Constitution trumps the Act.

In practice, the effect of this is that most HRA 1998 protections (including statements of compatibility with the Convention rights under section 19) will continue to be available. In particular, declarations of incompatibility will continue to be granted as at present by those courts having jurisdiction to award such relief. However, the Supreme Court is not subject to that limitation.

It should also be borne in mind that existing UK fundamental rights regimes are not necessarily confined to the ECHR. Such rights are sometimes given effect to (whether directly or indirectly) under the common law, and even by reference to customary international law, international human rights treaties and the European Charter of Fundamental Rights (EU Charter).

Article 179 is designed to address most of these regimes. In essence, it provides that any fundamental rights that are recognised in other existing UK legal rights regimes (including, most notably, EU law and the common law) remain in full force and effect save and insofar as they are incompatible with the Constitution.

International human rights treaties have sometimes afforded a basis for developing fundamental rights under the common law, and to that extent they continue to have identical legal effect under this Constitution. However, other than in respect of some rights under the ECHR which have not been incorporated into domestic law by the UK and other than in respect of the EU Charter, purely international obligations or other international provisions relating to fundamental rights have no separate force under the Constitution save interpretatively (and on the basis, of course, that they are not separately treated as binding under this Constitution).

The EU Charter is a proclamation rather than a source of legal obligations. However, it refers to a number of social and economic rights and it has been taken into account by the European Court of Human Rights and the High Court in England.

It seems likely, therefore, that the EU Charter will be increasingly relied upon before domestic courts and, in many instances, will be referred to by those courts. It contains a number of social and economic rights. As explained earlier, this is a logical development of the modern approach to human rights. For these reasons, this Constitution proposes to treat the EU Charter in the same fashion as the ECHR and to accord them equal status in the Constitution (see Article 176).

Three further issues merit brief mention. The first is devolution. As is made clear, nothing in the conferment of constitutional rights and recognition of civic responsibilities prevents additional rights from being conferred or additional responsibilities from being recognised through the devolved institutions of the UK acting within their jurisdictions.

The question of what role the devolved institutions might play in the creation of further fundamental rights (or responsibilities) raises difficult issues. One difficulty is that the current Convention rights do not include reserved matters (that is, matters over which power to legislate is reserved to the Westminster Parliament). However, at least some of the extended rights set out in this Constitution (or the UK Bill of Rights envisaged by the Joint Committee on Human Rights) are likely to intrude upon reserved matters. This Constitution does not confront these potential problems but leaves the way open for further discussion with the devolved institutions, which might even lead to some restructuring as to what might be included or excluded from the definition of 'reserved matters' in the context of fundamental rights.

The second issue is the question of restrictions on, and derogations from, the constitutional fundamental rights. This is linked to the last issue, which is concerned with the enforcement of the constitutional fundamental rights. As to *restrictions* on rights, Article 182 contains a general provision enabling those constitutional rights that can legitimately be restricted (an obvious exception is the right to life under Article 187) to be restricted by reference to the principle of proportionality. Some of these rights specify their own limitation provisions and it is for consideration whether such provisions – which follow the language of the ECHR – are from a drafting perspective now otiose or whether there is a rationale for retaining them given the full retention of the ECHR where it is compatible with the Constitution.

Third, a restriction on a fundamental right is to be distinguished from *derogation*. Derogation involves a breach of the right in question, whereas a legitimate restriction does not. It follows that derogation should only be permitted in very exceptional circumstances.

This Constitution envisages that derogation will only be allowed in a situation of true emergency.

Parts 6 and 9 of the Constitution are therefore necessarily connected. Thus, this Convention provides that the rights and freedoms may not be derogated from in the exercise of any emergency powers under Part 6 of the Constitution apart from those in time of war or armed rebellion. This goes further than Article 15 of the ECHR, which excludes derogation from the rights contained in Articles 2 (right to life – other than deaths resulting from lawful war), 3 (torture or inhuman or degrading treatment or punishment), 4 (servitude) and 7 (no punishment without law). However, the European Convention is the ultimate test of legitimacy.

There is an important debate as to the extent to which other essential freedoms such as the right to freedom of expression may be derogated from (as opposed to being legitimately restricted) even in time of war or other emergency. This Constitution proposes that the distinction between legitimate restriction and derogation is important and that the scope for legitimate derogation from fundamental rights should be curtailed. It is also for consideration whether the prohibition on derogation should be extended (as this Constitution does) to certain rights and freedoms such as, most notably, the fair trial rights set out in Articles 201–208.

Other constitutional rights may be derogated from where emergency powers are being exercised under Part 6 of the Constitution. The limited circumstances in which derogation may occur even then are set out in Part 6 of the Constitution.

The connection between, on the one hand, restricting fundamental rights or derogating from human rights and, on the other, enforcing compliance with fundamental rights is that without a clear enforcement process the restriction and derogation provisions arguably lack coherence. It is to be noted, in that context, that the Joint Committee on Human Rights would retain a provision in its Bill of Rights that allows Parliament to declare expressly in an Act of Parliament that the Act or any of its provisions 'shall operate notwithstanding anything contained in this Bill of Rights and Freedoms'. This is designed to preserve parliamentary sovereignty and is similar in nature to the mechanism detailed in the HRA 1998 which allows primary legislation to have full legal effect and validity notwithstanding that the Court has declared it to be incompatible with the ECHR.

However, as explained elsewhere, the concept of parliamentary sovereignty cannot stand beside a written constitution. It follows that a constitutional provision that adopted the Joint Committee's proviso by simply allowing Parliament to override the Constitution in the case of primary legislation would be logically inconsistent with the overriding nature of the Constitution itself. This is why if the Supreme Court finds a breach of a fundamental right, then – as with any other breach of the Constitution – it has a general duty to make a declaration of unconstitutionality, the effect of which is (see Art 5) that the Act in question is invalid to the extent to which it violates the constitutional requirement.

Scope and Content of a Domestic Bill of Rights (Arts 174–219)

There is considerable scope for debate as to the precise rights that should be included in the Constitution and how they should be formulated. The Joint Committee suggested an outline Bill of Rights in its report. However, the rights themselves – with a few exceptions – were not drafted.

In the main, the rights drafted in this Constitution have taken the ECHR and the EU Charter as their starting point. Developing things further, it is proposed that in a modern Constitution it is appropriate to include, for the reasons advanced earlier, a number of social and economic rights that do not appear in the ECHR, and many of these are derived from the EU Charter. The Joint Committee considered that a savings clause was needed for such rights and suggested a statutory formulation that would have weakened their effect by not allowing them to be enforced by individuals against the Government or any public authority. The reason for such a limitation is understandable and there is something to be said for it. However, this Constitution (borrowing from the South African Bill of Rights) proposes that instead of preventing legal enforcement altogether this class of rights should, rather, be qualified in two instances by requiring the state to progressively realise, within the state's available resources, these rights by legislation. It is perhaps undesirable to emasculate these rights further, especially with respect to free compulsory education and the very widely phrased series of environmental rights.

The Joint Committee on Human Rights considered the difficult question of whether a UK Bill of Rights should contain some pre-eminently 'British' rights,[201] such as the right to trial by jury in the Crown Court, and concluded that it should. That suggestion has not been adopted in this Constitution because the ancient right of trial by jury in serious cases is regarded by many as anachronistic and time-consuming. In 2009 the Court of Appeal (Criminal Division) made legal history by ruling that a criminal trial in the Crown Court could take place without a jury.[202] In such a climate, it is considered that it is unwise to entrench

[201] However, there are difficulties in categorising even this right as 'British', since there is no established right to a jury trial in Scotland. See generally the discussion of devolution below.

[202] *R v Twomey* [2009] EWCA Crim 1035.

jury trial as a constitutional right, whatever may be the merits of having separate laws that retain the absolute right of jury trial in the Crown Court.

However, this Constitution adopts the general approach of the Joint Committee, which suggests that there is a need for a few more modern rights than those contained in the ECHR and even in the EU Charter. Thus, for example, the Constitution proposes a wide right of participation in public service on general terms of equality, extensively-framed rights for children, persons with disabilities and victims of crime, a right to free social[203] (as well as health) care, and broad environmental rights. These rights are either not recognised in the ECHR or EU Charter or are framed in much wider terms.

Nonetheless, despite the importance of modernising rights and including, for the first time, specific social and economic rights, this Constitution does not, for the most part, go further and introduce so-called 'third generation rights', being rights which are internationally recognised fundamental rights (such as the right of self-determination). In this, again, the views of the Joint Committee are reflected. The inclusion of environmental rights in a UK Bill of Rights was treated by the Joint Committee as an exception to the omission of third generation rights. However, a level of environmental protection is recognised in the EU Charter and, indirectly, in the ECHR by means of the case law on Article 8; it is, I suggest, now more of a social right than a third generation right.

Given the specific inclusion of the ECHR and the EU Charter in the Constitution, the new rights introduced are relatively few, although the rights as expressed in the Constitution often differ considerably from one or both of the two European rights instruments.[204] The Table below sets out all the constitutional rights. These follow the general scheme of the outline Bill of Rights sketched out in the Twenty-Ninth Report of the Joint Committee on Human Rights, which is referred to above. Where the right in question derives from the ECHR or the EU Charter the source of the right is stated, along with any material differences. There is inevitably a degree of overlap, but incorporating the ECHR and the EU Charter into the Constitution should remedy any omission in the formulation of constitutional rights.

[203] The arcane distinction between health and social care has been the subject of a number of court cases and was greatly muddied by the introduction of community care (for which charges may be levied) in 1993. Many consider it unfair that free treatment under the NHS becomes chargeable as social care once an individual's health has stabilised and they leave a long-stay hospital (where formerly they would have remained) and move into a residential care home setting. This is a subject that, it is suggested, deserves a full public debate.

[204] A notable example is the new equality right. There is now significant evidence that inequality in society is responsible for many social ills: see Richard Wilkinson and Kate Pickett, *The Spirit Level – Why More Equal Societies Almost Always do Better* (London, Allen Lane, 2009) and *The Inner Level* (London, Penguin Books 2019). The Equality Act 2010 is a further advance in this direction. It reflects what Amartya Sen refers to as the 'capability approach' by focusing more on the redress of substantive differences than on an impartial equality of opportunity (see Amartya Sen, *The Idea of Justice* (London, Allen Lane, 2009) esp 291).

Should there be a Statement of Constitutional Responsibilities? (Arts 220–224)

A constitutional statement of responsibilities is to be distinguished from the normal duties that may arise under the criminal law or other discrete legal regimes such as those of tort or contract. The difference is that a constitutional responsibility is a normative statement suggesting how individuals ought generally to behave towards each other.

In that context, it is perhaps a truism to state that rights may entail a degree of responsibility, certainly in the manner of their exercise. This is expressly recognised in parts of the ECHR, such as in Art 10(2), which – before stipulating the restrictions that may be imposed on the different aspects of the right of freedom of expression – provides that 'The exercise of these [Art 10] freedoms ... carries with it duties and responsibilities'.[205]

Table of Constitutional Rights and Parallels in the ECHR and the EU Charter

Constitutional right (if any)	ECHR source (if any)	EU Charter source (if any)
Art 185: Equality. This provision is modelled on a similar provision in the South African Bill of Rights	No direct parallel but the ECHR recognises equality of arms under Art 6(1) and non-discrimination in the enjoyment of Convention rights under Art 14	Art 20. Chapter III contains certain other requirements relating to equality (see Arts 21–26) which – although some of these requirements overlap with other constitutional rights – automatically become part of the Constitution.
Art 186: Respect for human dignity	No direct parallel but many ECHR rights implicitly require respect for human dignity	Art 1
Art 187: Right to life (with specific exclusion of the death penalty)	Art 2. However, Art 2 includes lawful execution as an exception to the right to life	Art 2 (which excludes the death penalty)
Art 188: Respect for physical and mental integrity	No direct parallel but this is implicit in Art 8 (right to respect for private life)	Art 3. This also contains special provisions in relation to medicine and biology which are not included in the Constitution

(continued)

[205] See also the Preamble to the European Charter of Fundamental Rights.

(Continued)

Constitutional right (if any)	ECHR source (if any)	EU Charter source (if any)
Art 189: Freedom from torture, inhuman or degrading treatment or punishment	Art 3	Art 4
Art 190: Freedom from slavery and servitude including trafficking in people (excludes legitimate punishment such as unpaid work orders by the court)	Art 4. However, Art 4 does not include trafficking in people. Nor does it exclude legitimate punishment	Art 5. This does not exclude legitimate punishment
Arts 191–192: Right to liberty and security of the person	Art 5	Art 6. This merely states the right and is not elaborated further as it is in the ECHR
Art 193: Respect for private and family life, home and communications	Art 8. However, this refers to 'correspondence' rather than 'communications'	Art 7. There is also a right to protection of personal data which corresponds closely to the EU Data Protection Directive
Art 194: Right to freedom of thought, conscience and religion (including the right of conscientious objection)	Art 9. However, this does not ostensibly recognise conscientious objection as a right	Art 10 (which includes conscientious objection)
Art 195: Right to freedom of expression	Art 10	Art 11
Art 196: Right to freedom of association, assembly and peaceful demonstration	Art 11. However, this does not ostensibly recognise a right of peaceful demonstration	Art 13. However, this does not ostensibly recognise a right of peaceful demonstration
Art 197: Right to marry and found a family, including samesex marriage	Art 12. However, this does not ostensibly recognise a right to same-sex marriage	Art 9. However, this does not ostensibly recognise a right to same-sex marriage
Art 198: Right to peaceful enjoyment of possessions. Intellectual property is protected under the same terms	Art 1 Protocol 1. There is no express reference to intellectual property	Art 17. Intellectual property is protected
Art 199: Right to freedom of movement	Art 2 Protocol 4. The UK is not currently bound by this right	Art 45

(continued)

(Continued)

Constitutional right (if any)	ECHR source (if any)	EU Charter source (if any)
Art 200: Right to asylum	There is no right to asylum in the ECHR	Art 18
Arts 201–202: Rights of arrested and detained persons. The rights here are modelled on the South African Bill of Rights	There are no express rights of this kind in the ECHR, although Art 8 recognises a privilege against self-incrimination and Art 6 contains a number of relevant due process rights	There are no express rights of this kind in the EU Charter
Arts 203–204: Due process rights in civil and criminal cases	Art 6(1) (which Art 203 of the Constitution replicates) contains a general due process requirement in civil and criminal cases. Art 6(2)–(3) (which Art 204 of the Constitution replicates) contains specific safe-guards in criminal cases	Arts 47–48
Art 205: Principles of legality and proportionality of criminal offences and penalties. This is concerned with no punishment without law and also with the proportionality of criminal penalty	Art 7. However, this provision is not concerned with the proportionality of penalties	Art 48. This provision, which Art 205 of the Constitution mirrors, is also concerned with the proportionality principle in relation to criminal penalties
Art 206: Right to an effective remedy	Art 13. Art 13 is not, however, a 'Convention right' under the HRA 1998	Art 47
Art 207: Right of access to information. The right here is modelled on the South African Bill of Rights	This right is not recog-nised in the ECHR	Art 41 contains a right to good administration, which is partially concerned with a right of access to infor-mation. Art 42 is concerned with a right to access docu-ments of EU institutions and bodies, offices and agencies of the Union

(continued)

(Continued)

Constitutional right (if any)	ECHR source (if any)	EU Charter source (if any)
Art 208: Right to fair and just administrative action. The right here is modelled on the South African Bill of Rights	This right is not recognised in the ECHR	Art 41 contains a right to good administration
Arts 209–210 Democratic rights. Art 210 is taken almost directly from Art 25 of the International Covenant on Civil and Political Rights and includes not merely free and fair elections and the right to stand as a candidate and be elected but also the wider right to participate on an equal basis in the conduct of public affairs	Art 3 Protocol 1. This deals with free and fair elections	Art 40 deals with the right to vote and stand as a candidate in municipal elections
Art 211: Rights of the child. This statement of rights is modelled on the South African Bill of Rights	There are no express rights for children in the ECHR. However, Art 14 provides that there must be no discrimination in the enjoyment of Convention rights so that they apply equally to children	Arts 24, 32 and 33 contain a number of rights relating to children, although they are less extensive than the rights set out in Art 211 of this Constitution
Art 212: Rights of national minorities. This right is modelled on similar provisions in the Romanian Constitution	There is no express right of national and ethnic identity in the ECHR, although Art 8 (the right to respect for private life) has been held to include national and ethnic identity. Art 14 prohibits discrimination in the enjoyment of Convention rights on several grounds, including association with a national minority	Art 22 contains a provision respecting cultural, linguistic and religious diversity

(continued)

(Continued)

Constitutional right (if any)	ECHR source (if any)	EU Charter source (if any)
Art 213: Rights of persons with disabilities. This right entrenches Arts 19–20 of the UN Convention on the Rights of Persons with Disabilities, which was ratified by the UK on 8 June 2009	There are no express rights relating to disability in the ECHR. However, case law on Art 8 recognises the right of persons with disabilities to respect for their private life and the fact that this can create positive obligations. Art 14 implicitly encompasses such persons in the overall protection of enjoyment of the other rights	Art 26 contains a provision recognising and respecting the rights of persons with disabilities to benefit from measures designed to ensure their independence, social and occupational integration and participation in the life of the community
Art 214: Rights of victims of crime and abuses of power	There is no explicit right in the ECHR	There is no explicit right in the EU Charter
Art 215: Right to adequate standard of living. This right is based in large part on a similar provision in the South African Bill of Rights	There is no such right in the ECHR	Art 34 recognises a right to social security and social assistance
Art 216: Right to free health and social care	There is no such right in the ECHR	Art 35 recognises a right to preventative health care and medical treatment
Arts 217–218: Right to free, full-time education. Art 217 is modelled on the 1948 UN Declaration of Human Rights	Art 2 Protocol 1 recognises a right not to be denied education and the right of parents to educate their children in accordance with their religious and philosophical convictions	Art 14 contains a similar right to that contained in the ECHR but includes the possibility of free compulsory education
Art 219: Right to a healthy environment. This replicates a drafting suggestion in the Twenty-Ninth Report of the Joint Parliamentary Committee in its Outline Bill of Rights	There is no such right in the ECHR, although the case law on Art 8 has established certain rights of environmental protection	Art 37 requires merely a high level of environmental protection in accordance with the principle of sustainable development

There is, though, a wider sense in which responsibilities are linked to the idea of fundamental rights protection. It is not necessary to embrace wholly Aristotle's view that it is the responsibilities of citizenship that give the fullest expression to the concept of the state to understand that rights are not exercised in a vacuum. They are exercised in a social context.

Without state responsibility there would be chaos. The same would be true if there were a complete absence of individual responsibility. Thus, even though there may be no a priori first principle compelling either the state or individuals within it to assume particular responsibilities, as a self-organising societal principle it is probably to be treated as axiomatic.

But should such responsibilities be given explicit voice in a constitution? The main argument against so doing is that what are really moral responsibilities may be artificially limited by their being articulated. A linked argument is that moral responsibility may easily be confused with legal responsibility or, in a section of a constitution addressing fundamental rights, as a *quid pro quo* of those rights being conferred.

As against these objections, it may be thought that there is strong symbolic value in having a statement of responsibilities. The statement of responsibilities here emphasises an older (mainly Greek) conception of civic virtue that, with the rise of impersonal computerised forms of communication, the decline of religion and few clear reasons for social bonding, leaves modern society looking strangely atomised and incomplete. As explained earlier, there are real risks involved in seeking to set out a statement of values that will always be less than comprehensive. But a general statement of civic responsibilities can double as an implicit endorsement of particular values and an overall reminder of what we owe to each other as human beings.

So, although some dangers exist, this Constitution opts for a short statement of constitutional responsibilities and their proposed effect. The responsibilities themselves are expressed in the most general terms and cover both our relationships with each other and our relationship to the state as well as to more distant communities or bodies. Tragedies such as the Asian tsunami of 2004 provide exemplary reminders of the reciprocal relationships that we have with the global community.

The remainder of the 'responsibilities' section of the Constitution is concerned to ensure that the responsibilities there set out are treated not as creating mechanistic legal responsibilities or as giving rise to restrictions on fundamental rights, but as the basis of a symbolic moral code. This is the intent to be inferred from the section on responsibilities in the 2009 Green Paper *Rights and Responsibilities: Developing our Constitutional Framework*.[206]

[206] Green Paper Cm 7577 Chapter 2.

FUNDAMENTAL RIGHTS, FREEDOMS AND RESPONSIBILITIES: KEY POINTS

- **The case for a domestic Bill of Rights:** The need for a domestic bill of rights is by no means obvious. The main concern of politicians has been that the right wing of the Tory party was using a domestic bill of rights as an excuse to tear up our allegiance to the ECHR. But in recent times the higher standards enjoyed by the population have raised expectations beyond the simple 'bread and butter' approach dictated by the ECHR. Interestingly, the arguments of the proponents of a domestic bill of rights were the same, in essence, as those favouring a written constitution.
- **Constitutional mechanisms for a domestic Bill of Rights:** There seems to be general acceptance of the proposition that any new formulation of human rights should not affect our adherence to the ECHR. This is achieved by Articles 175–176, which permit, inter alia, for an interpretation of the ECHR which allows for increased human rights protection but not for less, and for the protection of the European Charter. Article 166 leaves the HRA 1998 in full force in so far as is compatible with the Constitution but not otherwise. Article 178 addresses other human rights regimes affecting the UK (common law, statute or international law) and proclaims that they are binding. Also binding are those rights recognised by the Constitution. Three other points merit brief mention: (i) devolution (the extent to which fundamental rights as defined could intrude upon 'reserved matters'; (ii) Article 182 includes a general restriction on those rights that can genuinely be restricted; (iii) derogation from fundamental rights – this is very exceptional.
- **Scope and content of a domestic Bill of Rights:** There is considerable scope for debate around this topic. The rights recognised in English law at the present time are in some need of modernisation. This Constitution accepts the need for some social and economic rights that are not contained in the ECHR. This Constitution borrows from the South African Bill of Rights by producing a clause that requires the State to pass legislation in the area complained of (and adjudicated as being lacking) subject to its own resources. There is a Table showing the majority of the relevant rights.
- **Should there be a statement of constitutional responsibilities?** Articles 220–224 set out provisions for a statement of constitutional responsibilities.

PART 10
THE CITIZENS' BRANCH (ARTS 225–229)

225. Subject to this Part, the Citizens' Branch shall consist of one person aged 18 or over from each of the constituencies of the United Kingdom's House of Representatives. Each serving member shall be selected at

random from the electoral register from those who are eligible. No person may be selected who is a serving member of the legislature, the executive or the judiciary under this Constitution or a serving member of the Scottish Parliament, the Welsh Assembly, the Northern Ireland Assembly or the European Parliament. The random selection of members of the Citizens' Branch, who will serve for a period of one year, will take place on an annual basis and no person may serve on the Citizens' Branch more than once unless they are elected as a member of the Citizens' Council. Any member of the Citizens' Branch who is elected to serve on the Citizens' Council may stand for re-election to the Council and is automatically a member of the Citizens' Branch if re-elected.

226. The Citizens' Branch chosen in accordance with this Part shall elect a Citizens' Council annually. The Citizens' Council shall be elected by the Citizens' Branch from those members of the Citizens' Branch who stand for election. Each member of the Citizens' Branch shall have one vote and the one hundred of those standing for election who receive the highest number of votes shall be elected. The Chairman of the Citizens' Council shall be elected by the members of the Citizens' Council by majority vote or, if the number of votes cast is the same, by agreement of the members of the Citizens' Council. Decisions relating to the organisation and operation of the Citizens' Council shall, subject to this Constitution, be decided by majority vote of the Citizens' Council.

227. The Citizens' Council shall be responsible, in accordance with this Constitution, for the discharge of all functions expressly assigned to it by this Constitution on behalf of the Citizens' Branch. The Citizens' Council shall have the general function of promoting and monitoring the fulfilment and implementation of the values of this Constitution, and in particular for promoting education as a process that helps to create better citizenship.

228. The Citizens' Council shall also be responsible for making recommendations to the legislature for amendments to this Constitution or other legislative change or to the executive for inquiries or hearings from time to time and for the organisation of referendums in accordance with this Constitution for the purpose of amending this Constitution, initiating legislation and initiating public inquiries and hearings into public bodies and their senior management.

229. The Citizens' Council shall be fully independent and shall enjoy operative, financial and administrative autonomy. To this end, it shall be allocated from the State budget a variable annual budget appropriation

> sufficient to enable it to be set up (including the costs of the election of the Council) and to discharge its functions. The budget shall not be less than the budget for the preceding year.[207] Each member of the Citizens' Council shall be remunerated for his or her services at the same rate as a member of the Cabinet. The initial budget appropriation and succeeding budget appropriations shall be determined by the Prime Minister in Cabinet with the agreement of the Citizens' Council once constituted in accordance with this Constitution. If agreement cannot be reached the Citizens' Council may apply to the Supreme Court for the initial budget appropriation and succeeding budget appropriations to be determined.

THE CITIZENS' BRANCH: OBSERVATIONS AND EXPLANATORY NOTES

Overview: Rationale for a Citizens' Branch

The term 'Citizens' Branch' is derived from the Venezuelan Constitution. However, the concept of citizens' power as developed in that Constitution is essentially state orientated and is very different from a muted version of the principle of direct or participative democracy with which Part 10 of this Constitution is concerned.

Direct democracy, in its purest form, is a form of democratic engagement in which sovereignty resides in a citizens' assembly in which all citizens are, at least potentially, eligible to participate (depending on the variant employed) in legislative, executive and judicial decision-making. It may have been practised to some extent in Athens in the fifth century BC and, to a lesser extent, in the Roman Republic as well as in a few other small states.

In a modern industrialised democracy, real, direct democracy is patently unrealistic. The overarching modern principle on which it may be thought democracy is best achieved is that of representative democracy in which the people, in theory, make decisions through elected representatives.

The dangers of a representative democracy being, in fact, thoroughly unrepresentative have been discussed in many sections of this Constitution and in Chapter 1 'Setting the Scene' above. The key principle underlying this Constitution is that of popular sovereignty, which entails the people having a true voice in political affairs.

In constitutional arrangements designed to give the people effective choice mechanisms, some form of popular participation is needed and this is what is sought to be achieved in Part 10.

[207] The term 'preceding year' is defined in Part 14.

Citizens' Branch and Citizens' Council (Arts 225–229)

The idea of a Citizens' Council selected annually by lot was practised in, amongst other places, ancient Athens. There, the *boule* (as it was called) comprised 500 male citizens but excluded females and slaves. In more modern times, a Citizens' Council of 500 sitting as an Assembly is unrealistic. This Constitution suggests a practical alternative, namely the creation of a Citizens' Branch from which a Citizens' Council of one hundred is chosen on an annual basis.

The proposed Constitution requires a random selection of people from the electoral register from each of the UK constituencies in order to form a Citizens' Branch. Tenure is ordinarily for one year. Although a year is a short time, any longer might unduly narrow the number of citizens playing a part in political affairs.

However, the Citizens' Branch of 650 people will do no more than select a Citizens' Council of 100 persons from those who put themselves forward for election. A Chairman is chosen from the newly elected members or re-elected members of the Citizens' Council.

Once elected, the Citizens' Council becomes more than merely symbolic. The work of the Council on behalf of the Citizens' Branch, as envisaged in this Constitution, encompasses three main elements: (i) the undertaking of functions designated elsewhere in the Constitution. The Citizens' Council is therefore – by majority vote – able to seek declaratory relief from the Supreme Court in relation to political parties and is also empowered to seek advisory opinions from the Supreme Court on issues of constitutional interpretation; (ii) the undertaking of wider, broadly monitoring and educative functions in respect of the constitutional values so as to ensure (amongst other things) a better appreciation of what citizenship entails;[208] (iii) the taking of organisational steps to initiate legislative change or public inquiries (including where appropriate seeking to trigger a referendum as provided for under the Constitution).

There is little danger of these powers being abused. The Supreme Court will have the power to refuse to allow the Citizens' Council to apply to it unless the matter in hand raises an issue of constitutional importance. The wider power of education and monitoring will itself be likely to be budget-dependent and the Constitution contains a mechanism for ascertaining the level of the budget. Finally, the power vested in the Citizens' Council to take steps to trigger the initiation of new legislation or public inquiries is no more than laying the ground for a referendum the result of which decides whether new legislation is to be enacted or a public inquiry held.

[208] The development of citizenship values may be better achieved by the Citizens' Council than by more formal political policy-making. A Citizens' Council might, for example, seek to promote the English language in a less controversial way than seeking to entrench it at a constitutional or legislative level as the language of the state. In this way the English language could be more subtly promoted to enable anyone resident in the UK to exercise more easily the full rights of citizenship.

The advent of a less deferential public makes it unsurprising that the Power Inquiry chaired by Baroness Kennedy made several specific recommendations encouraging more citizen power, in the light of its findings that many citizens felt that they did not have enough influence over political decision-making.

A constitution is an institutional framework rather than a detailed policy document. Thus, this Constitution has not proposed incorporation of all the Power Inquiry's recommendations in respect of greater citizen involvement.

However, under the Constitution, the Citizens' Council itself has power to recommend constitutional amendments and other legislative change. It is therefore able to consider each of the Kennedy recommendations (and suggest whether and how they should be implemented) over all areas of proposed constitutional reform, including reforms which further empower the people (such as citizens' juries) and the recommendation of the Power Inquiry that all public bodies should be required to meet a duty of public involvement in their decisionand policy-making processes.[209]

Citizen involvement of this kind has been attempted less often in recent times than in ancient times but it is not unknown. For example, in 2004 the province of British Columbia in Canada introduced a Citizens' Assembly on Electoral Reform, members of which were selected at random, which proved to be extremely successful.[210]

It is likely that persuading responsible members of the public to participate in a full-time role as a member of a Citizens' Council would require considerable incentives. The Constitution proposes a salary equivalent to that of a member of the Cabinet and an appropriate budget. In order to maximise on the experience of those who have already held tenure for a year, the Constitution also permits members of the Citizens' Council to stand for re-election.

THE CITIZENS' BRANCH: KEY POINTS

- **Rationale for a Citizens' Branch:** The term 'Citizens' Branch' is derived from the Venezuelan Constitution. However, the two versions are different and this Constitution advocates direct or participative democracy.
- **Citizens' Branch and Citizens' Council:** The Citizen's Branch envisages a random selection of people from the electoral register. Tenure without more is for a year. From the Citizens' Branch there is an election to the Citizens' Council which is a group of 100 persons from which the Chairman is

[209] The Liberal Democrats' proposal for a citizens' convention of 100 citizens to consider proposals for electoral reform (see Nick Clegg, 'Don't Waste our Time … Bring Forward Real Reform', *The Independent*, 16 November 2009) falls into this category of possible future recommendations, although it would probably be subsumed in the work of the Citizens' Council itself.

[210] For further detail see Bogdanor (n 183) 304–05.

selected, again by the Citizen's Branch. The term of office of a member of the Citizen's Council is for one year but any member may offer him/herself for re-election. The work of the Citizens' Council falls into three broad heads: (i) to seek a declaration from the Supreme Court on a wide host of constitutional issues; (ii) to participate in a wide variety of monitoring and educative functions; and (iii) to take organisational steps to ensure that there is legislative change, or a referendum or a public inquiry take place where necessary (Articles 225–229).

PART 11
OTHER ASPECTS OF GOVERNMENT (ARTS 230–242)

The Civil Service

230. Subject to this Constitution, laws shall make provision for the composition, recruitment and organisation of the civil service, except that this Part of the Constitution does not apply to the Secret Intelligence Service, the Security Service or the Government Communications Headquarters.

231. Such laws must, in particular, provide that recruitment to the civil service shall be solely on merit and on the basis of fair and open competition. They must also contain rules for a code of conduct in respect of members of the civil service and must prescribe as minimum requirements of that code of conduct that civil servants who serve an administration in the United Kingdom must carry out their duties for the administration as it is duly constituted for the time being, whatever its political complexion, and that such persons must carry out their duties with integrity, honesty, objectivity and impartiality.

232. Such laws may also make provision in relation to special advisers who are not subject to the recruitment provisions applicable to the civil service. Any laws made in relation to special advisers shall not affect the other provisions of this Constitution in respect of such special advisers.

The Armed Forces

233. The State shall make sufficient provision to ensure that the armed forces[211] are adequately resourced for the performance of their

[211] See Part 14 for a definition of the term 'armed forces'.

constitutional function. Laws must make provision for such resourcing of the armed forces and for the regular monitoring of that resourcing which must be required by law to be transparent and consistently exercised so far the facility of that person or persons appointed to act as in a supervisory role is concerned.

234. Laws may make further provision for the composition, recruitment and organisation of the armed forces.

235. The armed forces shall have the constitutional function of safeguarding the security of the United Kingdom but shall exercise that function only on the direction of the Prime Minister or any Supreme Commander appointed by the Head of State under this Constitution. Any such Supreme Commander shall be subject to the exercise of power by the Prime Minister under Article 100 of this Constitution or pursuant to the exercise by the Prime Minister of emergency powers under Part 6 of this Constitution.

236. The Head of State shall be the nominal Commander-in-Chief of the armed forces but shall remain subject to this Constitution and, in particular, to the powers exercisable in relation to the armed forces by the Prime Minister under Article 100 of this Constitution.

237. The Head of State shall, following any advice of the Prime Minister acting through Cabinet under Article 100 of this Constitution or pursuant to the exercise by the Prime Minister of emergency powers under Part 6 of this Constitution, appoint a Supreme Commander of the armed forces.

The Police

238. The State shall make sufficient provision to ensure that the police are adequately resourced. Laws must make provision for such resourcing of the police and for the regular monitoring of that resourcing which must be required by law to be transparent.

239. Laws shall also make provision for the establishment of police areas and for the maintenance of police authorities throughout the United Kingdom which authorities shall be charged with the constitutional function of securing the effective and efficient policing of their police areas.

240. Laws may make provision for the election of members of the police authorities.

Local Authorities

241. The State shall encourage by law the progressive simplification of the structure of local government institutions and the progressive strengthening of local government power.

242. To that end, the State shall pass laws with the intention of making local government institutions progressively self-financing and less dependent on central government.

OTHER ASPECTS OF GOVERNMENT: OBSERVATIONS AND EXPLANATORY NOTES

Overview

Part 11 of this Constitution covers a number of controversial constituent elements involved in or associated with the process of government. Each of them has generated recent political debate, with occasional polarisation of views amongst the main parties. For that reason, some care is needed in devising a constitutional mechanism to deal with them.

The Civil Service (Arts 230–232)

The regulation of the civil service is perhaps the least controversial of the four topics that are addressed in Part 11. This is because it appears not to be seriously disputed that the civil service should be regulated on a statutory basis, that there should be a core statement of values, and that recruitment to the civil service should be merit-based, competitive and transparent.

Stereotypically, perhaps, civil servants have been expected to serve the Government of the day with independent and objective advice whatever its political complexion. The nineteenth century Northcote-Trevelyan reforms, leading to the establishment of a Civil Service Commission in 1855, were designed to achieve just that.

Over the years the neutrality of the civil service has come under fire. Some view the Thatcher era as one in which the willingness of civil servants to challenge Ministers' views on policy was weakened by virtue of the Prime Minister's growing influence over senior appointments. But it was the Blair years that witnessed the burgeoning of special advisers and, with the appointment of such persons, the treatment of those pursuing careers in the civil service as 'simple subordinates with little or no recognition that they had a constitutional function of institutional scepticism, of speaking truth to power; of helping Ministers to ensure fairness in their decision-making, of legitimating that decision-making; of helping them to achieve objectivity and truth in their public statements and documents'.[212]

The need, in general, for modern reform of the civil service and, in particular, to make special advisers more accountable seems to be common ground amongst all political parties.

The Constitutional Reform and Governance Act 2010 (in this respect essentially repeating provisions contained in the 2008 Constitutional Renewal Bill) includes provisions which set out, amongst other things, a statutory code for the civil service and for special advisers, a series of recruitment principles, and a requirement for annual reports to be made to Parliament or the relevant devolved bodies from the relevant Minister in relation to special advisers.[213] The Institute for Government produced a paper in 2013[214] in which it observed that the evidence from elsewhere does not necessarily suggest that the UK should place more of the civil service in legislation. But it does suggest that the UK should explain more clearly and openly the relationships at the heart of government to enable a full and shared understanding of who is responsible for what and on the basis of which powers.

This Constitution accommodates these provisions whilst maintaining the entrenched constitutional scheme relating to special advisers.

The Armed Forces (Arts 233–237)

The problem here is lack of adequate funding and there is now widespread concern that troops are not adequately resourced. While British munitions and hardware are sent to Ukraine to aid in its fight against Russian invasion, the lack of backfilling of capabilities has placed the armed forces at a low state of readiness. The search for military capabilities is all the more acute because of heightened tension in Israel.

There are significant issues involving dilapidated military housing, depleted ammunition and poorly executed procurement programs. Meanwhile in 2023 'Defence's response to a more contested and volatile world' (DCP23) the Government noted that 'the transition to a multipolar, fragmented and contested world had happened more quickly than anticipated in IR2021'.

Incontestably, the armed forces require sufficient resources and the Government accepts this. This Constitution therefore creates an express constitutional role for

[212] Christopher Foster, *British Government in Crisis* (Oxford, Hart Publishing, 2005) 218.

[213] For their part, civil servants have argued that considerable further reform is needed to ensure that central government has 'a single coherent strategy for government'. See Simon Parker et al, *Shaping Up: A Whitehall for the Future* (Institute for Government, January 2010).

[214] Josh Harris, *Legislating for a Civil Service* (Institute for Government, September 2013).

the armed forces and mandates adequate resourcing as well as regular and transparent monitoring of such resourcing.

Nothing in the Constitution is designed to interfere with conventional statutory provisions, such as those contained in the Army Act 1955, on the general organisation of the armed forces. However, a new command structure is necessary because of the diluted role of the monarchy introduced by the Constitution.

The Police (Arts 238–240)

In relation to policing, we come up against the difficult question of whether the police force is sufficiently accountable to the electorate. It has even been suggested by some that there should be American style, directly-elected local sheriffs who could make decisions as to how their neighbourhoods are policed.[215] Other suggestions aimed at making the police more accountable involve a requirement that some members of police authorities are directly elected and the creation of a directly-elected police commissioner.

The last idea was taken up by the Conservative and Liberal Democrat Government in 2011. In the Police Reform and Accountability Act 2011 the Police and Crime Commissioner must in their area (there are currently 37): (a) secure efficient and effective police, (b) appoint the Chief Constable and if necessary dismiss him/her, (c) set the police and crime objectives for their area through a police and crime plan, (d) set the force budget and determine the precept, (f) contribute to the national and international policy capabilities set out by the Home Secretary, and (e) bring together community safety and criminal justice partners, to make sure local priorities and joined up.[216]

The underlying idea behind this Constitution is that, whatever form it might take, electors should be given a greater say in policing in their local areas, with the Home Secretary's power to control police forces' priorities being removed. As voiced by some critics of the present system, the concern is not whether or not *national* crime figures have or have not gone up but, rather, whether *local* crime has risen.

Although localism in certain areas such as local government (discussed below) is to be encouraged, a rather more complex question arises in relation to the police. It is not at all easy to see how elections for, say, a local sheriff would work in practice. It would be hard to guarantee against extremists standing for office or (perhaps similarly) a far-right party fielding local candidates. As against this, advocates of direct elections point out that policing has become

[215] See eg Douglas Carswell and Daniel Hannan, *The Plan – Twelve Months to Renew Britain* (2008), available on Google Books.

[216] Over recent years the statutory responsibilities have increased: see, for example, the Policing and Crime Act 2017. The statutory remit for three current authorities (Great London, Greater Manchester and West Yorkshire) fall within the jurisdiction of the elected Mayor but he/she is entitled to appoint a Deputy Mayor for Crime and Policing to carry out functions on the Mayor's behalf.

over-centralised with national targets and standards overriding local priorities and that the risk of extremist candidates standing for election is, in principle, no worse than at a general or local election.

There are powerful arguments both ways and it is probably too soon to seek to entrench direct elections into policing or even, perhaps, to introduce such legislation. This Constitution leaves open the possibility of future laws being introduced as well as present laws (which would not be entrenched).

Local Authorities (Arts 241–242)

Introducing more localism in local government is a rather different matter. It is hard to deny that the structure of local government has, to say the least, become unnecessarily complicated and that local democracy has all but disappeared. The reason for this is the increasing centralisation of government which has led to the financial expenditure of local authorities being controlled largely from the centre. This started with local authority capping in the 1980s and now some three-quarters of local government finance comes out of the central government purse, often with legal directions as to how it must be deployed. The topic is important too because it is related to devolution.

Articles 241–242 seek to simplify the structure of local authorities and (viewing it as a related matter) to enable local government to be progressively self-financing. The means by which this might be achieved are likely to be highly technical and the detail required is well beyond the scope of any constitution. This Constitution simply lays down a framework for laws to be passed which achieve both simplification and increased local authority self-financing. However, unlike some other constitutional provisions which *permit* laws to be passed, thus giving a 'steer' to the legislator, Articles 241–242 are mandatory in nature. This is because increased local democracy is one of the most politically 'tangible' elements touching our lives and needs a far greater emphasis than it has been accorded in the past. Reform of local government is also essential for federalism.

OTHER ASPECTS OF GOVERNMENT: KEY POINTS

- **The civil service:** It is, generally agreed that the civil services should be regulated on a statutory basis, that there should be a core statement of values and the civil services should be merit-based, competitive and transparent. The Constitutional Reform and Governance Act 2010 achieves all this – see the Notes above (and generally Arts 230–232).
- **The armed forces:** The armed forces currently lack adequate resources. The Constitution recognises this and requires the state to provide adequate funds. There is a revised governance structure which takes account of the diluted role of the monarchy (see generally Arts 233–237).

- **The police:** See generally Articles 238–240. Beyond a duty to provide adequate resources and to provide policing areas there is a permissive function to be able to pass laws dealing with elections to the membership of police authorities. This is a difficult area and very much down to party policy. The Conservative Party and the Liberal Democrats passed the Police Reform and Accountability Act 2011 providing for (see Notes) elected Police and Crime Commissioners.
- **Local authorities:** Local democracy is important and Articles 241–242 are mandatory in nature. There lay down a framework of laws to be passed which aim at increased local authority self-financing. This has become important at a time when some three-quarters of local authority finance comes from central government, often accompanied by legal directions as to how the money will be used. It is also relevant for devolution (see Notes on devolution).

PART 12

CONSTITUTIONAL CONVENTIONS (ARTS 243–245)

243. Constitutional conventions[217] that are incompatible with this Constitution shall no longer apply. A convention shall be deemed to be incompatible with this Constitution for the purposes of this Part of this Constitution if, amongst other things, its effect is to place any restriction on the exercise of a constitutional power, duty or right.

244. Constitutional conventions existing at the time when this Constitution comes into force shall otherwise continue to apply and form part of this Constitution except that such constitutional conventions shall no longer apply if the convention in question has been codified in this Constitution in whole or in part or if the subject matter of the convention has been provided for by this Constitution.

245. Nothing in this Constitution shall prevent a new constitutional convention from arising after the coming into force of this Constitution and forming part of this Constitution provided that what would otherwise have been a new convention is not incompatible with this Constitution and does not cover matters that have, in whole or in part, been codified in this Constitution or if the subject matter has been provided for by this Constitution.

[217] See Part 14, where the term 'constitutional convention' is defined and given an extended meaning for the purposes of the Constitution so as to include documents such as concordats or memoranda of understanding between government and third parties. This would encompass, for example, the 2004 concordat agreed by the Lord Chief Justice and the Lord Chancellor as to the intended separation of powers as between the government and judiciary.

CONSTITUTIONAL CONVENTIONS: OBSERVATIONS AND EXPLANATORY NOTES

Constitutional Conventions (Arts 243–245)

Articles 243–245 deal with the effect of constitutional conventions in a written constitution. Their brevity is deceptive, since the problems raised by unwritten 'conventions' arguably go to the analytic integrity of a written constitution and therefore make drafting this part of the Constitution rather more difficult than the drafting of entirely new and freestanding constitutional provisions.

Conventions, in their broadest sense, are unwritten agreements as to what particular procedures should be followed or how certain powers should be exercised in a constitutional arrangement. Where conventions are recognised as having arisen, they are treated in practice as binding. Although such conventions can exist in tandem with a written constitution, they are usually the product of earlier informal arrangements before the Constitution was set down in writing. In the UK, which has not had a written constitution since Cromwell, conventions find their place alongside a medley of statutes, court decisions, customary law and other sources of obligations and powers such as the (unwritten) royal prerogative.

In order to understand the drafting difficulties entailed in encompassing both substantive conventions and the very concept of conventions in a written constitution, three things need to be appreciated. First, the entire purpose of a written constitution is to reduce obligations and sources of power to writing. From that initial perspective, conventions outside the Constitution are both untidy and – worse than that – distort one of the purposes of the Constitution. They should, on this logic, *all* be reduced to writing or discarded. Second, however, conventions do not have the force of law. This means that the courts do not normally adjudicate on the meaning or existence of conventions. It follows that the act of reducing a convention to writing in a constitutional provision means that the meaning of what was once a convention but is now a constitutional provision becomes justiciable in the courts. This may (depending on the nature of the convention in question) be a reason *not* to reduce the convention to writing. Third, because of the need to entrench rights in a constitution rather than enabling them to be taken away by a strong executive, the process of amending a Constitution is intended to be difficult. This is a further argument for retaining at least the possibility of developing some types of conventions over time; otherwise, the vitality of the Constitution may become too dependent on straining the meaning of existing constitutional provisions to cater for new and unforeseen situations.

This Constitution seeks to preserve the fluidity of allowing new conventions to develop whilst, at the same time, not permitting unwritten constraints on power to continue to be exercised or new conventions to develop which could subvert constitutional provisions.

Some existing conventions have been expressly codified in the Constitution. For example, the convention that Money Bills must originate in the House of Commons is, *mutatis mutandis*, preserved. The convention *qua* convention therefore no longer applies but that is immaterial because it is now an express term of the Constitution.

Where there is no clear transposition of this kind, the first step is to ascertain whether an existing convention not expressly incorporated is incompatible with the Constitution. If so, it no longer applies. A convention is deemed to be incompatible with the Constitution for these purposes if, amongst its effects, it places a restriction on the exercise of a constitutional power, duty or right. This has to be read with the relevant part of the Constitution which stipulates that, otherwise, existing conventions shall continue to apply except where the convention has been codified in whole *or in part* in the Constitution or if the subject matter of the convention has been provided for by the Constitution.

A number of existing conventions (if not the majority) will, as a result of these provisions, no longer apply.

A concrete example will illustrate how the Constitution is intended to operate in terms of the incompatibility of current conventions. It would be incompatible with the constitutional power of the Houses of the Parliament to legislate for that power to be circumscribed by conventions such as the Sewel Convention, which entails the Westminster Parliament first having to seek the consent of the Scottish Parliament before legislating on devolved (non-reserved) matters. This Constitution therefore prevents such a convention from applying. But that does not mean that it is not still open to the Westminster Parliament to continue to seek consent from the Scottish Parliament before legislating on devolved matters. What it does mean is that any continued practice by Westminster of seeking the consent of the Scottish Parliament before legislating on devolved matters will not, no matter how long-lasting the practice, operate to create a new convention because the seeking of consent *as a constitutional requirement* is always incompatible with the Constitution. It will therefore always be open to the Westminster Parliament to enact legislation relating to devolved matters without seeking the Scottish Parliament's consent.

Similar principles cover those cases in which the existing convention, whilst not intrinsically incompatible with the Constitution, is nonetheless treated as being subsumed into the Constitution if the Constitution has wholly *or partially* codified it or if the subject matter of the convention has been provided for by the Constitution.

The same principles cover the creation of new conventions. The Constitution, for example, sets out an express requirement that war may not be declared without a majority vote of the House of Representatives. It follows since the Constitution already contains a provision encompassing this subject matter, such a practice involving, say, a higher measure of support from Parliament cannot legitimately develop into a convention.

It can be seen from the above that interpretation issues may arise as a result of these provisions. The process of identifying a convention is itself uncertain and, almost by definition, is fraught with ambiguity.[218] Once a convention has

[218] A graphic account of the possible difficulties is given in Bogdanor (n 183) 222–24.

been identified, the further process of deciding whether it is incompatible with the Constitution or whether its subject matter has been provided for by the Constitution may fall to the Supreme Court to decide on a constitutional reference or other application.

There is therefore some scope for debate as to whether the Constitution should seek to encompass constitutional conventions more rigorously, perhaps by itemising them, or whether they should simply not be included at all. The rationale for the drafting underlying the proposed draft Constitution is that, given the combination of express codification and wide exclusions, few former conventions will remain unscathed and the potential for the development of new ones will be limited though not precluded.

CONSTITUTIONAL CONVENTIONS: KEY POINTS

- **Constitutional Conventions:** Articles 243–245 address the subject of constitutional conventions. Conventions in their broadest sense are agreements as to what particular procedures should be followed or as to what should be the process of exercising certain powers in a constitutional arrangement. Three things need to be borne in mind: (i) the process of reducing things to writing means that all conventions should be reduced to writing or discarded; but (ii) the very process of reducing things to writing means that a few of certain conventions will not be the subject of legal resolution at all; and (iii) the fact that the process of an amendment of the Constitution is intended to be difficult may be regarded as an additional reason for not treating the subject of conventions as being coincident with a constitutional provision. Some conventions have been expressly incorporated in this Constitution. Some conventions have not been expressly incorporated and the next stage is to examine whether there is a necessary incompatibility with this Constitution. Incompatibility is assumed where the convention has wholly or partially been subsumed into the Constitution or if the subject matter of the convention has been provided for by the Constitution.

PART 13

CONSTITUTIONAL CHANGES AND REFERENDUMS (ARTS 246–252)

246. Subject to, and in accordance with, this Part of the Constitution, one or more provisions of this Constitution may be amended following the referendum procedure set out in this Part. Part 13 of the Constitution does not affect referendums the mechanics of which have been part covered separately by this Constitution.

247. Amendments to this Constitution following such procedure include the addition of provisions. Referendums may also be held on other matters not affecting this Constitution directly but affecting the implementation of matters covered by this Constitution (this is subject to any inconsistent Constitutional provision, or Treaty or Act entered into before the coming into one force of this Constitution) and this Part shall apply to those referendums as well as to referendums concerning amendment of the Constitution. Sometimes two referendums may be necessary where the first referendum is asking for approval in principle but there is debate about putting those principles behind the original approval.

248. No fundamental provisions[219] of this Constitution or rights protected under the Constitution shall be amended, nor shall their amendment be proposed except to increase their scope. The nations constituting the United Kingdom as described in Article 1 may only be altered following the referendum procedure set out in this Part applied to the part of the United Kingdom to which a proposed alteration relates.

249. After approval in a referendum (not expressly covered by this Constitution but dealing with constitutional issues) by a three-fifths majority of the people, conducted in accordance with this Part of the Constitution, a proposal to amend one or more of the provisions of this Constitution or on any other matter not precluded by this Constitution shall result in an amendment of the provision or provisions of this Constitution approved in the referendum or, as the case may be, adoption of the proposal the subject of the referendum, only with the agreement of the Houses of the Parliament sitting as a single assembly by a three-fifths majority.

250. Save where, subject to this Constitution, the executive Government offers a referendum to the people or to the registered voters of part of the United Kingdom, in which case the referendum must be organised and funded by the State, a referendum shall only be required to be held, organised and funded by the State where 20 per cent of the registered voters of the United Kingdom (or where the matter principally concerns a part of the United Kingdom, 20 per cent of the registered voters of that part of the United Kingdom) petition the Speaker of the House of Representatives calling for a referendum on a matter not precluded by the Constitution from being the subject of a referendum.

[219] This term is defined in Part 14.

251. A referendum result (whether offered by the executive or otherwise) shall not be valid unless forty per cent of the registered voters of the United Kingdom (or, as appropriate, forty per cent of the registered voters in the relevant part of the United Kingdom) vote in the referendum. A referendum result shall not be binding without a three-fifths majority of those voting in the referendum. Where a referendum is invalid or is not binding, a further referendum shall not be held without a new petition. No referendum may be offered to the people by the executive Government or proposed by the people on a matter principally affecting a part of the United Kingdom but may only be offered to that part of the United Kingdom principally affected or proposed by the people of that part of the United Kingdom principally affected.[220]

252. Laws shall be published setting out the same scheme for the various referendums. The same general scheme should extend to all referendums.

CONSTITUTIONAL CHANGES AND REFERENDUMS: OBSERVATIONS AND EXPLANATORY NOTES

Amending the Constitution (Arts 246–249)

Part 13 is concerned with changing the Constitution and changes affecting the Constitution as well as with the referendum procedure for these and other matters. The proposals relating to referendums treat proposed constitutional amendments and other matters in the same way, on the basis that if a matter is sufficiently serious to require a referendum, a high vote is needed for change to be effected.

In relation to constitutional amendments, a constitution seeks to *entrench* rights and obligations, as opposed to merely enacting laws, which can easily be changed by different policies of incoming governments. This means that a process of constitutional amendment must make changing the Constitution more difficult than it would be simply to change a law. This is why allowing amendment by majority parliamentary decision (the basis of primary legislation in the UK) would be unacceptable in relation to a written constitution.

However, this ought not to mean that entrenched provisions can *never* be changed. If that were the position, a constitution – far from being a liberating force – could become a straitjacket.

[220] This latter provision is intended to prevent the UK as a whole from being able to vote on matters that principally affect only part of the UK. Scottish independence is one such issue.

It is nonetheless suggested that there are certain provisions that should, in principle, be irrevocable.[221] This safeguards against the dangers of tyranny and subversion of the Constitution, as, for example, occurred in Germany in 1933 when a legitimate law – the Enabling Act – passed by majority vote in the Reichstag allowed Hitler to deviate from the Constitution and thereafter to suppress all political opposition.

At first sight there are problems with the suggestion that there may be constitutional principles which are prescribed in advance as irrevocable. The difficulty was expressed succinctly by Thomas Paine in *Rights of Man* (1791), where he observed that 'Every age and generation must be as free to act for itself, in all cases, as the ages and generations which preceded it. The vanity and presumption of governing beyond the grave, is the most ridiculous and insolent of all tyrannies.' This was part of his stinging rebuke of Edmund Burke, who had suggested that the 1688 Revolution had resulted in a permanent constitutional settlement whereby the people of England submitted themselves and their heirs and posterity 'to the end of time' to the power of the Crown.

Of course, in one sense Paine is right. No Government can, in practice, bind another or even itself, let alone a generation. Constitutions that are ostensibly watertight can simply be torn up, as occurred in Fiji in April 2009 when the President of the Republic, dissatisfied with a court judgment declaring his actions to be unlawful under the Constitution of Fiji, simply jettisoned the Constitution and ruled under his own 'emergency' fiat.

Moreover, there is a real danger of hubris in treating any underpinning constitutional 'idea' as irrevocable. If, to take a particularly apposite example, parliamentary sovereignty were to be declared irrevocable, the UK could never, as a matter of constitutional settlement, have a written constitution. Indeed, that is the subtext of Burke's view of the legal effect of the Glorious Revolution of 1688.

The difficulty is that the very logic of Paine's position can feed back into a profound relativism which, in political terms at least, is highly dangerous. As suggested in Chapter 1 'Setting the Scene' above, mankind has no tool other than reason with which to confront prejudice, greed, envy and all the other irrationalities and superstitions that have the potential to destroy us. There is no precise linear reasoning, comparable to a mathematical equation, that will solve the problems of humanity or even point towards a clear solution. But this does not mean that reason is not the underlying principle that should govern our actions and inform how we seek to address our political and constitutional relationships.

An important premise of this Constitution is that whilst reason might get things wrong, it can never be wrong to employ reason. Further, since reason is

[221] Certain Constitutions (such as that of India) contain such a provision.

the antithesis of blind, unquestioning belief yet supports a right to harbour any beliefs one wishes, this Constitution supports as axiomatic a pluralistic society in which mutual tolerance, including religious tolerance, prevails. Finally, consistently with that axiom and with the underlying significance of reason, ultimate constitutional power must reside in the people, whose collective reason is what informs everything in the Constitution.

Philosophically, these may at best be normative statements. But they are, even on that level, statements of practical intent and if the Constitution is to be based on them it is suggested that they should be expressed as permanent values incapable of change. That is why this Constitution operates to prevent the amendment of certain fundamental provisions as defined in Part 14. If they are to be changed, that may only be achieved by abrogating the Constitution itself. Yet that, too, is forbidden. It may, as accepted earlier, be true that ultimately nothing can be done in practice to prevent say a neo-Stalinist from tearing up the entire Constitution and even proclaiming a new one, but there will be a severe price to be paid in terms of loss of legitimacy. Ultimately, as James Madison observed, 'all governments rest on opinion'.[222] The apparent coercive power of the state is only effective if people believe in its legitimacy.

Constitutional amendment (where permitted) could be triggered by a large majority of Parliament without recourse to a referendum at all. However, a referendum or series of referendums coupled with a large parliamentary majority is probably more accurately reflective of principles of representative democracy. A referendum is a vote by the whole or a part of the electorate on a specific proposal or proposals. Few countries currently make extensive use of referendums (there are some exceptions, such as Switzerland). Whilst consistent with the doctrine of parliamentary sovereignty, but which can never allow a referendum to have legal effect because parliamentary sovereignty would allow a statute to override the creation of norms having legal effect, this is sought to be remedied in this Constitution since referendums are themselves a form of direct democracy of the kind encouraged by it (see Notes on the Citizens' Branch). The UK Government has rarely offered a referendum, and this has sometimes been criticised (take, for example, its failure to do so in respect of the Lisbon Treaty). It did offer a national referendum on the principle of continued membership of the European Community in 1975 and again in 2016 and a national referendum was held on the voting procedure in 2011. A few local referendums have also been held. For example, devolution was made the subject of local referendums in Scotland and Wales and independence from the UK was exercised in 2014.

[222] 'The Federalist', 49 in Alexander Hamilton, James Madison and John Jay, *The Federalist Papers* (Oxford, Oxford University Press, 2008) 251.

The Referendum Procedure (Arts 250–252)

In outline, the referendum procedure set out in Part 13 provides for an initial referendum (if offered by the Government or triggered by 20 per cent of the electorate or relevant part of the electorate) which mandates parliamentary consideration if adopted by a three-fifths majority. If Parliament (again by a three-fifths majority) sanctions the proposal, it is binding.

Articles 250–252 are concerned with the procedure for referendums for constitutional change and other matters. Like a recall referendum for the recall of elected representatives (albeit usually on a national level save where local interests are involved), it is suggested that the requisite proportion of the electorate needed to trigger a referendum for possible constitutional change in the form of constitutional amendment or relevant legislative change should be quite high. Twenty per cent of the registered electorate is suggested.

The detail of organising referendums is probably best a matter for the national Government; this is a matter entrusted to the executive Government or the Citizens' Council. The Government may offer a referendum at any time and no constitutional convention can constrain its power to do so. Nor will a prior 'trigger' be necessary for a Government referendum to be held.

The Constitution stipulates that – whether offered by the Government or triggered by the electorate – there should be a large majority vote in favour of change before further action is required under the Constitution. A three-fifths majority is suggested both in terms of a popular vote and a vote from Parliament. Further, a sufficiently high proportion of the registered electorate actually voting in the referendum is suggested as being necessary. Other countries have such a requirement. For example, Poland requires a 50 per cent turnout; in Denmark the threshold is 40 per cent. The size of requisite turnout suggested here is 40 per cent.

It should be noted that the procedure suggested for referendums (and their legal effect) apply equally to the referendums referred to in other Parts of the Constitution unless the mechanics have been separately addressed.

Separatism raises particular referendum/amendment issues. If part of the UK (such as Scotland) wished to separate from the UK, Art 239 makes it clear that a petition from 20 per cent of the registered electorate in (say) Scotland will be sufficient to trigger the proposal being debated in the Houses of the Parliament (which makes it clear that the Government can only offer the option of separation to the relevant part, as opposed to the whole, of the UK).

Special considerations may be thought to attach to Northern Ireland. Section 1 of the Northern Ireland Act 1998 requires only a simple majority of the people of Northern Ireland to vote for Northern Ireland to cease to be part of the UK. Parliament would then be required to give effect to that majority wish. Such a provision is incompatible with Part 13 of this Constitution, as currently drafted, which contains stricter criteria for separation to occur which is why inconsistent treaties have been noted as an exception to the general rule.

Experience of Referendums

The Conservatives have held three recent referendums (the first two in partnership with the Liberal Democrats).[223] These were:

(i) 2011: UK Alternative Vote referendum, binding (turnout 42.2 per cent; 32.10 per cent voted 'yes', 67.90 per cent voted 'no');
(ii) 2014: Scottish independence referendum, binding (turnout 84.6 per cent; 55.3 per cent voted 'no', 44.7 per cent voted 'yes');
(iii) 2016: UK European Union membership referendum, not binding (turnout 73 per cent for England, 'Leave' 53.4 per cent, 'Remain' 46.6 per cent; turnout 62.7 per cent for Northern Ireland, 'Leave' 44.2 per cent, 'Remain' 55.8 per cent; turnout 67.2 per cent for Scotland, 'Leave' 38.0 per cent, 'Remain' 62.0 per cent; turnout 71.7 per cent for Wales, 'Leave' 52.5 per cent, 'Remain' 47.5 per cent).

The first two went the Conservative Government's way. The third went the Vote Leave way. The three referendums now enable us to plot future referendums with care.

The main lessons to be learned are few but important.[224] Historically, national referendums have been rare. This is because of the long-standing principle of parliamentary sovereignty. This would be abandoned in the new Constitution but it does, perhaps, explain why we have failed to pick up vital starting and finishing posts of referendums as a piece of constitutional machinery.

The two vital starting and finishing points (apart from setting out the binding nature of the referendum) are: (i) the threshold required for the vote to be binding (including the vote, if required, by Parliament); and (ii) the break-up of the information for certain decisions (ie two referendums) to be made before binding the country into the make or break decision to break free of Brussels, for example.

[223] At present national referendums are governed by the Political Parties, Elections and Referendums Act 2000, which also regulates for regional and local referendums in England, Northern Ireland and Wales. Scotland has a separate Act (the Referendums (Scotland) Act 2020). Before the last two referendums, the only national referendum that was held was the one conducted in 1975 on whether the UK should stay in the European Communities. The UK has had a number of local referendums dealing with devolution, sovereignty and independence but these (save the vote on Scottish independence) draw on mainly local issues.

[224] Further detail is provided in Michael Gordon, 'Referendums in the UK Constitution: Authority, Sovereignty and Democracy after (2020) 16(2) *European Constitutional Law Review* 213–248, where Professor Gordon (in addition to a host of helpful materials) makes reference to the 2010 report of the Constitution Committee of the House of Lords *Referendums in the United Kingdom* published by the House of Lords on 17 March 2010, being Paper 99 12 Report in session 2009–2010, and the report of the *Independent Commission on Referendums* published by the constitution unit in July 2018.

A high threshold is needed for a decision of national importance such as Brexit because a low threshold leads to national discord, especially where two of the four constituent elements (Scotland and Northern Ireland) voted to remain and most of the elected Parliament voted to remain. Similarly, a relatively high threshold is required for turnout. As stated above, this Constitution adopts a relatively high proportion under each head for each referendum.

The second factor is one that has come to affect the perception of unfairness to, for example, the respective Brexit campaigns. How could the people know what the Government had in mind, a 'hard' Brexit or a 'soft' Brexit? How could the electors know what the terms meant, or what intentions the Government had in relation to each? Worse still, the Government had to negotiate with the European Commission and the result of that negotiation would not be apparent at the time of the referendum (or for a great many years thereafter). Similarly with the Scottish independence referendum. It is impossible to know in advance what the consequences of acceptance or rejection would be or, therefore, to know in advance the scope of the decision at the time of the referendum. All that one can say is that one is content with the principle of independence but that that will depend upon the terms negotiations produce.

What is the problem with setting two referendums?

CONSTITUTIONAL CHANGES AND REFERENDUMS: KEY POINTS

- **Amending the Constitution:** Articles 246–249 deal with amendments. The proposed Constitution covers referendums and other changes in the same way. Because amendments to a constitution raise serious issues, the proposal is that a three-fifths majority is needed both by the people and by its representatives in both Houses of Parliament.
- **The referendum procedure:** Articles 250–251 are concerned with the procedure for referendums and other changes to the Constitution. The proposal is either triggered by the Government or by 20 per cent of registered voters. Separatism raises particular issues because its localism means that only the relevant part of the United Kingdom affected is entitled to vote.
- **Experience of referendums:** There have been three recent referendums: (i) the 2011 Alternative Vote Referendum; (ii) the 2014 Scottish Independence Referendum; and (iii) the 2016 United Kingdom European Union Membership Referendum. The main lessons to be learned are few but important: (1) the threshold required for the vote to be binding should be relatively high; and (2) there may be a need for two (or more) referendums on the same issue to be held, where key information is lacking (as the last two referendums have clearly shown).

PART 14
INTERPRETATION AND FINAL MATTERS (ARTS 253–255)

253. In this Constitution unless the context otherwise requires:

'Appropriate Boundary Commission' is the appropriate Boundary Commission or Commissions established by law for the different nations of the United Kingdom or other body or bodies established by law[225] for those nations to create or review as the case may be constituencies in respect of elections to the House of Representatives and larger regional constituencies in respect of elections to the elected body of the Senate.

'Armed forces' means the Army, the Royal Navy and the Royal Air Force of the United Kingdom.

'Cabinet' means the collective decision-making body of the Executive comprising the Prime Minister and no more than 25 other Ministers occupying the most senior offices of State.

'Child' means every human being below the age of eighteen years.

'Civil list' is the annual sum voted by the Houses of the Parliament for the expenses of the monarch, the Royal Household and other members of the Royal Family.

'Constituency' is the electoral area electing, as provided for in this Constitution, a member or members to one or other of the Houses of the Parliament.

'Constitutional convention' is a well-established custom or practice that has evolved over time and is widely regarded as a fundamental aspect of government. For the purposes of this Constitution the term shall include documents such as concordats and memoranda of understanding that have been concluded between the Government and third parties.

'Declaration of constitutionality' and 'Declaration of unconstitutionality' is the name given to the remedies granted by the Supreme Court declaring that a law or other measure or state of affairs (including administrative acts and omissions) is (respectively) in accordance with this Constitution and therefore constitutional or is contrary to this Constitution and therefore unconstitutional with the effects provided for by this Constitution.

[225] At one stage it was anticipated (see the Political Parties, Elections and Referendums Act 2000) that the UK Electoral Commission would take over the work of the four Boundary Commissions for England, Scotland, Wales and Northern Ireland. This specific proposal has not been implemented but another body or bodies may, in time, take over the work of the present Commissions.

'Declaration of incompatibility' is the name given to a remedy granted by a court with the requisite jurisdiction that a law or other relevant measure is incompatible with this Constitution with the effects provided for by this Constitution.

'Fundamental principles' as referred to in Article 120 means the fundamental rights contained in Part 9 of this Constitution, and the values of liberty, democracy and popular sovereignty, fairness, civic duty and the rule of law.

'Fundamental provision of this Constitution' means any of the following provisions of this Constitution: Articles 2–5, 9, 112, 129, 136–140, 180–181, 246 and 248.

'Head of State' shall mean the person or body of persons exercising the functions of Head of State under Part 5 of this Constitution.

'In time of war' as used in Article 120 does not extend to acts of terrorism.

'Larger regional constituency' is the electoral area electing one member to the elected body of the Senate.

'Majority vote' means a vote in excess of 50 per cent of the votes cast.

'Multi-member constituency' is an electoral area electing more than two members to the House of Representatives.

'Preceding year' as referred to in Article 229 means the calendar year preceding the day of agreement or determination of the new variable annual budget.

'Primary legislation' means an Act or Acts of Parliament enacted by the Westminster Parliament.

'Royal Acts' means the Bill of Rights 1688, the Coronation Oath Act 1688, the Act of Settlement 1700, the Union with Scotland Act 1707 and the Succession to the Crown Act 2013.

'Secondary legislation' means a law made by an executive authority under powers conferred by primary legislation.

'The people' and 'the people of the United Kingdom' means, throughout this Constitution (including the Preamble), those persons who are, by law, eligible to vote at parliamentary General Elections in the United Kingdom.

'Two-member constituency' is an electoral area electing two members to the House of Representatives.

'United Kingdom' has the meaning given to it in Article 1.

254. The territories specified in Schedule [...] shall be consulted in relation to, and prior to, the coming into force of this Constitution. Special constitutional relationships may be entered into between the United Kingdom

and one or more of those territories which, if proposed to be entered into, shall be the subject of separate provision by law.

255. This Constitution shall come into force at the expiry of 365 days after approval by referendum following the referendum procedure contained in the Constitution of Britain (Referendums) Act. For the avoidance of doubt, the referendum procedure establishing this Constitution shall not be regulated by Part 13 of this Constitution and Part 13 has no application to the referendum procedure establishing this Constitution.

INTERPRETATION AND FINAL MATTERS: OBSERVATIONS AND EXPLANATORY NOTES

Interpretation and Other Matters (Arts 253–255)

Part 14 is devoted to practical matters relating to interpretation and implementation of the Constitution. Most constitutions require a section of this kind unless such matters are included in earlier parts of the Constitution as they arise.

As far as interpretation is concerned (see Art 253), general expressions have sometimes been used in the Constitution which, whilst they may trigger associations, may – unless defined more precisely – have the potential to confuse.

For example, a term such as 'the people' could mean anyone living in the UK, or it could have a more restricted meaning. Given that the Constitution represents a conferment of power from the people, and that the people have a certain measure of power under the Constitution (see especially Part 10), it is considered that this term requires precise definition and should be restricted to those persons who are entitled to vote at parliamentary general elections. Currently, these include UK citizens who are resident at an address in the UK, citizens of the Republic of Ireland and qualifying Commonwealth citizens aged 18 or over, or else living abroad and registered as an overseas voter and not legally excluded from voting.

Importantly, a number of such citizens are not currently entitled to vote at general elections. These include peers entitled to sit in the House of Lords and detained prisoners. In the case of *Hirst v United Kingdom (No 2)*[226] the European Court of Human Rights declared the UK ban on voting by detained prisoners to be unlawful and legislative change to comply with this ruling has now been published.[227]

[226] *Hirst v United Kingdom (No 2)* (2006) 42 EHRR 41.

[227] The changes are summarised in the House of Commons Briefing Paper *Prisoners' voting rights* published 9th August 2023.

Other general expressions of this kind which require precise definition in order to serve a sensible constitutional purpose are exemplified by 'Cabinet', 'fundamental principles' and 'fundamental provision of the Constitution'. There is obviously scope for debate as to which of these classes of terms need even more careful definition and what such definitions should be.[228] Although in a western liberal democracy the fundamental principles set out in the Constitution are probably uncontroversial, the term 'fundamental provision of the Constitution', from which emergency laws may not derogate, needs to be distinguished from those provisions of the Constitution that may not be amended. Whilst there is likely to be overlap between the two, they are not necessarily co-extensive.

Other expressions requiring definition are those which are terms of art and which are intended to be used in a specialised sense. Examples of these include 'appropriate Boundary Commission', 'constituency' and 'larger regional constituency'.

Articles 254 and 255 conclude the Constitution and deal with (respectively) the future constitutional relationships between the Schedule 1 territories and the UK (see also Art 1), for which separate provision will need to be made, and the date for the coming into force of the Constitution, which, if it is approved, will be dependent on the outcome of the referendum procedure contained in the Constitution of Britain (Referendums) Act (suggested text for which is in Chapter 3, below).

[228] For example, although the Constitutional Reform Act 2005 uses the expression 'rule of law' without defining it further, some may think that it should be defined more precisely. The contrary case is that it is fruitless to seek to define broad concepts such as 'rule of law', 'fairness' and 'democracy'.

3

The Constitution of Britain (Referendums) Act

An Act to make provision for the holding of referendums on the question of whether the United Kingdom should have a written Constitution and, if so, what form the Constitution should take and to make further provision, should the outcome of the referendum be that the United Kingdom should have a written Constitution, for the implementation of the Constitution in substitution for the present constitutional arrangements that prevail in the United Kingdom.

BE IT ENACTED by the King's most Excellent Majesty, by and with the advice and consent of the Lords Spiritual and Temporal, and Commons, in this present Parliament assembled, and by the authority of the same, as follows:–

PART 1
REFERENDUM ON A WRITTEN CONSTITUTION

1. A national referendum shall be held on whether there should be a written Constitution for the United Kingdom.

2. The question to be asked in the referendum and the front of the ballot papers to be used for that purpose shall be in the form set out in Schedule 2.

3. An Order under this section shall be laid before Parliament by the Prime Minister and shall:

(1) appoint a day for the holding of the referendum, and, subject to the provisions of this Act,
(2) make provision for the manner of holding the referendum, which shall be conducted on the same basis as a Parliamentary Election using the constituencies in existence at the time of the holding of the referendum.

4. An Order made under section 3 may make such further provision as may be necessary or expedient for the carrying out of the referendum including the funding of the referendum from money provided by Parliament and for the provision and funding from money provided by Parliament of a period of public education and debate preceding the holding of the referendum for the purpose of facilitating public understanding of the issues involved in the referendum.

5. No Order shall be made under section 3 unless a draft of the Order has been laid before, and approved by resolution of, Parliament.

6. Those entitled to vote at the referendum shall be:

(1) persons who, on the date of the referendum, would be entitled to vote as voters at a General Election in the United Kingdom;
(2) peers who at that date would be entitled to vote as electors at a local government election in any electoral area.

7. The result of the referendum to be held under section 1 of this Act is binding only if at least 60% of the validly cast ballots in the constituencies aggregated together vote the same way on the question that forms the subject of the referendum.

PART 2
SECOND REFERENDUM ON THE CONTENT OF A WRITTEN CONSTITUTION

8. Part 2 of this Act shall apply only if the outcome of the referendum held under section 1 is binding under section 7 and if it is in favour of a written Constitution for the United Kingdom.

9. If Part 2 applies, a second national referendum shall be held within [ ] of the date of the referendum held under section 1 of this Act, in which the question to be asked in the referendum and the front of the ballot papers to be used for that purpose shall be in the form set out in Schedule 3, and the draft Constitution in the form set out in Schedule 1 shall be attached to the ballot paper.

10. An Order under this section shall be laid before Parliament by the Prime Minister and shall:

(1) appoint a day for the holding of the referendum, and, subject to the provisions of this Act,
(2) make provision for the manner of holding the second referendum which shall be conducted on the same basis as a Parliamentary Election using the constituencies in existence at the time of the holding of the referendum.

11. An Order made under section 10 shall make such further provision as may be necessary for the carrying out of the second referendum including the funding of the second referendum from money provided by Parliament and for the provision and funding from money provided by Parliament of a period of public education and debate preceding the holding of the second referendum for the purpose of facilitating public understanding of the issues involved in the second referendum.

12. No Order shall be made under section 10 unless a draft of the Order has been laid before, and approved by resolution of, Parliament.

13. Those entitled to vote at the second referendum shall be:

(1) persons who, on the date of the referendum, would be entitled to vote as voters at a General Election in the United Kingdom;
(2) peers who at that date would be entitled to vote as electors at a local government election in any electoral area.

14. The result of the second referendum is binding according to the choice of a simple majority of the validly cast ballots in the constituencies aggregated together.

PART 3
IMPLEMENTATION OF THE SECOND REFERENDUM

15. If the outcome of the referendum in Part 2 is that the Constitution set out in Schedule 1 is approved, that Constitution shall come into force in accordance with Article 248 of that Constitution and from that date the provisions of that Constitution shall apply in their entirety.

16. If the outcome of the referendum in Part 2 is that the Constitution set out in Schedule 1 is not approved, then within three months of that binding outcome an Order under this section shall be laid before the House of Commons by the Prime Minister and shall make provision for the drafting of a Constitution for the United Kingdom and for its implementation in accordance with this Act.

17. An Order made under section 16 shall make provision for the following matters:

(1) the process by which the Constitution is to be drafted which must include full public consultation by those entrusted with the responsibility for drafting the Constitution;
(2) (without prejudice to the general need for public consultation) arrangements for citizens' councils and assemblies to participate in the process of drafting the Constitution;
(3) the persons or bodies to be entrusted with the responsibility for drafting the Constitution (including any necessary appointment process) which should include, in a proportionate manner, a mixture of persons qualified by reason of expertise and experience including one or more members of the Law Commission but which should also contain a small number of citizens of the United Kingdom without such expertise or experience;
(4) the time within which the Constitution is to be drafted which shall not be later than [ ] years after the making of the Order.

18. An Order made under section 17 shall make such further provision as may be necessary for the implementation of the second referendum including the funding of such implementation from money provided by Parliament.

19. No Order shall be made under section 17 unless a draft of the Order has been laid before, and approved by resolution of, each House of Parliament.

20. A Constitution drafted in accordance with the process contained in an Order made under section 17 shall come into force in accordance with the provisions of that Constitution and from that date the provisions of that Constitution shall apply in their entirety.

PART 4
SUPPLEMENTARY

21. No court shall entertain any proceedings for questioning the numbers, as certified by the Chief Counting Officer or any counting officer, of any ballot papers counted or answers given in a referendum under this Act.

22. The preceding provisions of this Act shall come into force on such day as the Prime Minister may order made by statutory instrument appoint.

23. This Act extends to England and Wales, Scotland and Northern Ireland.

24. This Act may be cited as The Constitution of Britain (Referendums) Act [ ].

SCHEDULES

SCHEDULE 1
[The Constitution]

SCHEDULE 2
Form of First Referendum Ballot Paper

Are you in favour of a written Constitution for the United Kingdom?

Put a cross (X) in one box:

YES ☐

NO ☐

SCHEDULE 3
Form of Second Referendum Ballot Paper

Do you approve the Constitution attached to this Ballot Paper in its entirety?

Put a cross (X) in one box:

YES ☐

NO ☐

Illustrations

THE EXISTING CONSTITUTION

The UK Constitution comprises statutes passed by Parliament, common law made by judges, and conventions and is not contained in a single document.

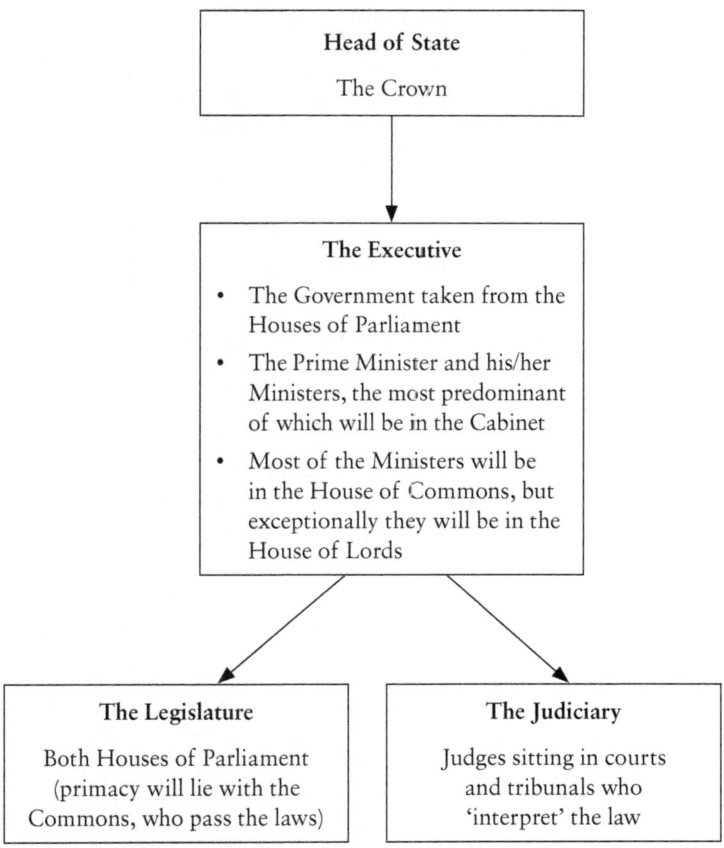

PROPOSED ALTERNATIVE CONSTITUTION

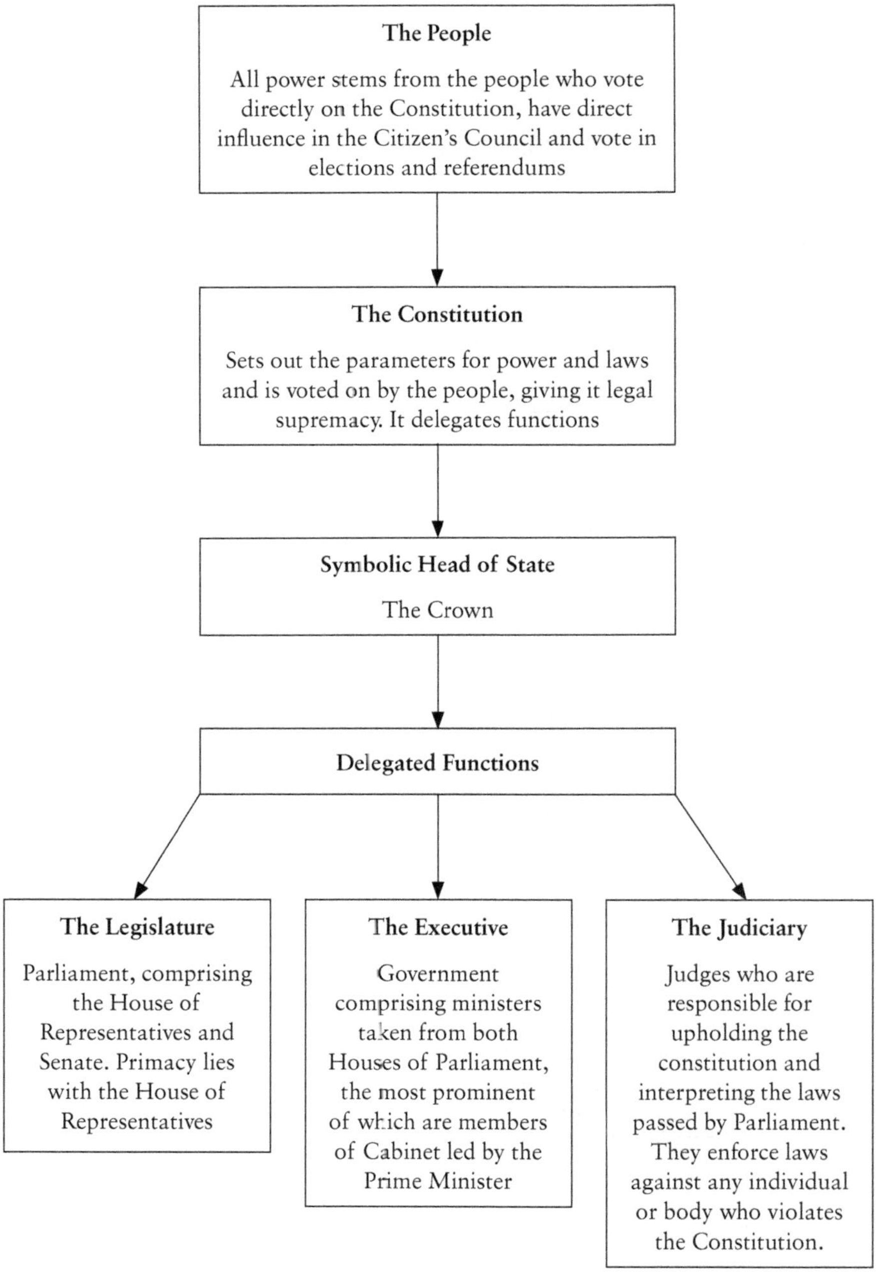

THE PASSAGE OF A BILL THROUGH PARLIAMENT

A Bill can start in either House of Parliament but most generally originates in the House of Commons. Money Bills are an exception – they always originate in the House of Commons. The procedure is essentially the same.

House of Commons or House of Lords

First Reading

Formal introduction and Order for Bill to be printed. No debate at this stage.

Second Reading

Once the Bill has been published, the Minister responsible introduces the Bill, providing an opportunity for MPs to debate the main principles.

Committee Stage

When in committee, each clause and amendment to the Bill is considered line by line.

Report Stage

The Bill returns to the floor of the House for further debate and voting on the proposals and amendments. This stage can take several days.

Third Reading

Usually immediately after the Report Stage. A short debate is held limited to the contents of the Bill.

Bill moves to the other House

It follows the same procedure.

Bill returns to the first House

After the Third Reading in the other House the Bill returns to the first House where it started and any amendments are considered.

Ping Pong

Occurs if either House disagrees with the proposals or amendments made by the other House. The Bill travels to and fro until there is agreement.

Royal Assent

Once the exact wording has been agreed the Bill receives Royal Assent and is made into an Act of Parliament which becomes law and is put on the statute book.

EXISTING DEVOLUTION LEGISLATURES IN THE UK

Parliament in Westminster

Westminster controls through the principle of Parliamentary sovereignty the process of devolution and determines which powers are to be reserved or delegated.

Scotland

The Scottish Parliament has executive and legislative powers.

(Scotland Act 1998, Scotland Act 2012, Scotland Act 2016)

Devolved Matters:

- Agriculture, forestry and fisheries
- Education and training
- Environment
- Health, care and social services
- Housing and land use planning
- Law and order
- Local government
- Sport, arts and tourism
- Parts of social security
- Some forms of taxation
- Many aspects of transport

Reserved Matters:

- Broadcasting
- Constitution
- Defence and National security
- Immigration
- Energy
- Employment
- Equal opportunities
- Foreign affairs and international relations
- Macro-economics and fiscal policy
- Pensions and party of social security
- Trade, including international trade

Northern Ireland

The Northern Ireland Assembly has executive and legislative powers.

(Northern Ireland Act 1998, Northern Ireland Act 2006)

Devolved Matters:

- Agriculture
- Economic development
- Education
- Employment and skills
- Environmental issues, including planning
- Health and social services
- Housing
- Local government
- Social security
- Pensions and child support
- Transport
- Culture and sport
- The Northern Ireland Civil Service
- Equal opportunities
- Justice and policing

Reserved Matters:

- Firearms and explosives
- Financial services and pensions regulation
- Broadcasting
- Import and export controls
- Navigation and civil aviation
- International trade and financial markets
- Telecommunications and postage
- The foreshore and seabed
- Disqualification from Assembly membership
- Consumer safety
- Intellectual property

Wales

The Welsh Assembly has executive and legislative powers.

(Government of Wales Act 1998, Government of Wales 2006, Wales Act 2014, Wales Act 2017)

Devolved Matters:

- Agriculture, forestry and fishing
- Education
- Environment
- Health and social care
- Housing
- Local government
- Highways and transport
- Some control over income tax, stamp duty and landfill tax
- Welsh language

Reserved Matters:

- Constitution
- Defence
- Energy
- Financial and Economic Matters
- Foreign affairs
- Home affairs
- Public service
- Political parties
- Single legal jurisdiction of England and Wales
- Trade and Industry
- Transport
- Tribunals
- Social Security, Child Support, pensions and Compensation
- Professions
- Employment
- Health, Safety and Medicines
- Media, Culture and Sport
- Justice
- Land and Agricultural Assets

(continued)

No thought was given to England as part of the devolution settlement. England continues to be governed by central government and local authorities with no intermediary level.

England

There is no equivalent parliament for England. Metro mayors and the mayor of London have only executive powers. Combined authorities and the London Assembly have executive powers but can only scrutinise legislation.

The majority of functions are agreed by deals made between central government and the local authorities concerned.

Cities and London Local Government Devolution Act 2016

Levelling Up and Regeneration Act 2023

VOTING SYSTEMS

Voting System	Advantages and disadvantages
First-past-the-post (FPTP): winner-takes-all in single-member constituencies in which a single vote majority is all that is required to secure victory in a parliamentary seat	A: Guarantees a link between the constituency and its MP; Suited to a two-party system and generally produces single-party governments D: Smaller parties tend to be ignored
Party list: A form of proportional representation (PR) by means of which parties provide candidate lists for the whole country which are then matched to the percentage of the votes cast	A: Small minority parties get access to parliament D: Breaks the constituency link
AV (Alternative Vote): A PR system which permits voters to cast votes for candidates in in each constituency in order of preference. The candidate is elected who has received the most first preference votes (that is, more votes than the other candidates combined).	A: Combines the potential for strong government with greater equity between all competing political parties; Supporters of losing candidates do not waste their vote, as their later preferences are relocated; Keeps the constituency link with the MP. D: Can skew the results resulting in greater inequity than the FPTP system.

(continued)

(Continued)

Voting System	Advantages and disadvantages
AV+ (AV Plus): A form of PR whereby most MPs are elected by AVin each constituency. An additional small percentage (15–20%) are elected from regional top-up lists.	A: Retains the electoral advantage of the two main parties while introducing an element of proportional representation. D: Breaks the constituency link
Single Transferable Vote (STV): A system of PR whereby single votes may be transferred to different candidates. Votes cast for unsuccessful candidates are then re-allocated to the other candidates according to voters' preferences until all but the most successful candidates are eliminated. Quotas for candidates are arranged by central government.	A: Better representation for minority parties; Voters can choose among party candidates D: Breaks the constituency link